MY 13th STATION

MY 13th STATION

A memoir by

Theresa Anthony

Copyright © 2019 by Theresa Anthony

ALL RIGHTS RESERVED. This book or any portion thereof may not be reproduced or used in any manner whatsoever without the express written permission of the publisher, except for the use of brief quotations in a book review.

ISBN: 978-0-578-52976-9

Library of Congress Control Number: 2019907700

Cover design by Emma Anthony
Cover art by Emma Anthony

Author's note: This is a non-fiction memoir. All names and some identifying characteristics have been changed to protect the anonymity of the individuals who are included in the narrative.

Printed in the United States of America

25 24 23 22 21
7   6   5   4   3

www.TheresaAnthony.com

*This book is lovingly dedicated
to my granddaughter, Grace*

and

*Our Lady of Fatima
Saint Anthony of Padua
Alcoholics Anonymous*

Contents

Introduction xi
Chapter 1: Life Extinguished 1
Chapter 2: The Pietà 5
Chapter 3: Enter Matthew 13
Chapter 4: The New House 23
Chapter 5: The Petersons 35
Chapter 6: Our Lady of Fatima 41
Chapter 7: Events 47
Chapter 8: Fatima, Portugal 53
Chapter 9: Divorce 65
Chapter 10: The Foothold 69
Chapter 11: Events Continue 75
Chapter 12: Matthew Changes 81
Chapter 13: The Enabler 95
Chapter 14: Enter Amanda 101
Chapter 15: Hope and Heartache 109
Chapter 16: Escalation 119
Chapter 17: Crescendo 131
Chapter 18: Saffron September 151
Chapter 19: Devastation 181
Chapter 20: Colorado Redux 199
Chapter 21: Fr. Matthew 223
Chapter 22: Hope 229
Chapter 23: Rehab Revisited 249
Chapter 24: Loss 269
Chapter 25: Grief 287
Chapter 26: Return to Fatima 313
Chapter 27: Lindsey's Story 317
Chapter 28: Spiritual Warfare 323
Chapter 29: God's Plan 335
Chapter 30: Matthew's Legacy 339

Afterword 347
Endnotes 351
About the Author 353

Saint Michael the Archangel, defend us in battle

Be our protection against the wickedness and snares of the devil.

May God rebuke him, we humbly pray

And do thou, O Prince of the heavenly host, by the power of God,

thrust into hell Satan and all the evil spirits

which roam about the world seeking the ruin of souls.

Amen

Introduction

HOW CRYSTAL CLEAR THE MEMORY IS—the kind of potent memory that you don't merely recollect but can still physically *feel* decades later. I was ten years old. There I was on the super tall swingset at the local park, pumping my long, skinny legs with all my might. With the wind sweeping across my face and tossing my hair, I flew through the air feeling sheer exhilaration and joy, as if anything in the world was possible. In that moment, the sense of flight and freedom so intoxicating, the rush of life itself so palpable, that the swing felt like the catalyst to my future—the launching pad. As a young girl, I saw the world as one big prize, full of opportunity, promise, and beauty.

Who knew what that wide-eyed girl's world would actually end up looking like! Had I known what lay decades ahead I would have run and run to the ends of the earth to avoid my future at all costs. To think that the pivotal event in my life, aside from having my children, would be losing one of them would have been unthinkable in my youth.

Yet here I sit, five years after the tragedy at age sixty-two, still reeling. My son died. There are moments, sporadic and unpredictable, when this reality hits like an anvil, leaving me feeling I might crumple to the ground under the weight of it, the loss of my only son.

Amazingly, when I allow myself to ponder the plot points along the timeline of my life, I can see how God's hand was evident all along, rearranging my sensibilities and taking a blowtorch to my once hardened heart. He was ever so gently guiding me towards the day when, at age forty, I would invite Christ to take over, to right the sinking ship of my life and take the helm.

For the next twenty years, He set about fortifying me, introducing me to the vast treasures of the Catholic faith in sacred Scripture, the writings of the great Doctors of the Church, the catechism, and the awe-inspiring lives of the holy saints. Acquiring a deep devotion to the Blessed Mother gave me the ultimate role model to aspire to while also finding cozy security beneath her loving mantle. As the cumulative base of my knowledge and exposure to truth and goodness expanded, God was preparing me to not only survive such profound loss, but to someday be strong enough to tell this story.

In fact, in the last few years I have come to realize that sharing my son Matthew's* life story has become a vocation of sorts, some kind of calling that I simply cannot turn my back on. I approach the writing process in the form of a humble pencil, to be held and guided by God's loving hand as an instrument used to accomplish a goal He has directed me toward. In the pages ahead, I will share openly about my beloved son, recounting in detail the events surrounding Matt's eventual battle with depression, anxiety, and alcoholism. Although there is a measure of discomfort in this level of transparency, I believe in my heart that this information will serve others.

In preparation for this undertaking, powerful emotions resurfaced while reading through my handwritten journals from 1997-2003, the typed journal entries from 2010-2014, old emails, texts, and even the calendars I had saved spanning 2007-2013. Angst, sorrow, helplessness, anger, despair, frustration, and abject fear were once again at my doorstep. As difficult as it was to relive the painful memories, these documents served to form the foundation of this book—the hard truths to be set down now in stark black and white.

To say that the preparatory process was hard is a serious understatement. The word "hard" shellacs over a myriad of intensely gut-wrenching emotions evoked as I read through the pain and suffering Matthew described in his rehab therapy notes, or the heartbreaking emails from his friends following his death. My journal entries from that period depict a mother's sorrow dripping off the pages, emotions that had to be summoned back to the present for the purpose of writing a story that is honest and genuine.

Because the actual words articulated in the documents reveal the pure expression of emotion, I will intermittently insert key excerpts directly into the narrative of the story, including my son's own words, rather than attempting to restate or rephrase them. In fact, one particularly powerful chapter will shift entirely over to my journal entries.

As hard as it was to revisit these memories, to rip the scabs off the wounds that had been in the process of healing, albeit at an excruciatingly slow pace, I recognize that for this book to have merit, to accomplish the goals that drive me to write it, I must share an honest accounting of Matt's battle. The raw edges of pain that, as his mother, I had to endure are as much of the story as is his battle with a dual diagnosis. I cannot spare the reader from the sheer magnitude and potency of those emotions while I stood in his corner with him, attempting to help him slay the monster. To do so would make me a fraud, someone hiding the ugliness and absolute devastation that accompanies addiction and mental illness.

Although I am writing this book from my own personal perspective, a mother's perspective, I do not hesitate to recognize the intense pain that Matthew's daughter, father, sisters, relatives, former wife, and friends have also endured in losing him. When he died, giant, aching holes were left in all our hearts, wounds that I strongly doubt will ever heal up. To us all, Matthew was a treasure.

As important a story that the scourge of addiction has become in recent years, and as much as I want to inform the reader about the disease and its profound impact across all aspects of life, I have a more important mission in writing about my son's battle. At its core, this is a story about spiritual warfare. While understandable that some may view me as a pitiful mother seeking to pin the blame for her son's issues on an influence other than his own free will, I will only encourage the reader to consume this story with an open mind.

I do not ask the reader to accept any of the events I relay as having caused my son's fate. It is not necessary for the reader to accept the idea that there is a God or a devil or that an ongoing invisible war is going on around us to still be deeply affected by Matthew's story. I will only hope that by the end of this accounting of true events—and allow me to emphasize that word again: *true*—corroborated by numerous people whose recollections, articulated independently of each other in recent months at my request, will be interspersed throughout—that the skeptical reader at least gains a sense of wonder as a result of reading it. Better yet, that the doubters might begin to investigate matters related to spirituality, possibly culminating in a renewed desire to seek the solace of God in their own lives.

For those readers who already come from a place of belief, but with perhaps a lukewarm devotional life, hopefully this story will inspire a deeper commitment. Too many Christians of all denominations rest in a false, but eminently easier, imagining of faith as a rainbows-and-butterflies state of serenity and sweetness. Angels and saints, Jesus and Mary only, thank you very much. Of course those are indeed sources of serenity and sweetness, but there is more to the metaphysical story than that, no matter how resistant believers might be to accepting that truth. Scripture is loaded with references to the demonic. In the end, I can only present the events that happened as something to ponder; conjecture versus scientifically proven fact.

The reader is absolutely free to come to their own conclusions based on his or her own perspective, worldview, and beliefs.

As Matt's mother, I share here my own story alongside his, my personal faith journey as well as revealing the unwavering love and devotion I had and will always have towards my son. I am a mom who never gave up on her boy. I suffered right along with him, as did the rest of our family, hanging on with a vise grip to hope while being simultaneously pummeled by the ferocity of the foe. My strong Catholic faith acted like scaffolding throughout, preventing me from sinking into a crumpled pile of despair. I feel richly blessed that God, Who knew that my son's life would be difficult and short, prepared me along the way to survive such a tragedy.

I actually first attempted to write Matthew's story three years ago. I thought it was time, that I could handle it. I completed only five hundred words and had to stop, completely overcome with emotion. But since then God has worked on me, holding me close, building me up, and spurring me on to increase my involvement in devotional practices and prayer. Prompted by the Holy Spirit, I made a renewed commitment to a weekly hour in Adoration and began a new habit of starting each morning with one page of Scripture. I didn't start out the year saying that I would write a book in 2018. But in hindsight I can see how God's influence throughout the year provided me with the inner strength to be able to tell my son's story.

The title, "My 13th Station," refers to the Stations of the Cross inside the perimeter walls of Catholic churches, or as framework for outdoor meditative prayer walks, depicting the way to Calvary the day that Jesus was crucified. The 13th Station is often expressed as an image of the grieving Blessed Mother cradling her deceased son. My personal devotion to this image, initially inspired in 1979, ended up being providential. The number 13 weighs significantly throughout my journey, as does the story of Our Lady of Fatima.

Today, as I begin to write about this immensely difficult chapter in my life, I pray:

Dear Jesus, Blessed Mother,

St. Monica, and St. Anthony

Please guide me as I attempt to write a story that

will inspire belief in God; instruct others about the

threats to our spiritual wellness by spirits unseen;

inform people about addiction and mental health disorders,

and, ultimately, stir hearts and increase faith.

Guide the words that flow from my heart to my mind

and through my fingers as I write this story of a mother's

love for her son. Help me craft something beautiful

that honors God, as well as my son's memory.

Amen

*Disclaimer: I have recreated here in this book events, locales, and conversations from my memories of them, as well as the recollections of others involved in the events I portray. In order to protect anonymity I have changed the names of individuals and places, as well as most identifying characteristics and details such as physical properties, minor details and dates, occupations, and places of residence. Masking and protecting identities has allowed me to tell this true story without reservation.

CHAPTER 1

Life Extinguished

I PASSED THROUGH THE DOOR held open for me and entered the emergency ward, holding my breath and trembling. In my hand, I clutched the Divine Mercy prayer book that I keep in my car in the event I am ever called to someone's deathbed. Surely, I surmised, I won't actually need it today, unless maybe just to pray for his strength to get out of that hospital bed.

Before me, I saw the eight or so cordoned-off bays, side curtains separating one bed from the other, and blue curtains drawn across each bay in various states of closure. Among the sea of blue was one black curtain, hand-picked just for me. This black curtain was my calling card, saying, "Come in, Theresa, your deceased son awaits."

I swept the curtain aside, the volunteer grief aides who had met me in the lobby following my lead as we entered his bay. And there he was, my beautiful son, my precious Matthew.

At the head of the bed stood the priest I had asked my daughter, Sarah, to beckon. He introduced himself as Fr. William. He was young and dressed in the long black formal cassock priests wear for such occasions. At the foot of the bed, slumped over in a chair, sobbing, was Matthew's father, John.

I approached my boy with a sense of ownership. 'Move out of the way, his mother has arrived,' my demeanor seemed to command.

But gazing at his face, with a small breathing tube still inserted in his mouth, I immediately went into a state of shock.

"I'm here now, Matt, you can open your eyes," I announced authoritatively. "I'm here to save you, Matt, I always save you. Open your eyes."

He lay still, unmoving, eyes shut with no hope of ever opening and looking at me again. Those big, brown eyes would never smile at me again, shed tears again, gaze at his daughter's little face again.

As my mind began making the sorrowful connections that he was really gone, my body began to shake violently. My teeth chattered. Through my tears I started loudly commanding him to breathe, to wake up.

"Wake up Matthew!" I shouted. I stomped my feet. I started to sob uncontrollably, convulsing, as it sunk in that this time, on this day, October 23, 2013, I had failed. This time I couldn't save my son.

Joel, one of the two grief volunteers who had been called to our aid, offered me a chair, which was positioned next to Matthew's right hand. I managed to take the two steps to get to the chair, and I sank into it, the prayer booklet lying forgotten across my lap. Instinctively, I picked up his hand. I curled my fingers around his still warm, but unresponsive fingers. I noted the medical tape on his wrist and a tiny incision. I moved as close as I could to his hand, leaning over and kissing it. As I hunched over his hand, my tears rolling over it, I had a sudden impulse to capture this tender moment. I wanted one last image of our hands together, and my phone was there on a vacant chair where I had tossed it upon entering the room.

"Ruth, can you pick up my phone and take a picture of our hands?" I quietly asked.

Ruth was the other volunteer there to help us in this sad, dark moment. She picked up my phone from the chair behind me and snapped a photo that I now consider a treasure. In the shot she captured not just our hands, but also the full length of my son lying in the bed, head to toe. Our last photo together depicts a weeping mother leaning over her dead son while clutching his lifeless hand. This image will forever preserve the punctuation point in the years-long struggle of Matthew's life. It was *my* 13th Station; me, the sorrowful mother with my deceased son stretched out before me.

I managed to choke out some words, using his nickname, Blue, telling him how much I loved him. How I had always believed in him, in his goodness. I had difficulty processing the reality of this crushing blow, as if my brain simply refused to accept that his battle was really over. His beautiful face, his perfect profile, was now at solemn rest. My Little Boy Blue was fast asleep.

After uttering my final goodbyes to Matthew I joined John and Sarah in the lobby to complete the coroner and hospital paperwork. Sarah was so distraught she was not able to endure seeing her deceased brother. John and I had yet to inform our youngest daughter, Emma, who was off at college, that her big brother was gone.

As the reality of the day's events sunk in, I realized, cringing, that I would have to notify his estranged wife, Amanda, to inform her that Matt had not survived this suicide attempt. Their sweet little girl, Grace, no longer had a daddy. I plunked myself down on the curb outside the emergency room to make the call, fighting off nausea. Amanda was devastated, and we both sobbed imagining how this news would impact darling Grace who adored her daddy so.

After completing that very painful phone call to Amanda, I realized I needed to call my mother to notify her of the tragic loss of her beloved grandson. Together we wailed. Eventually, I realized I had to return home to face the scene of the tragedy, so my mom and I said goodbye. I asked both Sarah and John to accompany me, as there was no way I could handle going home alone.

We arrived at the house to find the sheriff deputies and someone from the coroner's office still recording notes at the scene in my garage where Matt's green Jeep still sat. It was a disturbing sight, my home invaded by these officials preparing their routine paperwork about a twenty-five-year-old young man's death—my child!—with their stony, expressionless faces. But just then, as one of the officers turned around, I recognized him as the same officer, Officer Jaime Gonzales, who had assisted Matt and me just seven weeks prior. He walked over to me and, with obvious sincerity, told me that he was the first to arrive on the scene, and how hard he had tried to revive him.

At my request, John entered the house first. I was afraid of what I might find and was too shaken to process any more trauma; my reserves thoroughly depleted. After six years of experiencing my son's pain as if it was my own, I was spent. When John came back out front he said there was nothing noticeably out of place, but said there was a letter to Grace on Matt's desk.

As John left to go home, Sarah and I grabbed each other's hands and tentatively entered the house together. Inside, it felt exceptionally silent and empty, like a tomb.

We climbed the stairs side-by-side, holding on to each other, and then took the short walk down the hall to his old room, which he had inhabited for the last two months. Sarah entered the bedroom first and as she walked through the doorway, I saw it. *It was back.*

> "Be alert and of sound mind. Your enemy the devil prowls around like a roaring lion looking for someone to devour."
> 1 PETER 5:8

CHAPTER 2

The Pietà

AS A TWENTY-THREE-YEAR-OLD college graduate I had successfully assimilated the vastly liberal ideals and secular humanist worldview of my undergraduate and cultural experience. The seventies were marked by aggressive efforts, through the curricula and modern media, to promote abortion, contraception, and freewheeling sexual practices while eschewing the whole concept of biblical truths and God. I was swept up in that misguided thinking and now blanch when re-reading essays I'd penned for my college sociology and psychology classes. In those writings, I earnestly make the case for free love and peace for all, while simultaneously exposing myself as a true Maslow adherent obsessed with self. These cringe-worthy writings reflected the unfortunate fruits of the brainwashing that was just beginning to find a footing among my generation.

I had bailed on my Catholic faith right out of high school, pridefully convincing myself that I didn't need some authority figure telling me what I could or couldn't do with my life. By the time I got through four and a half years of liberal indoctrination in college, I was about as far away from my Catholic heritage as one could be.

My grandfather had always promised me a trip to Europe if I completed my education, so in the summer of 1979, at age twenty-three, I headed off on a twenty-five-day sprint across Europe with my girlfriend, Liza. We would spend eighteen days on a guided tour, and one week on our own flitting about the U.K. on trains.

When the tour brought us to Italy, our itinerary, obviously, included a stop in Rome. As an avowed secular humanist I cared not a lick about any of the Christian highlights of this portion of the trip, but rather preferred to focus on the historical ruins, beautiful scenery, and, of course, shopping at the Spanish Steps. For me, it was all about picking up a cool Gucci wallet. But, alas, the day arrived when we would tour the Vatican.

I approached this leg of the journey with a bad attitude and a sneer on my face, telling myself I would go along with the group, but only reluctantly. Our tour group assembled outside in St. Peter's Square, ready to file in to the compound to tour the basilica, the Sistine Chapel, and the grounds. As we entered St. Peter's Basilica, there, in a chapel to our right, was the most beautiful thing I had ever seen in my life: Michelangelo's famous marble sculpture, the Pietà.

I stood there with tears welling up in my eyes, transfixed by the potent depiction of pure love, grief, beauty, sorrow, and acceptance emanating from the Virgin's face as her deceased Son lay draped across her, this imagery often depicted in the 13th Station of the fourteen Stations of the Cross. Amazingly, this work of art managed to break through my thick wall of stubborn defiance and touch my heart deeply. While standing there in awe of it, the image became etched into the fabric of my heart, unbeknownst to me for many years, like a seedling just waiting for the perfect moment to sprout.

I remember the day like it was yesterday, the moment when I submitted my life to the will of Christ. It was 1995 and I, then just shy of forty years old, was driving home to the East Bay from San Francisco, feeling broken in spirit and out of options. I was extremely unhappy in my marriage, my career had taken a recent hit, and the financial strain of raising three children while living in one of the most expensive regions in the country was causing intense stress. I had just crossed the bridge when I began to cry uncontrollably, hands tightly gripping the steering wheel. Through my tears I suddenly, without warning, implored Jesus to come into my life and do with me what He will. I completely relinquished my own failing agenda for my life and turned it entirely over to God—Thy Will be done. And so, just like that, my whole world changed.

For about a year leading up to that day, I had been feeling pangs of guilt that my children had not been instructed in the Christian faith or had ever attended church. Thankfully, for some reason, I had responded to some innate calling to have them each baptized as babies at our local Catholic church, but it was more out of a sense of duty than any outward approval of the Church of my childhood. But as the years passed, I began to feel, as a parent, that I was neglecting an important part of their development, the teaching of basic Judeo-Christian beliefs regarding right and wrong. Of course, in hindsight, it was clearly the Holy Spirit tapping me on the shoulder.

After my conversion day, I wrestled with where exactly I would find our future faith community. I had residual negative feelings about the Catholic Church, so began to explore the other Christian churches in our area. John, also a fallen-away Catholic, was antipathetic towards any form of structured religion, or any religious or spiritual expression whatsoever, so he was not at all on board with my desire to find a church for the family. This meant it would be up to me to make that important decision.

Over the next year, I dipped my toe into four other churches, including a Presbyterian church, a Calvary Chapel, a Methodist church, and a Lutheran church, none of which resonated with my heart. I found each one to be lacking in some way that I couldn't quite put my finger on, but would dismiss through some superficial flaw. The Presbyterian church, for example, had stark white walls, no statue of Mary, and no Corpus on their cross, so to me it felt sterile; this, despite a great choir, friends who were congregants, and a very popular youth group. The Calvary church practiced a more vocal form of praise and worship that felt foreign to me, just not a fit. The other two churches lacked something, too—what I didn't really know at the time—but I just felt it in my gut that, they, too, were not the place for us.

Having run out of local options, one Sunday I decided that I would give the local Catholic parish a shot. I arrived at the 11:00 a.m. Mass not knowing what to expect. Many liturgical changes had been woven into the Mass since I was an eighteen-year-old so I decided to play it safe and sit in the very back pew so no one would notice that I had no clue what to do or say during the liturgy. And then the craziest thing happened.

From the time the priest made the sign of the Cross, until he recessed out of the church an hour later, I wept. I wept and wept and wept. I didn't attempt to go up to receive Holy Communion, having somewhere deep in my memory been taught that I would first need a good confession before taking that step. Aha! Bingo! It was the *Eucharist* that was missing at the other churches I had visited.

I continued to wipe away tears, soaking the one single tissue I had in my purse, and found myself longing for the day I could again receive the Eucharist. Sitting there, I prayed with my whole heart that Jesus would forgive my sins. I prayed that I wished I could rewind the tape of my life and start over, to live a life that would be more pleasing to Him. Departing the church that day, I knew I was home.

After Mass I felt emotionally spent with only one thought guiding me as I drove home, how soon could I enroll the kids in the faith formation class (C.C.D., as we once called it)? I signed them up the very next day, and for the next two years Sarah and Matthew prepared to receive the sacrament of Holy Communion.

A close friend of mine, Jo, encouraged me to go make a good confession at the Institute of Christ the King in San Jose where the priests take such things extremely seriously and are methodical in helping you examine your conscience and identify past mortal sins. Because I had twenty-two years worth of muck to review, my confession lasted about thirty minutes—a deeply emotional and exhausting experience. I felt ashamed going through the litany of sins I had committed over those two decades. But when that priest, in Latin, pronounced the absolution of my sins, his words gave me such comfort that I nearly burst into tears. I felt about ten pounds lighter. Emotionally spent, I drove up to visit my mom and shared with her my re-initiation back into the state of grace.

I came back to the Church with fervor. I devoured books about church teachings, the lives of the saints, church history, and began to read the Bible. I couldn't learn fast enough, and usually had three or four books going at once, parked in various parts of the house. I knew that my husband was appalled to witness me voraciously reading such books. He had married an agnostic, fallen-away Catholic and must have wondered, who *was* this strange person? Thankfully, he did not object to our kids being enrolled in faith formation class or proceeding with the sacraments, and I was grateful for that.

Being an introspective person, I had been an avid fan of journaling for years. There is something so therapeutic about getting stuff out of one's head and on to paper. From 1997 on, after returning to the Church, I methodically chronicled my faith journey through journaling, the entries becoming increasingly deep and substantive as time went on.

One evening, while relaxing in a bubble bath on an ordinary summer evening in 1999, I was suddenly inspired to discover Eucharistic Adoration. That day my journal entry read:

> **7/18/99:** At 8:15 p.m. I had a compelling thought, like a directive, to go to the Adoration chapel at our parish, even though I had never been inside that little chapel before. Responding to this unusual prompt, I got out of the tub and found [daughter] Sarah [age 13] in her room and asked if she would go with me. She agreed, so off we went to the church to spend about an hour in the presence of Jesus exposed on the altar.

Thus began my love affair with Jesus, visiting Him every Wednesday from 5:00-6:00 p.m. for the next six years. Over this time period, I filled up several journals, jotting down raw emotions, musings, petitions, contrition, summaries of my children at various points in time, and sheer praise and thanksgiving as I progressed in my relationship with Jesus.

Along with my growing devotion to Christ came a strong sense of duty to make sure that I attend Mass every Sunday. I admit, this didn't happen immediately, but developed as I became more educated about the Eucharist and the Mass itself. This meant that even when we were out of town on vacation, I would seek out the local Catholic church and attend Mass. Invariably, whenever I entered a Catholic church I had never been to before, I felt compelled to seek out their "13th Station" from the Stations of the Cross that adorn the interiors of most Catholic churches. For some unknown reason, I seemed to be obsessed with the sorrowful imagery of that Station.

Because this practice involved churches I would attend or visit while on a trip somewhere, I always made sure to snap a photo (back then with a camera) of each of these 13th Stations. As a result, I have literally dozens of images taken within church interiors in various countries, as well as different states, and assorted California missions I have visited since my conversion back to the faith. Over the years, each time I ordered my vacation prints I would pluck the photo of the 13th Station out of the packet and add it to a little collection kept in an envelope that I still have to this day. In recent years, having switched to digital photography, the newer 13th Station photos I've snapped are saved in a file on my hard drive.

Why the compulsion to locate and document this image of the Blessed Mother with her deceased Son in every church I have visited since 1997? I believe it is an outward reflection of how deeply I was affected in viewing the Pietà in Rome all those many years ago as a then a worldly, cynical, agnostic young adult. I had become strangely drawn to this image of a mother's unimaginable pain in losing her precious Son. In hindsight, I now see that my attraction to it was prophetic.

CHAPTER 3

Enter Matthew

WHEN BLESSED WITH MY FIRST CHILD, a daughter, in 1986, I quickly learned what life was all about. When Sarah was just 9½ weeks in utero, I had my first ultrasound. My heart exploded when I viewed the image of a fully formed little baby, legs kicking and heart beating, measuring just over an inch in length. Seeing a glimpse of my daughter with all ten fingers and toes residing inside my womb was literally the turning point in my life. At that instant, I changed. I became a mother. That is a *baby*!

Although, during the early years of motherhood, from 1986 until my conversion in 1995, my secular worldview had stubbornly persisted, something deep inside was definitely shifting. As a mother, I now saw the world through different eyes. The degenerate things in our culture that I had once laughed off, or worse, embraced, suddenly seemed appalling to me. It was a slow, simmering crockpot-like process that would take nearly ten years to coagulate into a renewed version of myself that God was methodically and patiently crafting.

Because we were new parents trying to manage the many responsibilities and financial obligations related to childrearing, John and I were fine with waiting a few years before having a second child. That plan allowed us to stabilize financially and be able to enjoy quality time with our adorable daughter. What a shock it was to learn, soon after Sarah's first birthday, that baby number two was on the way, far ahead of schedule. Well, this certainly threw a monkey wrench into our perfect plan. Ha! God has such a way of humbling His creatures. Not only was this second child blowing up our timetable, but an additional layer of angst was added when I went into labor almost six weeks before my due date.

On that cold, stormy February night in 1988, defying all attempts by the doctor to stop the labor, our beautiful son entered the world just after midnight. We were torn between two boy names, so had decided to just wait and see which name would best suit the baby once we met him, should it be a boy. Matthew it was. He was shriveled and beet red, with various health concerns due to being early, so he was swept away immediately to head to the neonatal intensive care unit (NICU). This broke my heart. The woman I shared a room with had her baby alongside her, yet there I was, lying empty-handed in my bed.

Once they had run some tests and stabilized his glucose they allowed me to go to the NICU to hold my baby boy, after scrubbing up like a surgeon. There was my infant son, lying in his incubator with various pads and wires attached to his little body to monitor his body functions. It seemed surreal, seeing him lying in that Plexiglas box looking so fragile and alone.

The nurse took Matthew out of the incubator and gently handed him to me. As long as I live, I will never forget the overwhelming love I felt for my baby boy in that moment, accompanied by an inexplicable sense of foreboding, a fear that something bad would happen to him. In an instant, this precious baby, who resembled a wrinkled little old man at the time, grabbed on to my heart and never let go.

Only years later, after I had returned to church and began studying Scripture and praying the rosary, did the significance of his birth date, February 2nd, gain deeper meaning. The Church celebrates

MY 13th STATION

February 2nd as the Presentation of the Child Jesus, and, included in that event, Simeon's prophecy. Simeon was the devout man at the Temple who would fulfill the requirements of the Law of Moses and formally present the child to the Lord God. Simeon approached the Blessed Mother who was cradling baby Jesus in her arms and spoke these words:

> "Behold, this child is set for the ruin, and for
> the resurrection of many in Israel,
> and for a sign that shall be contradicted; and
> *thy own soul a sword shall pierce,*
> that out of many hearts thoughts may be revealed."
> LUKE 2: 34-35

Twenty-five years after Matt's birth, those words, "Thy own soul a sword shall pierce," and the Virgin's sorrowful face as depicted in the 13th Station, would coalesce to represent, in a loosely figurative way, my own maternal agony.

Raising Matt was easy. He was at once mellow, funny, thoughtful, loving, and all boy. He was the kind of kid you never had to ask twice, always compliant and respectful. Mostly, Matt was kind. He was the little boy who, on the way to school, veered off the sidewalk and up the bordering hill to pick some bright yellow daisies to take to his first grade teacher. These kinds of sweet and thoughtful gestures came naturally to him. He was every parent's dream child.

In 1996, when Matt was in second grade, his teacher asked the kids to write a little note about themselves, a time capsule that was not to be opened until 2004 when they'd be sophomores in high school. Long forgotten and still sealed, I came upon the envelope one day in 2011 in a tub of mementoes, several years past that 2004 date. Matt lived out of state at the time, so I asked him if I could open it. He said, "Sure," so I did. Here is what he had written all those years ago:

> Dear Self,
> I hope you can still play baseball and I hope you are on the Cincinnati Reds [he draws logo]. I hope you are still naughty, muscular, and athletic. I wonder if you will still like baseball and animals.

The rest of the page was dominated by a his childlike self-portrait on the pitcher's mound winding up for a toss under a big, oversized sun. By the time I opened this in 2011, his life was in complete disarray, making it very sad to see how hopeful and positive he was at age seven, and to recall just how much he loved baseball even at that young age.

And, yes, he did love animals. One day when Matt was nine, he and I were taking a walk down our street. He spotted a common garter snake on a neighbor's front lawn and said he wanted to keep it for a pet. Ugh, really? A *snake?* He already had a pet rat, but what the heck, he's a boy and he wants a pet snake.

We went back to the house and grabbed a box from the garage and rounded up the snake. After providing a bed of grass, twigs, and leaves, Matt asked me what to feed it. I had no idea, so off we went to the local pet store to ask them. The pet store employee blithely told us we could feed the snake either baby mice or goldfish. Well, Matt couldn't bear the idea of feeding the snake mice because they were too similar to his pet rat, so he opted for a bag of twelve goldfish.

When we returned home, he approached the snake holding the bag full of fish, preparing to net one to feed to the snake. He hesitated.

Finally, he said, "Mom, let's just let the snake go, okay? But, can I get a tank for the fish?"

So with that we freed the snake and headed back to the pet store to buy the supplies we would need for a dozen pet goldfish. Matthew had a big, squishy heart.

God blessed us with happy, delightful children. Each of our three children had their own unique personality and gifts. Raising them will always be the most meaningful thing I have ever done with my life. I often wrote about the kids in my journals during my Adoration hour. In the stillness of that little chapel, I could really ponder my love for them, and would note the little things about each of them that I found so endearing. One day in 1998 I wrote short summaries about my children. Here is what I wrote about my then ten-year-old son:

> **11/21/98:** Matthew warms my heart. He is unique and wonderful. He is masculine and athletic, but also sensitive and kind. He is such a GOOD guy. He is levelheaded, but also fun. He is popular and I think this friends look up to him. Sometimes my love for him overwhelms me. Since the first time I held him I felt two things, 1) that he is special in some way and, 2) a fear that something will happen to him. I still feel these two emotions, although I don't yet understand why.

One of my favorite memories of Matthew and I together was a road trip we took that same year. I often traveled out of state for business and enjoyed taking one of my kids along with me when I could. These three-day journeys gave me special alone time with one child at a time, something that is next to impossible to grab during the commotion of daily life. On this trip to neighboring Nevada, Matt and

I enjoyed listening to my favorite oldies, like Credence Clearwater Revival, the Eagles, the Beatles, and a great classic rock station we found along the way. While flipping around on the radio dial we came across a pop station that was playing Seal's current hit song, "Kissed by a Rose." We both already loved that song, but somehow when listening to it together on that road trip, just the two of us captive in a car motoring across the desert, that song forever became associated with my son. To this day, I place a single red rose on his grave when I visit.

The bond between us was incredibly strong. Matthew and I were wired much the same, both of us wearing our hearts on our sleeves, with generous, sentimental, open, and loving natures. He rarely ever elicited parental wrath; Matthew was simply a joy. I kept a model of a red '65 Mustang on the bookcase next to my bed; the kids knew it was my dream car, and still is. One day, when Matt was about twelve, he was in my room chatting with me. He pointed at the model car and stated, "Someday I am gonna buy you one." I knew in my heart that he sincerely intended to do that for me some day.

As a boy, Matt would summon me to come out front to witness his tricks on his new GT BMX bike, and other times ask me to join him and his buddies in the adjacent hills where they performed jumps on their bikes. It was obvious to me how much it meant to Matthew that I was interested and involved in the activities he loved. He clearly sought my approval and admiration. After doing a trick, he would immediately turn to me, then light up when he saw me smile or give a thumbs up.

Matthew was an outstanding baseball player. He played pitcher and shortstop in Little League, and made All-Stars three times. His dad was instrumental in teaching Matt the proper fundamentals, and always coached the All-Star teams. John spent many an hour playing catch with Matt out in the street and pitching to him for batting practice at the nearby middle school's ball field. Between his dad's instruction and, later, private lessons with a professional baseball player, his mechanics were smooth and nearly flawless. In high school he played Junior Varsity as a freshman, and was brought up to Varsity in his sophomore year.

Matt acquired a passion for skateboarding back when he was about thirteen, and would often ask me to take him and his friends to the local skate park. There I would stand with clenched jaw and fists as I watched him jump off stairways and do other crazy tricks, sometimes crash landing. He revered skater Jamie Thomas and regularly collected skate videos to study and learn tricks from. Sometimes I would hang out with Matt and watch the skate videos with him. I have poignant memories of that, sitting side by side with my son watching skate videos together and enjoying the classic rock that accompanied the skater's tricks.

His dad and I were not totally on board with his love for skateboarding, however, somewhat worried that the edgy culture that surrounded skate might be a bad influence. I remember finding the graphics on the skate decks, clothing, and marketing materials decidedly worrisome, with some brands employing gothic symbols and imagery. But his feelings about skateboarding were intense and unshakable, regardless of how we felt about it, so John and I tentatively supported his passion. Matt's favorite birthday parties as a young teen were the trips to the big skate park that his dad would haul him and his friends to.

All through high school Matthew was just a really great kid. He was responsible and never gave us any reason to worry. He excelled at his chosen sport. He did well academically, with an aptitude for math and science. He was well liked in school, developing friendships that he cultivated and maintained for the rest of his life. Matt was fun, with a quick chuckle and sense of innocent mischief about him. Mostly, though, Matthew was a gentle soul who formed tight bonds with the people he loved, cleaving wholeheartedly to friends and family members.

As is common with teens, I was aware that he and his friends, who were at our house so often they were like additional sons to me, occasionally dabbled in alcohol consumption, starting in their junior year of high school. The occasions were few, but did increase by the end of their senior year, as parties became the primary venue for socializing. Thankfully, the demands of baseball kept the boys in line for the most part and there were never any issues related to alcohol abuse. The times I suspected they were drinking inspired my occasional mom-lectures, but the boys never raised any unusual red flags to cause serious concern. Matt and his friends were good kids.

When Sarah turned eighteen in 2004, I decided to start a tradition for my kids and write them each a personal letter on their eighteenth birthdays. In 2006, it was Matt's turn to get the letter. Here is what I wrote to him:

Dear Matthew,

Today you turn eighteen—a huge milestone for both you and me. I want to take a few minutes to express my feelings to you.

When I look at you, now a grown man, I still see the little guy who excitedly put on the Batman cape that I'd sewed him. In your eyes I still see a sweet, sensitive soul, and it warms my heart.

In all those eighteen years I think I've been mad at you maybe five times. You were a joy to raise, a great kid. Your mellow nature makes you easy to be around—a good buffer between your two sisters. I have always loved being with you. I have nice memories of driving out to Nevada with you and playing music on the radio really loud. Certain songs still remind me of that trip with you.

I know you may doubt the value in the four years we homeschooled, but I sure don't. To me, those were the best years of my life. I got to spend all that time teaching you, loving you, forming your character, and truly enjoying you. I got to experience the essence of motherhood in those years—mainly showing you the path to Heaven. There is no more important job for a mom.

I pray that you stay strong in your convictions, always seeking to please God above anyone else. I hope that when you have questions and doubts that you will come to me for guidance. There is nothing on earth that you cannot talk to me about. I will always be here for you. I will always be honest and truthful with you, and I will always be your biggest fan.

From that first stormy night when you came into this world, all through these eighteen wonderful years, I have loved you with all my heart, my precious son.
Love,
Mom

CHAPTER 4

The New House

IN THE FALL OF 1991, when Sarah was five and Matt was three, I was enjoying that wonderful little window of time when toddlers have evolved into cool little kids who are much more self-reliant. I envisioned going back to my career and having some more free time to pursue interests now that the kids were not as needy. I would join a gym and paint my toenails. I would take up photography and redecorate the master bedroom. I had my girl, my boy, a neat little family of four that barely squeezed into the small two-bedroom home we owned in a quaint neighborhood that we loved. Life was good.

Alas! Along comes baby number three to take a torch to the master plan yet again! Oh, let me tell you, I sobbed. I grieved. I mourned for the loss of that now vaporized reemergence-of-me I had set my sights on. Once I processed this new reality and settled down a bit, the next question became: Where the heck will we even put this child, the garage? So, the wheels were set in motion to put our charming little two-bedroom on the market and search for a nice, new roomy home for our growing family.

On the opposite side of town, a new subdivision was going up in a quiet area that rested at the base of the foothills. The Mediterranean styling was de rigueur for the early nineties, uninspiring beige stucco cookie cutter homes that would serve our needs just fine. The homes were close to schools and were tucked into a thriving family community. We sold our little place quickly and soon found ourselves leafing through escrow papers and closing the deal.

What's nice about buying a new home is that all the neighbors are in lockstep, decorating the interiors, designing and installing the landscaping, and making new friendships as we shared ideas about things like window treatments and palm tree selections. The kids were happy to find new playmates right away on our street, Meadow Lane, and soon there were birthday parties and backyard barbeques providing opportunities for the neighbors to get to know each other better.

On one side of our house lived a nice young couple that had purchased the large floor plan in anticipation of starting their family. On the opposite side of our home lived a couple, in their mid-thirties, who chose to primarily stay to themselves, not socializing with the neighbors at all. The husband, Brian, was quiet and reserved and seemed pleasant, but the wife, Andrea, had a strange off-putting personality. The first thing I noticed about her was the ebony color of her eyes, just a shade off of black. She was openly hostile towards children, even stating once that she "hates" kids. When I heard her say that I wondered to myself, why on earth would they have purchased a house in a suburban neighborhood chock full of children? She had a detached, yet angry, demeanor that made us uncomfortable, so we were grateful that she kept to herself. Both she and her husband traveled extensively for work, which was fine with me.

One day, while I was sitting on the sofa against the living room front window, reading and simultaneously keeping my eye on my two oldest kids playing on the driveway, I spotted Andrea out watering the small palm tree in the front corner of her yard. This tranquil scene was suddenly disrupted when I heard her shout, and when I turned to look at her I witnessed her sticking out her tongue at my two little kids! Who does that? But, I guess just the sight of them out there playing irritated her. I decided not to confront her, but instead just called the kids into the house to ask why she yelled at them. The kids, who were six and four years old, had absolutely no idea why "the mean lady" was mad at them.

Meanwhile, during that first year in the new house, the neighbors who lived on the opposite side of Andrea and Brian, the Petersons, had their own run-ins with her. She apparently hated dogs, too, and one day had found some dog droppings on her front lawn. She made the leap that it must have been left there by the Peterson's dog, although how she came to that assumption I have no idea. There are myriad dogs in the neighborhood and any one of them could have been the guilty party. That day, when the mother, Suzanne Peterson, opened her front door to get the mail she was greeted with dog feces smeared across her door.

Andrea was absolutely livid a few months later, when we constructed a small playhouse in a niche tucked into the side yard of our backyard. This was a small playhouse, the kit type you buy at Home Depot, with a floor plan that measured all of five feet square. You would have thought we built a three-story tower based on this neighbor's reaction. She was so incensed, spewing her fury that we had built a horrible eyesore, that she even filed a complaint with the homeowners association. To her chagrin, the representative pulled up our approved backyard design plans, showing a space labeled "future playhouse," which Andrea had signed off on.

By this point, the local kids knew to steer clear of Andrea, as her foul temper had become a matter of public knowledge on the street. The adults just ignored her whenever possible, knowing that being friendly with her was just a wasted effort.

One day in early 1994, the kids were all playing ball out in the street when at some point the ball ended up rolling onto Andrea and Brian's lawn. Six-year-old Noah Nichols, who lived four doors up and had become my son's best friend, walked over to retrieve the ball from her lawn, but not quickly enough to avoid Andrea's wrath. She was standing in her garage when she witnessed the ball land on her lawn and bolted out to yell at poor Noah as he attempted to grab his ball. Because her shrill voice caused me to come to the window, I saw the altercation and wondered what the kids could have possibly done to set her off. The boys then headed up the street to Noah's house, a decidedly safer place to play.

Within five minutes my attention was again directed to the window by a loud ruckus happening out front. Noah had apparently informed his mother of what had just occurred in front of the "mean lady's" house. Linda Nichols was a fiery, passionate, moody woman, and a fierce protector of her three children. I heard Linda using some choice language while yelling at Andrea, loudly threatening to call the police on her if she ever verbally abuses her child again. I smiled. Good—someone needs to stand up to that awful woman, I thought.

It was a beautiful afternoon in June 1994. One of those perfect bay area days where sunshine seems to take on an iridescent quality, sparkling across the landscape and bringing everything it touches to new, radiant life. Other than the unusually lovely weather, it was just a non-descript day. My usual afternoon routine was to push the stroller containing my two-year old daughter a few blocks to the local elementary school to claim brother, Matt, from his first grade classroom. On our way back home, as we approached eyesight of our house, I noticed someone standing on our driveway. It was Steve Nichols, Noah's dad, seemingly agitated and yelling something toward me that I couldn't make out. Sensing urgency, I began to run with the stroller, Matthew jogging alongside us.

"She did it! She did it!" Steve hollered frantically while pointing toward his home up the street. He was holding his young daughter's hand, and Noah stood bewildered at Steve's side.

"Steve," I nervously uttered, "what are you talking about?"

"She killed herself, go see, she killed herself," he fervidly stated, "Go see, she's in the bedroom."

"What? no way," I said, "Take the kids into my house. I will be right back," and as he ushered the four children into my house, I began to march up the street to the Nichols' house.

I was always very comfortable in the Nichols' home, as I was in and out of it several times a week retrieving Matt for dinnertime. The first thing I noticed when I entered their home, however, was that is was an utter mess. This was surprising, as Linda was a meticulous housekeeper with never a thing out of place, even with three little kids residing there. That day, seeing the chaos—piles of laundry on the couch, toys strewn everywhere, dirty dishes on the table—I knew immediately something was very wrong.

The house was eerily quiet. I began ascending the steps to the second level, my breathing slow and heavy and my feet feeling like I was wearing lead boots. Slowly, methodically, I climbed the stairs and turned to the master bedroom, expecting to find Linda passed out on the bed with a bottle of pills on the nightstand, you know, one of those attempts for attention you read about. When I got through the bedroom door, I saw no one on the bed. No pill bottle, no sign of Linda.

Suddenly, spotting the bathtub full of water just around the corner on the right, I shuddered. As I slowly, tentatively approached I could see that, although the tub was full of water and there was a razor sitting on the ledge, Linda was not in the tub either. While standing there next to the tub an overwhelming feeling of dread came over me. I noticed some specks of something at my feet, but of what I did not know. In the next instant my peripheral vision caught a glimpse of Linda's legs lying on the floor in the walk-in closet directly to my left.

I turned just enough to see her torso. With an eerie calm, I remember standing there, mentally willing her abdomen to rise and fall. God had protected me from the horror of what had happened, as the self-inflicted gunshot had caused Linda to fall back, her head covered by the clothes hanging on the lower rod and not visible to me. Thankfully, I could only see her from the collarbone down, a trickle of blood descending down her chest. I immediately connected the dots and realized that the small bits on the carpet were fragments of brain tissue. Fighting the urge to vomit, my heart pounding violently, I fled the house as fast as possible, detouring to another neighbor friend's house for help.

Banging on Debbie Miller's door, I yelled, "Debbie, help, help! Debbie, please open the door!"

She answered the door, took one look at my face, and knew something horrific had happened on our quiet little suburban street. As I relayed to her what I had witnessed across the street I was hyperventilating and shaking, completely traumatized.

I asked Debbie to please come back to my house with me, as I knew I could not face those children alone after just seeing their dead mother. Debbie and I proceeded to cross the street to my house. After calling my husband to tell him what had happened, and asking him to get home as soon as possible, I was somehow given the grace I needed to, with Debbie's help, make peanut butter and jelly sandwiches for the four kids while Steve returned to his house to meet the coroner and sheriff. For the next forty-five minutes Debbie and I somehow managed to put up a false front for the children, getting them involved with games and putting on a Disney movie until Steve's parents arrived to retrieve their two youngest grandchildren before picking up their older brother at school.

The suicide traumatized us all. Our children had played together at each other's homes, and the families had enjoyed birthday parties, cul-de-sac potlucks, attended school events together, and generally bonded over these past two years. For three nights I was unable to pass by my own closet, so shaken was I. For a year, I couldn't even glance toward the Nichols house. Our serene little Meadow Lane now had an ugly scar, and it was incomprehensible to us why Linda would have taken such a drastic step. Yes, there was marital discord. Yes, she had a history of mood swings and depression. Yes, she had even once, years ago, made a half-hearted suicide attempt by gulping down a few pills in a cry for attention. But this? This violent death was just unfathomable, that she had shot herself dead leaving three beautiful children and a good man behind.

The lingering shock of the suicide impacted all of us in some way or another. I was jumpy, and for a year felt the fight or flight response rise up in me spontaneously whenever something triggered a memory of that day. Steve decided to gut and remodel the bedroom so the family could remain in the home. He felt it was important to ensure stability for his children, and we were very grateful they wouldn't be moving away, especially Matthew. We attempted to recapture the fun vibe we had cultivated on the street during our first couple years living there, but things were just never quite the same.

Lindsey Miller, Debbie and Jason's youngest child, was a year younger than Sarah. Sarah, Ashley Peterson, and Lindsey Miller, all roughly the same age, played together often, taking turns hanging out at each other's homes, skating in the cul de sac, holding their Hummingbird Club meetings in the playhouse, or making crafts in our garage. For the most part, the girls were a compatible threesome. Lindsey was a quiet, passive kid who kind of hung back.

About a year before the suicide, I remember being startled hearing a very loud commotion coming from Lindsey's open bedroom window across the street. It took me a few seconds to realize that what I was hearing was a raging tantrum. Not your normal run of the mill six-year-old outburst, but a full-on blast of venomous anger being directed at her mother, Debbie. I remember being really flummoxed in hearing this because Lindsey was such a mellow, soft-spoken girl.

These highly charged emotional outbursts happened with some regularity. Once, confiding in us neighbor moms over a bottle of wine, Debbie asked if we had ever heard the commotion coming from their house. Well, I couldn't lie, so I told her yes, in the warm weather when her window is open I had heard several of these mega-tantrums. Debbie was obviously embarrassed, and shared that at one point she literally had to crawl on top of her daughter to settle her down, even being tempted to choke her to quiet the noise and get some control over her daughter. She admitted that she didn't know what to do. Apparently, her husband, Jason, was battling depression and had taken to drinking gin every evening until he passed out in his recliner, so she felt totally alone in trying to parent Lindsey through these intense rages. She made an off-the-cuff comment that when Lindsey was in the midst of these events she looked like she was possessed.

One day in 1995, I was driving home toward my house when I spotted a moving van on Andrea and Brian's driveway. As I approached my home I noticed Suzanne Peterson standing with Brian next to the moving van, so after parking my car I walked next door to get the scoop. I asked Brian if someone was moving in, and he responded, no, that he was actually moving out.

Suzanne said, "Brian, tell her what you just told me."

Brian looked at me and said, "Well, I am actually afraid for my life."

He did not elaborate and Suzanne and I both felt a little awkward. The scene was quite surreal, and Suzanne and I gave each other a sideways glance, wordlessly communicating our own safety concerns about this seemingly emotionally unbalanced woman. Unfortunately, the wrong person was leaving the neighborhood.

Later, my husband also stopped by and asked Brian if he had a contact number where he could reach him if needed. He proceeded to write down a phone number, stating that he would be staying with a friend in Sausalito and under no circumstances should he give this information to Andrea, who was out of town on business at the time. Basically the gist was that Brian was fleeing his marriage while his wife was not around in order to avoid her possibly inflicting some type of harm on him.

"What's burning?" asked Sarah, now nine years old, in 1995.

We walked around the house trying to locate where the smell of something burning was coming from. It was a school day, and this strange smoky smell greeted us early in the morning, around 6:00 a.m. while we were all in the process of getting ready for the day. The smell of smoke wafted through our open windows and seemed to be emanating from Andrea's property. From my upstairs bedroom window I could see smoke rising from the far right corner of her backyard. My first thought was, who burns their mail in this day and age? But my next thought was, hey, that doesn't really smell like paper burning. The smoke had an acrid odor, something I couldn't put my finger on. She most definitely was not barbequing at that hour, so what the heck was she burning in her backyard?

This was only the beginning of what would become years of burning smells arising from Andrea's backyard. She seemed to have designated that corner of the property as a pyre of some sort, where she regularly burned things. Sometimes the smoke did smell like burning paper, but other times it had an indescribable scent. Whichever the case, the fact that this bizarre woman was burning items in her yard, versus inside her wood-burning fireplace, was beyond comprehension. To this day, my daughters and the Peterson girls all have very clear memories of the strange burning smells from the neighbor's yard, as evidenced by their recent 2018 recollections.

> *Sarah (Anthony) Donahue, age 32*
> I remember always smelling things burning from her yard. Sometimes it smelled like paper, and sometimes it just smelled meat-ish, but not like beef, chicken, or pork ... something strange.
>
> *Bethany (Peterson) Marquez, age 28*
> I remember that the new owners found a pile of burnt papers in the corner of her planter.
>
> *Ashley (Peterson) Walters, age 31*
> We always thought it strange when she [Andrea] would incinerate her pruned vegetation instead of just using the green waste receptacle, especially when it smelled like some type of meat.
>
> *Emma Anthony, age 26*
> Bethany and I snuck back into the yard once when the house was sold, before the new owners moved in. We found a pile of burned papers in the back planter.

The new owner, Lauren Mitchell, relates discovering the buried remnants of burned papers in the planter upon taking possession of the property as well.

Lauren Mitchell, July 2018
My husband found a thick pile of buried burnt papers in the planter along the back wall of the yard.

During about an eighteen month period starting in 1997, a series of strange events occurred in our house, although each one was separated by several months. One Sunday, after returning from a four-day mini-vacation to Lake Tahoe, we entered the house to begin the unpacking process, each of us bringing in a bag or two from the car. For some reason, I always seemed to be the first person to head upstairs with luggage in hand. As I ascended the stairs towards the landing at the second floor there was a strong, putrid smell that I attributed to a dead rat. The neighborhood did have rat issues every so many years, so that day when I smelled the disgusting odor of a decomposing rat I cringed to think of the dead rodent inside the wall at the top of the stairs. Then, off I would go to begin the unpacking and laundry routine that took my mind off it.

It may have been six or eight months later that, again, we were returning home from a long weekend in Tahoe. As I got to the top of the stairs, I was greeted with that same disgusting scent of a dead, rotting rat apparently stuck inside the wall. Since it had been several months since the last episode, enough time had passed that I didn't make any kind of mental connection between the two events. Again, I got distracted by all the commotion of unpacking after a family trip and didn't give it another thought.

Approximately six months later, we came home from yet another three-day trip only to encounter the same awful odor at the top of the stairs. How could this be happening again, I wondered? Why always when we returned home, and always in the same spot? It was perplexing enough that I paid closer attention that time, noticing that within a couple of minutes the strong stench had suddenly disappeared. In fact, I now realized that in all three of these "dead rat" events, the odor had disappeared soon after we had entered the home.

Later that day I walked down to Suzanne's house to share with her my experience with the unnerving dead rat smell at the top of my stairs. She, too, had numerous concerning events to share, such as hearing sounds upstairs when the whole family was downstairs, and the side door to the garage shaking and rattling late at night, with no sign of wind or earthquake to cause the movement. As both of us were Christians, we decided to take proactive measures to rid our homes of any possible dark spirits.

I filled a bottle with holy water from the local Catholic church and then splashed it all through my house, dousing windows, corners, and doorways while casting out any demonic beings in the name of Jesus Christ . . . loudly. I literally felt like I was on a mission to save my family, as crazy as that sounds.

CHAPTER 5

The Petersons

BY 1997 THE PETERSON FAMILY HOME was like my daughters' second home, as our girls had become close friends over the five years as neighbors. I always felt perfectly comfortable in their house, as they did in ours. The girls spent copious amounts of time together, my youngest, Emma, hanging out with their youngest daughter, Bethany, and my oldest, Sarah, close friends with their oldest, Ashley. Theirs was a Christian home, with Scripture verses taped to the wall in the kitchen nook and Christian music playing softly in the background whenever I visited. Suzanne spearheaded the spiritual upbringing of the kids, as Dave was not really all that religiously oriented. He was a hard-working man, with his own construction company, who might enjoy a beer or two after a long day's work. Everyone liked Dave; he was a man's man, a friendly, likeable guy. Suzanne didn't imbibe at all; alcohol just was not her thing. She was a devoted daughter of Christ who spoke the Word with passion and did her best to cultivate a godly home, including being a brave, dedicated homeschool mom.

In 1997, it became apparent that there was strife in the Peterson home. At first I sensed a change in Suzanne's usual sunny demeanor, with a newly acquired look of worry on her face and a crease in her brow. She had seemed preoccupied the last few times I had visited.

Eventually, she came over to my house to visit and, weeping, shared that her husband had, out of the blue, become a drug addict. It made no sense. Why would this family man in his mid-forties, with a beautiful wife and two lovely daughters, suddenly succumb to a crack cocaine addiction? It made no sense.

But the sad reality was that he was at the mercy of the drug and it was resulting in serious financial and emotional consequences at home. Suzanne said she had been praying nonstop for Dave to snap out of it, to come to his senses before any lasting damage was done. But Dave, initially at least, was not at all interested in going into treatment for the addiction. He was still too beholden to his drug of choice to consider giving it up. Suzanne seriously contemplated leaving him, wanting to shield their daughters from the devastating impact of drug addiction.

Suzanne continued praying for her husband to go into rehab, to throw off the addiction and right his relationship with God. It was Christmas time and there was no money for gifts. In fact, she confided that they were in default on their mortgage, with a good possibility of losing their home. I had just closed one of my retail stores, so I told Suzanne to come over and select some items from my inventory to give as gifts, since she was in such bad straights. She was immensely grateful, and took me up on my offer.

One day, Suzanne appeared at my door looking shaken. She had come over to share with me what her daughter, Ashley, then twelve years old, had experienced the night before. This riveting account, which I will never forget, is best told in Ashley's own words, based on her recollections shared with me this year, nearly twenty years after it happened. Her words today align exactly with the notations I made after hearing her mother's account back in 1998 when this disturbing event occurred.

MY 13th STATION

Ashley (Peterson) Walters, age 31, 2018
I know my mom tried to shelter us kids as much as she could from our dad's addiction to drugs, so there was a lot I was naïve about until I was much older . . . but his lifestyle began to bring so much spiritual darkness into our home it in some way affected each of us. I will never forget that night when it all became so real. The night I knew without a doubt that I wasn't crazy and that everything I feared to be true was waging war on our family. It was late and everyone in the house was asleep—except my dad. From what I understand now, it wasn't uncommon for him to go downstairs and into the garage late at night to get high. He would often stop in the kitchen for a glass of milk or a quick snack before heading back up to bed to try to sleep it off.

    I remember waking up that night and hearing him in the kitchen. I wasn't startled or scared as it was a familiar series of sounds. My mom was already in my bed from an earlier request to lie with me until I fell asleep, and as she often did, she'd fallen asleep in the process. My bed was situated to have me facing my bedroom doorway, which gave me a view all the way down the hall to the top of the staircase and then down a little further to my parents' room. I could hear him slowly stomping his way back up the stairs like he had a hundred times before. It wasn't until he was nearly to the top, just as his head came into view, that my heart stopped.

    As he continued up the stairs and my eyes adjusted to what they almost couldn't believe they were seeing, I couldn't move—I became paralyzed with fear. Part of me wanted to yell out to my dad and hope the dark shadow vanished from behind him, but somehow I knew that wouldn't be enough. The other part of me was terrified that whatever was enveloping him would come after me if I acknowledged it.

My chest pounded so hard I was afraid anyone in the house could hear it! I lie there still as I watched my dad turn the corner and slowly head toward his room. What I saw was nothing I could have dreamed up in my wildest imagination. My dad was completely surrounded by a demon. Its eerie shape lurched over him from about mid-waist to clear over his head. It hunched over him like a beastly robe and ran completely down the backside of his body, trailing on the floor behind him like the train of a veil. It's translucence allowed me to fully see my dad, yet I remember many details reminiscent of a creature from what you would see in a horror movie. After he walked out of view into his dark room, I lie there frozen, praying, because I knew my dad's life depended on it. Part of me wondered if my dad would still be alive the next morning, but as he settled into sleep and his loud snores echoed back down the hallway, I started to breath again. I didn't hesitate to tell my mom in the morning what I had seen, and to my surprise she confirmed what I hoped was a nightmare telling me she had woken up and had seen exactly what I saw.

One day in 1999, in the late morning, I was reading the newspaper in the living room. This was one of my guilty pleasures, taking a break from the business of being what amounts to the C.E.O. of a family, and devouring the whole paper in one sitting. This lazy indulgence was suddenly interrupted when my daughter, Emma, along with Bethany Peterson stormed through the front door shrieking. They were young kids, Emma, age seven and Bethany, eight and a half, and always looking for adventure. I just assumed they had discovered some cool treasure or found a snake slithering through the grass or some such thing that might excite a little kid.

Seeing their crazed state it was hard to imagine what could have sparked this frenzied outburst. Then out it came, each of them chiming in, filling in the gaps so the whole story was delivered intact. As I had been doing for a while, I made sure to note each detail that these two girls relayed to me that morning. Recently, I reached out to them separately, my daughter, Emma, and her old neighbor friend, Bethany, to ask them what, if anything, they might remember as an unusual event in their childhood. Here are excerpts of their replies:

Emma, age 26, 2018:
I remember Bethany and I were walking home from her house one day after I had spent the night there. As we passed by Andrea's house we saw that her trash can lid was open. It must have been trash day, and for some reason the lid was up. Inside the trash can we saw blood-soaked paper or gauze, what appeared to be animal fur, and a bag of what looked like guts. There were small, empty vials, too, several of them.

Bethany, age 28, 2018:
As Emma and I were walking up the street to your house we noticed the mean lady's trash can was open and couldn't resist looking inside. There was a lot of what

looked like raw meat, bloody gauze, and bloody Q-tips. Really disgusting.

While their accounts today of the contents viewed inside Andrea's trash can in 1999 do vary slightly some nineteen years later, these recollections align exactly with what they told me that morning—that there were bloody guts and bloody rags and animal parts inside that can. The fact that, after all these years, something they witnessed at such a young age had been so indelibly imprinted on their memories is testament to the intensity of the grotesque sight.

CHAPTER 6

Our Lady of Fatima

ONE DAY IN LATE 1999, there was a notice in our church bulletin announcing that the traveling statue of Our Lady of Fatima was coming to our parish. I pondered, what *is* Fatima? Somewhere deep in the recesses of my memory I had some glimmer of recollection about a movie I saw about Fatima as a child, but could not recall anything about the story. Ever inquisitive, I decided to go home and Google it (Google was a cool new toy back then).

When I entered "Our Lady of Fatima" into the search engine over 200,000 results popped up. I realized that this Fatima thing was bigger than I thought. I selected a webpage at random on the first page of search results, and when it loaded the first thing that jumped off the page was the date July 13th, wow—that's my birthday! I saw the depiction of the Virgin Mary with three little children in what appeared to be a field somewhere in Portugal. This also drew me in, as our family has Portuguese roots. And I smiled when I saw that one of the apparitions occurred on June 13th, 1917, the Feast Day of Saint Anthony of Padua (who was Portuguese by birth), who I had recently claimed as my favorite saint while learning about various saints' lives. This all triggered a sense of familiarity and interest in me, so I began to read about the story of these events that occurred in Portugal in 1917.

To say that I was captivated by the story of the Blessed Virgin making six appearances to these three simple little children in a remote area of central Portugal is an understatement. The weight of the messages conveyed to the children, their experience in being scorned and ridiculed as a result of their claims—even thrown in jail, and the amazing miracle performed at the final apparition, completely enthralled me.

This amazing story compelled me to learn more, so I ordered a book about Our Lady of Fatima. I devoured that book and ordered another one. Eventually, I would consume five books relating to the miraculous events that occurred on the 13th of the month for six consecutive months (with the exception of August when the children were being held in jail, delaying their visit with Our Lady until August 15) in Fatima, Portugal.

In learning about the Fatima events I grew to have a particular fondness for little Jacinta, the youngest of the seers who, as a result of the experience, developed into a holy, saintly child. The tales of her acts of pure love and sacrifice touched me deeply. For example, Jacinta gladly wore a rough rope around her waist under her clothing so that the painful sores and scabs that formed would remind her to pray daily for sinners, and for the souls suffering in Purgatory. She happily gave up her lunch, intended to sustain her for the long day of tending the sheep, to offer to village children who were less fortunate than her.

The list of Jacinta's selfless acts of love and sacrifice is long, especially considering her short life. She died in 1919 at age ten. The child's body was found to be incorrupt when exhumed sixteen years after her death, while her brother, Francisco had decomposed naturally. Incorruptibility is a rare occurrence when a body, not embalmed or preserved, does not decay; a rare condition associated with sanctity. The children were both canonized as Saints on May 13th, 2017 by Pope Francis during the centennial celebration of the famous apparitions.

The number thirteen was there again, beckoning me as the common denominator in my faith journey. One day during my hour in Adoration I began to make a list in my journal of all the number 13s among our family members' birthdates—we have five family members with Fatima birthdates and several others with thirty-one and twenty-six (13 reversed; 13 x 2), as well as family member's addresses. Added to the list of the significance of the number thirteen is my obsession with the 13th Station, and that Saint Anthony's Feast Day is on the thirteenth. For whatever reason, this number seems to be woven into my personal faith journey.

After learning so much about Fatima I felt compelled to go on a pilgrimage trip to Fatima, Portugal. I wanted to be physically present among the thousands of other pilgrims who flock to that special place on the thirteenth day of the month between May and October. So, I began to hatch a plan to visit this amazing place for which I had acquired such a deep love and reverence.

Catholics are not beholden to accept or believe any supernatural or mystical occurrences, even if these events have been approved through a long, arduous process conducted by the Vatican, as Fatima was. But after seeing the actual photographs of the 70,000 eyewitnesses who gathered on October 13, 1917 to witness the miracle promised by Our Lady, The Miracle of the Sun, it gave the story significant credibility. Reading the news stories written by the staunchly secular press of the day, and learning how the prophecies spoken to the children all came to pass, I became utterly convinced that these events in Fatima did indeed take place.

By the year 2000 I had become an advocate for Eucharistic Adoration. Each Wednesday I would meet up with Jesus in the Blessed Sacrament, laying my troubles at the foot of that little altar. Struggling with an increasingly tortured marriage in which I felt my husband despised me, I would drag my weary heart there to seek Divine solace every Wednesday. One elderly priest often joined me during that hour, and would console me and give me pep talks when I shared with him my sorrows regarding my marriage.

When I happened to find myself alone in the little chapel, I didn't hesitate to weep and wail aloud, enjoying the sense of relief by expressing my emotions to Jesus in such raw form. One day, on October 14, 2000, I was sitting there in the Adoration chapel as usual, writing away in my journal, and documenting an interesting dream I had had the night before (on October 13th):

> **10/14/2000:** What an odd dream I had last night! I dreamt that (now this is very weird, I warn you) someone, a voice, was telling me that the Ark of the Covenant was Christ's chest (ribcage) and the covenant was His heart. Now in addition to the voice telling me this, in my dream I saw the actual image . . . a simple set of white ribs, black inside with an oversized deep red heart within. It was as clear as day! It was almost juvenile in its rendition. I wish I could draw well, but this is kind of how it looked [drew an illustration of the image]. I have not been able to shake this image all day.

This dream and multiple other inspirations I was experiencing told me I was on a spiritual journey that, no matter how much I prayed for his conversion, would not be shared, understood, or appreciated by my husband. To his defense, the person he'd married all those years ago in a civil ceremony was no longer present in our home, having been replaced by this new model who now placed Jesus at the top of the totem pole. I was now, as he sneeringly referred to me, a "church lady," and he was clearly disgusted by that.

So my reversion back to Catholicism only added more distance between the two of us, setting up a palpable sense of spiritual warfare within the home about this time. My husband was not on board with attending Mass with our kids and me, and would often deride my efforts to teach them the faith. When I'd apply some pressure to get him to come, he would purposely make us late and would punish me with a petulant, negative attitude. Although I found this demoralizing, I continued to pray fervently that his heart would soften and at some point he might begin to participate in the faith formation of our kids, including willingly joining us at Mass on Sundays.

As painful as the marriage had become, I did not consider divorce to be an option. I convinced my husband to allow our priest to convalidate the marriage, and he agreed to participate. So on the Feast Day of St. Francis of Assisi, October 4, 2000, we renewed our vows on the altar, with our kids and some close family members witnessing. This gave me hope.

I located a Catholic pilgrimage tour company and made the travel arrangements to visit Fatima, Portugal the next year, on my birthday, July 13, 2001. It would be so incredible to spend my forty-fifth birthday there in Fatima. I was delighted when my husband agreed to my request to take fifteen-year-old Sarah along on the trip. I looked forward to begging for special graces there, in hopes of my husband's conversion, and to receiving much needed blessings for our marriage.

CHAPTER 7

Events

RIGHT ABOUT THIS TIME, in mid-2000, Andrea sold her house. By this time, she was simply loathed by the neighbors so seeing that "Sold" sign on her front yard was cause for celebration. We looked forward to meeting the new next-door neighbors, the Mitchells, a family with two young sons. By now, Meadow Lane was teeming with kids, so adding two more boys made everyone very happy.

One day that summer, about a month after the family had moved in, the dad, Bruce, knocked on my front door. He asked me if I would like to see what he had just dug up along our mutual property line while he was planting some new landscaping.

I followed Bruce with some trepidation to their house next door. There, lined up against their garage door on the driveway, were four or five small objects. As I approached the garage I could see that these items were carved idols, like pagan gods or voodoo dolls. My breath caught in my throat at this sight. They resembled ugly little monsters. I had an immediate visceral reaction knowing instinctively that whatever or whomever these items depicted was of an evil nature. I don't recall if the idols were made from carved wood or were cast of some resin or ceramic material, as I didn't want to look at them too long.

On a subconscious level I had always known that the chilly, soulless woman, Andrea, was evil. First of all, you could sense it; those eyes, nearly black as coal. Then there was the ongoing ritual burning of unknown items in her yard, and the trashcan contents described by the girls. But to see actual evidence of ritualistic practices, possibly casting curses or hexes on us, or at minimum summoning dark spirits to our general location, was incredibly disturbing.

I told the new owner that we had suspected she might be doing something sinister there on the property. He shared that, in addition to unearthing the idol figures, he had also uncovered large piles of burnt papers buried in the planters. I told him about the unusual burning smells we neighbors had noticed coming from that yard over the past few years, strange odors we never could identify. Could it be that the paper was used to conceal whatever else she had burned in that planter?

Ashley, age 31, 2018:
When our new neighbors moved in it was quite interesting when they came over asking about the previous owner while holding what appeared to be two adult and four child voodoo dolls they found buried in the yard.

Bethany, age 28, 2018:
When the Mitchell family moved in the dad was redoing the landscaping and found multiple idol-like voodoo statues buried around the property.

Lauren Mitchell, 2018:
Bruce remembers finding two or three statues (he called them Mayan looking idols) in the front of the house by the

water tap for the hose and Alex [son] remembers some buried in the backyard along the fence as well. And we collectively remember the piles of burnt papers buried in the planters around the back of the yard.

Back in 1998, I had taken the huge leap into homeschooling the kids. This important decision came about because our public schools at the time were abysmal, using the "whole language" reading methodology, not teaching grammar or cursive handwriting, not requiring the students to memorize basic math facts — having them rely on calculators instead, not correcting spelling errors (following a program called SPEL is a four letter word), emphasizing art projects in lieu of writing assignments, and using curriculum filled with political messaging that was in direct opposition to my values. Although I had enrolled them at a local Christian school the year before, a recent career setback made tuition payments untenable. My neighbor, Suzanne Peterson, was successfully homeschooling her two children, so I picked her brain and decided to give it a whirl.

I will always value those years while home with my children as the most important thing I have ever done with my time and skill set. To be able to actually parent my children, to show them the world through amazing field trips and nature outings, and to teach them the Catholic faith as part of our school day, was fulfilling beyond description. Hard, yes, but worth every single sacrifice that was made in order to fulfill the roles of both mom and teacher.

I took the job seriously. I attended conferences, read books about homeschooling, and interviewed homeschool veterans. While in college, I had considered becoming a teacher, so the various internships in elementary schools I had completed equipped me with some basic skills.

Our family is chock full of teachers, so homeschooling came naturally to me; teaching was in my DNA. I made sure that the kids would continue to participate in sports and clubs—Little League, Girl Scouts, music lessons, AYSO soccer, private horseback lessons, Little Flowers Club, and softball. The kids had all their friends in the neighborhood available for socializing after 3:00 p.m. each day, and had plenty of group activities and classes offered through a large homeschool umbrella organization of two hundred local families.

One day, Matthew and Sarah were sitting with me at the dining table while we completed a math lesson. One of the benefits of homeschooling is the ability to adjust the curricula to the skill set of each child. As for math, Matthew was gifted and Sarah struggled, so they used the same program. At the time, Sarah was fourteen and Matt was twelve. That morning, I put a problem up on the white board and asked who felt they could solve it. Sarah jumped up to beat Matthew at this challenge, and headed toward the white board. Before reaching the board she suddenly stopped dead in her tracks and grabbed her ear. She got a strange look on her face, visibly upset, and then crumpled into the chair, still holding her ear and with tears streaming down her face. I documented this event in my journal that evening:

> **1/24/01:** Interestingly, Sarah had a third "angel" (?) event yesterday. We were in the middle of our math lesson and we were having fun. The kids both "got" it. Suddenly, Sarah, who was approaching the white board, said, "It just happened again—just now!" and she started to cry from fear. She said it was someone whispering in her ear. As I had before, I asked her if she might have an earache or fluid in her ears, or maybe a bug flew by her ear. But she was emphatic and said, "No, it was a voice saying words I couldn't understand." Who was speaking to Sarah? Was it

MY 13th STATION

You, Lord? Was it her guardian angel? I think I will go with her to the see a priest next week.

Based on my journal entry, apparently there had been two other incidents where Sarah experienced this phenomenon, which had escaped my memory until I recently reread the old journals. Notice that I placed the word angel in quotation marks, followed by a question mark. This is exactly the way it was written down by me that day in Adoration. I was obviously concerned about it, hoping that these strange occurrences where from a holy source, but worried that they may not be. After all, this happened just months after the new next-door neighbor, Bruce Mitchell, showed me what he had excavated in his yard.

CHAPTER 8

Fatima, Portugal

FINALLY, THE TRIP I HAD BEEN PLANNING for a year was about to become an amazing reality. All of the research I had done in advance of the trip to Fatima filled me with a deep sense of connection to the Blessed Mother and those three children, as if they were members of my own family. I was about to set foot on sacred ground, where about five million pilgrims come to pay homage each year. I was overcome with emotion just anticipating the moment I would stand upon the same spot where the miracles had taken place all those decades ago.

When beginning the packing process I found that we didn't have enough luggage for the two of us, so I asked my mother-in-law if we could borrow one of their suitcases. After getting the suitcase to our house, I took it to Sarah's room so she could begin packing. That afternoon she came to me holding a pretty necklace that she said was in one of the side pockets of the suitcase. It was a gold-toned necklace with green enamel Miraculous Medal charm.

I assumed that my sister-in-law must have borrowed the suitcase and inadvertently left the necklace in the bag. When I called to tell her about the necklace, she said she had never borrowed her mom's suitcases. So, I called my mother-in-law and asked her if she had lent the bag to anyone else, and described the necklace I had found. I assumed it didn't belong to her because she was not a Catholic, and didn't practice any religion. When she replied no, that she had never lent the suitcase out before, I was flummoxed.

That night, while processing my day as I drifted off to sleep, I thought about the necklace. Suddenly, it dawned on me that the image struck on this medal was the result of an apparition of the Blessed Virgin Mary witnessed by a young nun named Catherine Labouré in Paris in the early 1800s. I got a shudder when I remembered that this is Sarah's confirmation patron saint, and that we will be visiting the very church in Paris where this event had occurred, and where St. Catherine Labouré is lying incorrupt in a crystal coffin. Was this just a strange coincidence? Where did the necklace come from?

On July 7th, my daughter and I trekked for a total of twenty hours before finally reaching our first stop on the trip, São Miguel Island in the Azores. Why the Azores? At the suggestion of my mom, she thought it would be wonderful for us to visit our ancestral home, and even generously paid for this side excursion. The Azores are a Portuguese archipelago, or cluster of islands, that sit off the northern coast of Africa. My maternal grandfather's ancestry was from the island of São Miguel.

Sarah and I arrived at the hotel fairly late that night, about 10 p.m. We were utterly exhausted from the very long day of travel, first to Munich, then to Lisbon, and finally to São Miguel. We were so tired we went straight to bed. In the darkness, in my little twin bed, I pondered our day, replaying in my head all our little experiences while traveling this long distance. Sarah was in her twin bed to my left.

To my amazement, while staring at the ceiling and processing my day, I saw, out of the corner of my eye off to the right near the bathroom, a vapor-type cloud, about four feet off the ground, slowly moving toward our beds. I lay there frozen, holding my breath. I figured it was a hallucination due to my extreme fatigue, that I was just imagining this thing approaching us. The cloud drifted across my bed and then hovered in the center space between the two twin beds. Out of the darkness I heard, "Mom, can you see that?! Apparently, not only was Sarah not asleep, but she, too, witnessed the cloudy phenomenon. A ghost? An evil spirit? An angel? We will never know. This "being" did not visit us again over the next two nights.

After three days on the ethereal São Miguel Island, we flew to Lisbon where we would spend the night before meeting the tour group the next afternoon. In the morning, while having breakfast in Lisbon, Sarah shared an interesting event from the night before. We had gotten in late, so it was about 11:30 p.m. when we finally went to bed. She told me that while she was lying in bed, not yet asleep, she had seen a vision of a white rose suspended above her head. She described it as a shrub-type rose with a short stem, leaves, and thorns, versus a long-stem variety. Sarah said the rose hovered over her, almost laying down flat, with the petals pointed towards the wall behind the bed. She said she watched incredulously as the rose began to rise nearly upright and then slowly disappear into the wall behind her, petals first.

Later that day, she mentioned the rose vision again, and how she had wanted so badly to hold it. I wasn't really sure what to make of this, whether it was a dream or an authentic vision, but it was significant enough that I documented the event in my journal. It seemed to me like a sign from above that we were being lovingly watched over. But honestly, with all these strange events happening, I really didn't know what to think.

After checking in at our hotel on Rue de Jacinta (how perfect), Sarah and I immediately made a beeline for the sanctuary just a few blocks away. Walking past the little souvenir shops, I felt dismay at the tacky evidence of blatant commercialism, sullying such a blessed place. We arrived at the entrance to the enormous quad, which was the designated area for accommodating the large crowds that regularly descended here. A ribbon of tile cut through the expansive space upon which pilgrims, many of whom had traveled from a great distance, would make the final leg of their journey on their knees. Slowly, with rosaries in hand and faces set in expressions of fervent prayer, these souls inched their way toward the destination, the Chapel of the Apparitions (Capelinha das Aparicões)—the actual spot where Our Lady had appeared to the children.

Sarah and I slowly descended to the sanctuary grounds and were both overcome with emotion, especially Sarah. It was a profoundly emotional moment in my life as well. I looked around me and conjured up a mental picture of the area as pastureland, with sheep grazing under the hot sun. I imagined being a simple child, going about my daily chores tending to the sheep, and then suddenly witnessing the glowing, bright white image of "the lady" hovering atop a small holm oak tree. What a gift! What a grace!

Sarah and I roamed around, exploring the beautiful Capelinha, which Our Lady had asked to be built, although the original chapel had been destroyed in an explosion in 1922. The 1920 original statue of Our Lady of Fatima inside the Chapel is adorned with a crown into which Pope John Paul II had the bullet inserted that had nearly taken his life on May 13th in 1981. He attributed the protection of Our Lady of Fatima as the reason he was not killed that day, and remained devoted to her for the rest of his life.

We then wandered over to the basilica, completed and dedicated in 1953, which was adorned on its facade with enormous banners on either side, one depicting Jacinta, and one depicting Francisco—who had both been beatified the prior year on May 13, 2000 by Pope John Paul II. Inside the beautiful basilica were the tombs of these two venerated children, which brought tears to my eyes. After so much study, I felt I knew them personally, these sweet children with hearts of gold; visiting their final resting place was very touching. Sarah had a special affection for little Francisco, who Our Lady had promised would go to Heaven after he prays many rosaries. We nicknamed him Frankie.

The following section here will be taken directly from my journal entries while in Fatima in July 2001.

7/12/01: After a great dinner (Sarah even ate the fish!) we returned to the sanctuary for the prayer vigil and candlelight procession in preparation for the Feast of Our Lady of Fatima tomorrow. The huge asphalt area was filled with pilgrims holding candles—an incredible sight to behold. The multi-lingual rosary was an amazing experience, with people all around us saying the prayers in their own language. I detected Portuguese (of course), Spanish, Italian, German, and English just in my little space, but the square was filled with people of all ethnicities from around the world. Between the decades of the rosary was the most gorgeous music, a rich, beautiful chorale that was so moving and powerful.

After the rosary, the procession of the statue of Our Lady of Fatima began on the other side of the huge quad. People sang along—Ave, Ave, Ave Maria—and waved their white hankies in farewell as the statue processed by, a tradition started decades ago. When the statue was within eyesight, I could see that it was placed on a bed of white roses that looked exactly like the type of rose Sarah had seen in her vision two days ago. Wow. I am realizing that our faith is deepening and our love for Jesus and Mary is growing by the hour. Only three days into the pilgrimage and already I can't imagine a day without praying the rosary. I can see that this experience will change our lives forever.

7/13/01: My birthday! Sarah had made a big 'Happy Birthday' sign and taped it up on our mirror in the room so it would be the first thing I'd see this morning. She gave me a beautiful rosary box containing a lovely necklace with medals of Our Lady of Fatima and Jacinta attached. Of course I cried—I was so touched by her thoughtfulness. I just cannot describe the effect of the Mass this morning— this is the actual Feast Day—I just can't find the words. It was two hours long and just absolutely gorgeous. There were about a hundred priests, a dozen bishops, and an archbishop from Brazil present. The Mass was spoken in four languages alternately. It was a high Mass, with the prayers and readings sung. The music was so incredible it made you cry—the songs were sung in Latin.

When it came time for communion, I was overcome with emotion, fighting to keep control from just sobbing. After communion, while we were kneeling on the asphalt, the sun suddenly broke through the clouds and a fairly strong breeze kicked up. I looked up to see the beautiful golden Sacred Heart of Jesus statue, arms outstretched, in the center of the square, and I just "got it." *Our Blessed Mother wants to bring her children to her Son—it is as simple as that.*

Earlier in the Mass I was deeply moved by a young pilgrim shuffling in his bare knees, in obvious pain, along the tile. He barely scooted an inch at a time and clutched his rosary, praying for strength. His friend walked next to him, consoling him and encouraging him to continue. Several times he stopped and leaned over on all fours, as if he couldn't continue. I prayed for him to make it and I cried watching his pure devotion and humble demonstration of

MY 13th STATION

penance. He finally did make it to the apparition site, the Chapel of the Apparitions.

The following morning, we all boarded the tour bus to our next destination, Burgos, Spain. Later on the itinerary was Lourdes, France and Paris. As we were pulling away from the Fatima site, I glanced out the window one more time at the basilica with the images of Francisco and Jacinta and tears stung my eyes. I was so emotional. I honestly didn't want to leave this amazing place, feeling as if I was leaving part of my heart here. As the bus began to drive away, I vowed that I would return to Fatima for the one-hundred-year anniversary in 2017.

We had been home from our pilgrimage trip for a couple of weeks, having time to process the wondrous sites we saw and enjoy the photos I had picked up from the drug store. Of course, these included several new pictures of the 13th Station to add to my collection.

I had purchased yet another book about Fatima, now even more intrigued after having been there in person. In my journal that day I wrote:

8/1/01: Today something weird happened. I have been reading a little book on the Third Secret of Fatima. In it the author speculates that the third secret has to do with the book of Revelation, chapters 11, 12, and 13. So I got out the old Bible that Grandpa had passed down, which my mom had given me earlier this year. As I was reading these passages I became distracted by the bad condition of the cover and wondering how I could get it rebound somehow. I then opened the back cover to see how it was attached, when out fell a paper. I opened it up and I could not believe it—it was a flyer from 1981 that was announcing the pilgrim statue of Our Lady of Fatima coming to the archdiocese of Los Angeles. I sat there, slack-jawed. Of all the things that I could have found in that Bible, it was a 20-year old flyer about the Fatima statue coming to town that Grandpa had tucked inside. Amazing.

Well the happenstances that seemed to be like little clues from heaven did not end there. The next one occurred a week later when I was visiting my mother. During our time together, she said she had something to pass down to me, this time from her mother. So, my mom went upstairs to retrieve the item. Again, I will refer to my journal entry that day:

> **8/8/01:** . . . It was a small navy blue plastic folder that held a picture of St. Anthony of Padua alongside a little card with my great-grandmother's name and address on it. Mom told me this little token belonged to my grandmother's mother and that now it was time for me to have it. I was thrilled to be the new owner of this little antique family heirloom.
>
> When I first returned to the Church, I loved to read about the saints. St. Anthony became my favorite saint. I was captivated by his story, his work with St. Francis, and how his sermons attracted thousands. I was also pleased to spot so many little familiarities when learning about him. He was born on August 15th (Feast Day of the Assumption—and my grandpa's birthday), he was from Portugal and his mother's name was Teresa (the same as me and my grandmother).

MY 13th STATION

So, my Irish great-grandmother carried around a little pocket shrine of St. Anthony, and her only child, my grandmother, Teresa, would someday marry a Portuguese man born on the same date as St. Anthony. How cool.

On August 15th, I stopped at the Adoration chapel for a short visit before Mass. That day in my journal I wrote:

8/15/01: I am sitting here today with Matt adoring the Lord. How nice it is to have him here sitting with me. We prayed the rosary and now he is reading a book about Francisco. Last week as I was gazing at the Blessed Sacrament, I thought I saw the image of the Holy Face of Christ in the Host! I squinted at it, blinked my eyes, looked away and then back, but really thought I had seen that image—the one taken from the Shroud of Turin. Today here with Matt, amazingly, it seems even clearer, kind of like this [I draw an image]. I must be going nuts. My eyes are playing tricks on me with the lighting inside the tabernacle or the reflection of the windows or something. But it is very nice to look at, though. Ok, off to Mass.

During August and September 2001 my journal entries were angst-ridden, as both Sarah and Matthew were looking forward to going back to regular school. The four years that we homeschooled together were so special to me, but the two oldest were ready to move forward into their next chapter of life and I knew I had to let them go. I struggled terribly, however, as my journal entries reveal, worried about them being exposed to worldly things or possibly losing their faith. My marriage was in bad shape, only adding to my worries. I didn't know what to do about it anymore, but the upcoming renewal of our vows in the presence of a priest offered me some hope. With enough grace and prayer, hopefully my husband would begin to embrace the faith and support my efforts to teach our kids about it. Mostly, I hoped he would be kinder and more attentive to me.

> **9/5/01:** . . . So now my job is to pray that God leads us all where He wants us. I will try with all my might to trust in Him. He has a plan, I just know it. Tonight at Adoration I could see the Holy Face of Christ so clearly—it gave me goose bumps! At certain times, while praying the rosary, the image almost looked like a hologram (3D) and I was afraid to blink. I stared at the Blessed Sacrament through most of the rosary, not wanting to take my eyes off His face. I love Him so much. How can I serve Him better?

Those past four years were marked with intense spiritual growth, which I attributed to my devotion to Our Lady of Fatima and Saint Anthony. While homeschooling my kids and teaching them the faith, I was learning much of it right along with them. I had not been well catechized as a child, as most kids in my generation hadn't. As a child my mother was divorced and no longer practiced the faith, so my sister and I, although making our First Communions and sporadically attending CCD classes, had only a minimal connection to the Church while growing up.

My mom remarried when I was twelve, and my new stepdad, who was also a Catholic, made Sunday Mass a priority for the family, which was admirable. However, by that point I was entering my rebellious teen years and wasn't very receptive, usually daydreaming during Mass about this cute boy in my seventh grade science class. When I left the church at age eighteen I had not forged a close bond with Jesus and, ignorantly, didn't yet understand the need for Him or the Eucharist in my life.

So now, forming my own children in the faith was a wonderful experience that added an extra layer of purpose to my life. I was a wife, a mother, a homeschool teacher, and a faith formation teacher—what a beautiful job description! I realized how important my role was in instilling the faith in my kids, providing a solid foundation upon which they could shape their own faith experience in later years. I knew that this was the most important job a parent can do, to pass on the faith to their children, arming them for the trials and challenges that would surely come their way in the journey of life.

Teaching the kids about the saints, reading the Bible together, and sharing sweet stories from old traditional Catholic storybooks, I hoped to instill in each child a sense of joy about the faith, and a love for Christ. I remember reading to them one day from *Story of a Soul*, the autobiography of Saint Therese of Lisieux. The copy had been handed down to me from my mother, a souvenir from a trip to Lisieux in 1952 when she was nineteen. I had developed a special devotion to the Little Flower, and I remember getting all weepy while reading her sweet words to my kids that day. I wanted them to know how easy it is to please Jesus through small, humble acts of charity done out of love for Him—the Little Way. The memories I have of homeschooling the three kids over that four-year period will always be precious to me.

CHAPTER 9

Divorce

SADLY, THE HOPES I HAD PINNED on the effects of having our marriage convalidated did not pan out. As my marriage continued to erode, I found my spirit flagging right along with it. I felt as if I had no option but to just accept the cross that I would have to bear in in order to keep my family together. The tension in the house incrementally increased with each passing year.

My husband and I were on completely different wavelengths. He never did accept my return to the church or the changes in my worldview that had resulted. I was increasingly frustrated at his stubborn refusal to join the kids and me at Mass. By his actions and attitudes, he seemed to be regressing into adolescence instead of progressing as a man, to act as the head of our household. He was emotionally unavailable, shutting me out by simply ignoring me much of the time. This hurt terribly. In my marriage I felt so deeply alone, abandoned and alone.

In 2004, the marital situation had deteriorated to the point that it began to take a terrible toll on both my emotional and physical wellness. I remember that summer sharing with my mother how miserable I was, describing it as feeling like a starved dog, wanting so desperately to feel loved by my husband, but feeling loathed instead. I began to sink into the depths of depression as the emotional abuse

I experienced at his hand continued to escalate. It literally felt like I was under diabolical attack.

My Catholic girlfriend, Jo, in whom I had confided, suggested I meet with a priest to discuss the struggles in my marriage and to ask for a referral to a Catholic or Christian marriage counselor. My husband had steadfastly refused to go to counseling over the years, but, at the very least, if the counselor could just help *me* that would be better than allowing the depression to swallow me up. As it was, I had lost my appetite, lost weight, had sleep difficulties, and had lost all interest in even getting out of bed in the morning. So, I took her up on her suggestion and made an appointment to meet with a priest at the Institute of Christ the King in San Jose, a forty-five-minute drive, but well worth it, as I valued these priests for their traditional views on the faith.

During our meeting Fr. Justin asked me for a summary of the issues in our marriage. I relayed five or six major problem areas, all serious issues. After hearing the description of the problems the priest was not very encouraging in his assessment. He suggested that things would likely continue to worsen, and that, based on the things I had shared, it might be necessary to end the marriage for my own health. He saw little hope in my husband changing his ways even with therapy, but told me to insist that he join me in therapy anyway, as a condition of the marriage continuing at all. He gave me a referral for a psychotherapist and offered to provide me with spiritual counseling as needed.

When I proposed these terms to John, he actually agreed to go to marriage counseling with me, finally, as he could see that I was serious about leaving him. Since the early days of our marriage I had been pleading with him to accompany me to marriage counseling, but he'd adamantly refused to go. So, I made the appointment and tried to manage the cold awkwardness between us until we could begin to work on our marriage with a professional.

Unfortunately, a 'final straw' episode occurred before we ever made it to the first therapy appointment, creating a situation that was irreparable. I asked him to move out of the house and I then filed for divorce a month later. The situation had devolved to the point that I no longer could emotionally endure being married to him. I had no option but to sever the marriage bond.

There is good reason why God hates divorce. Throughout Scripture there are clear and undeniable admonitions regarding the subject of divorce. Divorce is highly disruptive to everyone involved, regardless of who was at fault. Mostly, it impacts the sense of stability in the home that all children deserve to feel. Suddenly, nothing is as it was. Holidays are forever tainted with a patchwork quilt of feeble attempts to normalize what is just not normal. The entire ebb and flow within the home and daily schedule of life becomes unmoored and unfamiliar. Emotions are raw as the strife and anxiety caused by the tense divorce proceedings bleed into the fabric of home-life.

My family was no different than any other family struggling with the aftermath of a divorce. It was very sad. All those years of fervent prayer had not changed my husband's heart. Although I knew I had no option but to end the marriage as a matter of self-preservation, it was very difficult for the kids to accept that their family was torn apart. As most divorced adults do, I suffered terrible guilt because I knew how much this impacted our children, then ages twelve, sixteen, and eighteen. I felt I had failed. No matter how much I had prayed about it and begged God to heal our marriage, I was not able to salvage it, fix it, or to survive it. Soon after the divorce, I met with a priest at Christ the King for his representation in seeking an annulment.

Slowly, the kids and I adjusted to our new normal, broken as it was. I was very grateful for three well-adjusted kids who managed to carry on for the most part. Yes, there were tears and pain and a sense that things were just "off." Generally, we all did our best to move into this new chapter, often limping along with our dignity barely intact.

One early evening, in the late fall of 2004, my daughter Sarah, then eighteen years old, suddenly came running into my bedroom very upset and distraught. I asked her what was wrong and she breathlessly told me, "I was in the bathroom putting on mascara and when I looked up to the mirror my pupils were like vertical slits! Like cat's eyes! It was so freaky, Mom, I had cat eyes!"

I walked down the hall to the kid's bathroom to check this out, Sarah at my heels. I looked in the mirror and my eyes looked totally normal. I told Sarah to come into the bathroom and look in the mirror, and her eyes, too, looked completely normal. I calmed her down, assuring her that she probably just imagined it, but she was very adamant that what she saw was not an illusion. She described the effect again, exactly as she experienced it. I didn't want her to think I might not believe her, but at the same time I wanted to calm her down, to reassure her that all is fine. Deep down, however, I knew it was not.

One night that same year, Sarah was awakened from her sleep by the sound of her sister's bedroom door opening and closely repeatedly. She said she knew she wasn't dreaming, that this commotion was actually happening. So, she got out of bed and opened her bedroom door, only to see Emma's door wide open and Emma snoozing away, oblivious to the racket. Sarah, I feared, was under some kind of attack.

CHAPTER 10

The Foothold

LOOKING BACK NOW, as I try to gain some sliver of understanding as to why my son might have fallen victim to some invisible dark force, one clear possibility emerges. A spiritual foothold, which can be the result of habitual sin, anger, dabbling in the occult, rebellion, and any manner of points of weakness, can provide an entry point for demonic oppression and torment. Once the demon has exercised a spiritual foothold, it proceeds to draw the victim into deep despair and discouragement, sometimes even sparking addiction, mental health issues, and self-loathing.

Back in 2002, when Matt was about thirteen, he shared with me a cover of Chris Isaak's "Wicked Game" by a band named H.I.M. We were big fans of Chris Isaak, my husband and I having seen him perform live three times. We had all his music and played it often in the house. I had never heard of H.I.M. so I asked about the band. Matt told me they were really cool, from Scandinavia, and had a unique sound they called Love Metal. In fact, he said he had first discovered them on one of his skate video soundtracks.

The first thing I noticed when seeing the album imagery was the band's logo, called a "Heartagram," which borrowed heavily from the pentagram, stylizing the occultist image to resemble a heart. The letters H.I.M. stood for His Infernal Majesty, an unveiled reference to the devil. Although a bit concerned that the band might be messaging something disturbing through these outward trappings, after reading the lyrics to some of the songs and listening to three or four tracks, I couldn't identify anything that I would call dangerous or worrisome enough to warrant forbidding it. But, oh, the slippery slope.

Over the next year, Matt became totally obsessed with H.I.M., listening to the music pretty much nonstop. One day my youngest daughter, Emma, told me that her brother had etched the H.I.M. Heartagram logo onto his wrist in a makeshift tattoo using a safety pin and ink. I was alarmed. I had him remove as much ink as possible and eventually the image faded as the scabbed healed and peeled off. I tried not to overreact about this event, remembering firsthand how passionate adolescents can be about their rock idols.

That same year, Matthew discovered the British 80s band, Iron Maiden. One look at the album artwork featuring Satan and entitled *Number of the Beast*, and then reading the title song lyrics with 666 references sprinkled throughout, was enough to trigger in me a sense of dread. But the horse was already out of the barn as he and his friends were now big fans of "Maiden," unbeknownst to me.

In 2003 he asked permission to go to an upcoming Iron Maiden concert, and my response was an emphatic "No way." Even though, as Matt assured me, the band members were not actually *practicing* Satanism, just the imagery and sketchy lyrics of their songs were enough to wake up the Holy Spirit in me and emphatically forbid this—especially at the age of barely fifteen. A metal concert would not be a safe place for my son, with drugs and head-bangers, in addition to the images of the occult integrated into the staging of the show.

That weekend I had a scheduled business trip to Nevada. When I returned home my then husband informed me that, in my absence, he had decided to overrule my objections and allow Matt to attend the concert with his friend. I was furious. Matt then showed me a band t-shirt he purchased with the money his dad had given him. I was horrified; the t-shirt was entitled "Dance of Death" and featured an orgy scene of bare-breasted women in gothic masks, small children depicted seductively, a man with a ram's head, dark demonic figures in the background, and a hideous grim reaper (Eddie, the band's mascot) at the center of the group of decadent characters, all placed atop a satanic pentagram. I grabbed the shirt from him and hid it from him, forbidding him to wear the disgusting shirt. Matthew was very angry with me, and his dad just rolled his eyes as if I was crazy. He made no apology for overriding my objections about the concert, leaving me to look like a crazy, overprotective mother and him as the cool dad. Matt continued to listen to Iron Maiden against my wishes.

The following year my marriage was over and I would be attempting to manage everything myself. The sheer energy involved in the divorce proceedings exhausted me, and on top of that stress I took care of the daily needs and demands of three kids, their schooling, shuttling them to practices and games, car problems, the finances, and maintaining the family home and yard. I admit I didn't follow through with the policing of Matt's music because I was distracted and simply spent. Over the next three years he and his friends saw Iron Maiden at least three other times in concert.

Aside from his unfortunate musical tastes, Matthew was never a problem, never got in trouble. He excelled at baseball, got good grades, and had quality friends. But the music . . . One day in early 2006, when Matt was eighteen, I was upstairs in his room, which faced the driveway, putting laundry away. I heard him drive up to the house, windows down and music blaring. But the sound of this music was very different from his Iron Maiden music—at least Maiden's music involved melodies. What I heard bellowing loudly through his car windows sounded like demons screaming at the top of their lungs. Never had I heard anything remotely close to what was emanating from the speakers in Matt's car.

I met him downstairs as he came into the house and confronted him about the "music" he was listening to. He called it Death Metal. He seemed totally nonplussed about the fact that it sounded satanic, so I told him in no uncertain terms that he was to never play that music in our home. Ever. Further, I warned him that it was likely a source of evil and could harm him. He scoffed at that and carried on with his mission to get a snack in the kitchen.

> *From the Wikipedia description of Death Metal:*
> Death metal is an extreme subgenre of heavy metal music. It typically employs heavily distorted and low-tuned guitars, played with techniques such as palm muting and tremolo picking, deep growling vocals, aggressive, powerful drumming featuring double kick and blast beat techniques, minor keys or atonality, abrupt tempo, key, and time signature changes, and chromatic chord progressions. The lyrical themes of death metal may invoke slasher film-stylized violence, religion (sometimes Satanism), occultism, Lovecraftian horror, nature, mysticism, mythology, philosophy, science fiction, and politics, and they may describe extreme acts, including mutilation, torture, rape, dissection, cannibalism, and necrophilia.

Over the next six months I became aware that this music had been embraced by not only Matt but also many of his friends, kids I have known since they were in grade school. The bands they followed were branded with the names Lamb of God, Iced Earth, Children of Bodom, and In Flames. This revelation, that my son was immersed in music that carried violent, satanic messaging and occult-inspired imagery, was highly distressing. I honestly didn't know what to do, other than to warn him of the danger to his soul, to forbid it in the house, and to pray for his protection.

Lest the reader consider me just an overwrought mother, I defer to the famous Vatican exorcist, Fr. Gabriele Amorth. In his book, *An Exorcist Tells His Story*, Fr. Amorth devotes a section to discussing the various ways the tools of Satan influence the young. Included in the list, Fr. Amorth notes, "And we cannot omit mentioning the growing popularity of a type of music that is almost [diabolically] obsessive; I refer in particular to satanic rock."[1]

I was deeply concerned about the effect this death metal would have on my son's soul. While some may reject the idea as wild conjecture, I believe that Matthew's sudden affliction with alcohol and mental illness, which would surface within the year, was caused by demonic oppression—and that this music, with its ugly, angry vocals and violent, anti-religious, anti-Christ messaging, provided the foothold through which my son would ultimately be destroyed.

CHAPTER 11

Events Continue

WHEN WE WERE SHOPPING for the new house way back in late 1991, the tract was still under construction. The model homes were very lovely, tastefully decorated and with soaring ceilings and huge windows throughout the models. After living in a small starter house that always felt hemmed in, these big sunny windows lending spacious hillside views were what sold us on the house.

Back then we drove to the latest phase of construction to select the lot. After walking up and down the street and wandering into the framed buildings, we agreed on a west-facing lot that had lots of light and a nice breeze wafting through the still unfinished walls. I fell in love with the open floor plan and the gorgeous view of the hillsides from the upstairs deck. This would be our new family home. Here we would make wonderful, lifelong memories together.

Over the many years we lived on Meadow Lane we hosted many events and parties. Neighbor children, school friends, and homeschool groups on a regular basis inhabited our home. I must have inherited my grandmother's flourish for throwing parties because, like her, I made our gatherings sunny, colorful, joyful events. Music often filled our home, being a passion of mine. The kids thrived, growing to be strong, healthy, stable little people. In the hot summers they enjoyed our spacious backyard, playing with squirt guns, water balloons, and Slip 'n Slide. The playhouse in the backyard became alternately a clubhouse for the girls and their friends, or a little schoolhouse where Sarah would try out her teacher kit we got her one Christmas, roping little Emma in as her "student." Matthew and his buddies enjoyed putting up a target in the backyard and shooting B.B. guns when they weren't out front sitting on the curb playing their Gameboys or practicing their latest BMX tricks in the cul-de-sac.

Never in a million years would anyone who entered our home have known that, though spaced out over a span of many years, strange, supernatural occurrences had taken place there. Sometimes a year or two would lapse between these odd events, long enough for each of us to briefly forget about them—until the next one occurred. However, at some juncture the events reached critical mass, making it impossible to explain them away or deny them anymore. 2005 marked that juncture.

It had been five years since the new next-door neighbor asked me to come over and see the small idol figures he had dug up on his property. That June day in 2000 was a turning point, helping to explain the creepy events that had been popping up intermittently from about 1994 until that point. In these ensuing five years, there was the torment targeted toward Sarah—the buzzing words in her ear, the cat-shaped eyes in the mirror four years later, and her sister's bedroom door slamming during the night. That period, 2000-2005, was also marked by intensifying marital strife that seemed to ramp up in proportion to my deepening faith and devotional life. In addition, these were the years when Matt became infatuated with dark, disturbing music, culminating in his embracing of death metal in 2006.

2005 was the year of our divorce, marking a significant pain point in our lives. I began to see a Christian therapist who helped me resurrect my broken spirit and taught me how to set healthy boundaries for future relationships. The first day that I showed up at her office I was a pathetic shadow of my former self, pummeled emotionally, underweight, and physically weak. I cried while filling out the intake paperwork, trying to put into words the reason for my visit. The year was marked by intense emotional pain, anxiety, worries about finances, and apprehension about the impact of the divorce on the kids.

One night in 2005, while fast asleep, I was suddenly awakened by the feeling of physical weight on my thighs. I was sleeping on my back and vividly experienced the sensation that someone was sitting on my thighs. Suddenly, whatever it was sitting on top of me began to push down hard on my upper chest, choking the air out of my lungs. Gripped with fear, and terrified to open my eyes, I instinctively began to pray the Hail Mary. In an instant, the being vanished. Poof. Gone.

> "The demons are very anxious in their pursuit of souls, yet they quickly abandon their prey merely at the name of Mary."
> SAINT BRIDGET OF SWEDEN

I jumped out of bed and flipped the light on, hoping to find some physical evidence of what I had just experienced. I knew without a doubt I had not dreamt it. Whatever it was, I knew it was evil. Somehow I was able to settle myself down and eventually drifted off to sleep while reciting the Hail Mary.

In the morning I called my friend, Jo, who happens to know a lot about the paranormal. I shared my experience with her and was surprised to hear that the exact experience had happened to her then nineteen-year-old daughter a couple of years before. The only difference between our events was that the demon had choked her daughter's neck, where in my case it pushed down on my chest—either way the objective was to disrupt airflow. Jo suggested I get some blessed salt and holy water and do a cleansing of the home, casting out demons in the name of Christ. I reminded her that I had done a similar cleansing about seven years before, but she assured me I needed to repeat the process, but to add the blessed salt this time. She knew of a source for the blessed salt and was kind enough to procure it for me.

I shared this creepy experience with my neighbor, Suzanne Peterson, that same day. She, too, got me up to speed about a variety of odd noises that they continued to experience in *their* house, and how the youngest child, Bethany, would tell her mom she felt someone was watching her as she slept. She decided, after hearing about the occurrence in my bed the night before, to also repeat a spiritual house cleansing. The two girls revisited these memories recently:

Bethany, age 28, 2018:
During the night I would hear multiple squeaks and sounds as if someone was rummaging about in the house. On multiple occasions the garage door on the side of the house below my window would sound like it was shaking and rattling, as if someone was violently trying to break in, but when I looked out the window it would stop and there was no one there. I also remember being woken up in the middle of the night on numerous occasions with the feeling that someone was watching me, so I would run and sleep in my parents' room.

Ashley, age 31, 2018:
I would hear what sounded like footsteps upstairs when no one was up there. Doors would slam shut without any sign of a draft. Windows rattled and occasionally an item would just fall off the bookcase. Each time these things happened

MY 13th STATION

I tried to tell myself that there must be some reasonable explanation behind the occurrence, convincing myself it was all in my head or that I might be going a little crazy.

It was unnerving to have to continue living in my house, but I didn't know what else to do. Initially, after the divorce, I considered downsizing, thinking it might relieve my financial situation somewhat. However, the market was sky high, making it impractical to sell a house with low property taxes (California Proposition 13) just to double my tax bill. Mostly, though, I worried that uprooting the kids would add one more traumatic event they would have to endure. This had been our family home for thirteen years, where so many beautiful memories had been made, regardless of marital strife and supernatural events. Emma had never lived anywhere else. I decided that, after doing the spiritual cleansing, we were safe to stay. All would be okay.

CHAPTER 12

Matthew Changes

MATTHEW GRADUATED HIGH SCHOOL in June 2006. Sitting there in the bleachers under the blazing sun while snapping photos of my handsome son, a lump in my throat and tears in my eyes were testament to the overwhelming love I had for this young man.

As his mom, of course I was very proud of his athletic accomplishments. He was honored at the baseball awards banquet just two weeks before, receiving a prestigious award, and was selected as one of just two players to participate in a tournament with the league's top talent, where they would be playing for scouts. I was proud of his academic accomplishments as well, and happy that he had surrounded himself with a wonderful group of friends.

The years Matt and these buddies spent playing Little League baseball and eventually playing high school ball together are treasured memories. As a baseball mom I sat there on the bleachers cheering on my son and his friends with gusto. We baseball moms bonded over the years, and to this day share a common attachment to those memories. We truly loved each other's kids, rooting passionately for each player's at bats, pitching prowess, and exciting plays. Each RBI was cause for high fives and strikeouts invoked real heart pangs. We parents sat there wrapped in blankets during chilly, windy games and passed around the squirt-fans when our boys played during blistering heat waves.

When the kids were eleven, Matt threw a wild pitch that managed to hit the batter hard in the chest, a scary moment for sure. I ran over to the opposing side to locate the mom of the injured player to offer my apologies for Matt's errant pitch while Matt apologized to the injured player, Justin. Her grace in accepting my apology was such a relief to me. And wouldn't you know it, not only did she and I become friends, but our sons eventually formed a close friendship that lasted until the end.

Through his high school years, Matt was lucky enough to have two really nice girlfriends. I remember being impressed with how kind he was when talking on the phone with them, when I happened to be within earshot. He was respectful and engaged in these conversations, and his romantic relationships were healthy. This was a relief, as I couldn't help but worry that the dysfunctional marriage he had grown up witnessing might mess him up.

The kids continued to attend Mass on Sundays, sometimes with me, other times with friends. They made their Confirmation. During their childhood I wanted to instill in our kids a heart for giving, so acts of charity were always a part of our family life. Whether it was selecting special gifts for the names of the needy on the community Giving Tree at Christmastime or donating food items at Thanksgiving, the kids grew up experiencing the joy of giving. As teens, they joined the church youth group and helped out with construction projects that benefited the less fortunate. Matt would also volunteer to help set up the large Christmas trees in the church sanctuary during Advent.

Matthew had a very well formed conscience. I remember one day in 2006 when I was in the backyard watering a dead zone in the grass with a hose, standing in the middle of the lawn. Matt, who was eighteen, had come back there to ask me for something, what I cannot recall. He wanted permission for something and I turned him down for whatever reason. He was angry and spouted off at me, which was a rare occurrence. I was stung by his hurtful words and bad attitude, but didn't relent on my decision. He stormed off. I just licked my wounds and kept watering the grass. About ten minutes later, Matt returned to apologize for how he had spoken to me. That is who my son was. He was thoughtful and caring, even when he was mad at me.

In late August, it was time to help him pack and get settled into a college dorm at Cal Poly San Luis Obispo where he would major in engineering. I was pleased that he selected a school that was only a few hours away, but even so I was on the brink of tears all summer. I truly enjoyed having my son around. He had been the man of the house for the past couple of years, helping me put Christmas lights up on the house and taking care of various home repair projects. I tried to prepare myself for this transition in our relationship, where he would be away at school, for I would miss him terribly.

When selecting his bedding for the dorm room I remember how much attention I paid to picking the coziest items. I bought him a thick ultra-soft red blanket, a down pillow, and high thread count sheets, a subconscious attempt to ensure creature comforts for my son. I realize how silly that must sound, being that this was a 6' 3" grown man, but that was just me being a mom.

I will never forget the day he left for college. We drove the four-hour trek to SLO and, together with his roommate and his parents, we got the boys' dorm room all set up. We all spent the day together, enjoying a nice lunch and then making a final Walmart run for the last minute items we discovered they needed. His roommate, Mitchell, was a close friend throughout his childhood and a teammate from high school baseball, someone I loved and trusted like a second son. It gave both us moms a sense of calm knowing that they would watch each other's backs as they adjusted to campus life.

When all was done, that moment arrived when I would have to leave my son and make the drive home alone. I clearly remember willing myself to be strong in front of Matthew, not wanting him to see me break down on this special day. He walked me to my car, we hugged and said, "I love you," while I managed to remain totally in control, not shedding a tear. The minute I pulled away from the parking lot, however, the waterworks began and, boy, did the tears flow. When I finally got back home the first thing I did was walk upstairs to his room. I stood in his doorway and just sobbed.

In my mind, I played the movie reel of his childhood, having spent his last fourteen years in that room. I envisioned him in his little twin bed with the blue comforter clutching his polka dot doggie, a plush toy that he never let out of his sight as a child. I imagined him sitting on his bed playing video games or rifling through his Pokémon collection. I saw him in his steady stream of Little League uniforms. I imagined him nailing his broken skateboard decks to the wall as a badge of courage. I saw him dressed in his tux before picking up his prom date. In my mind's eye I watched him grow from a small child into the handsome young man he had become. I walked over to his bed, sat down, and wept.

All parents have to cycle through the difficult separation that comes with the end of high school and the beginning of college if their son or daughter picks a college out of the local region. My oldest was commuting to a local college so I hadn't yet crossed this bridge. For me, having my child leave home was very painful. I just had to keep reminding myself that this is the natural order of life, that we raise them to be independent, functioning, responsible adults. After that, when they leave the nest, all we parents can do is pray for their protection and hope for the best.

Matt and I stayed in touch as he settled in and started his classes. He shared funny stories about his teachers and details about his suitemates. There were a total of eight young men in his apartment—imagine the chaos. He mentioned that one of the roommates was from Tennessee and began each day by drinking alcohol. I repeated my worn out mom-warnings about avoiding falling into the party scene, to keep his head on straight. I was well aware of the many kids who get sidetracked by the party atmosphere in college and can end up flunking out or getting into trouble. He assured me that he wasn't like that and not to worry. I looked forward to our chats and texts; it helped me feel less anxious about his wellbeing.

It was late November, Thanksgiving break, and Matthew was home for the week. He stayed busy visiting friends and family, which I had expected. To my relief, after a three-month absence he looked perfectly healthy. It was wonderful to have him take up temporary residence in his old bedroom; our house felt complete again.

One night during his visit, Matt woke me up at 1:00 a.m. asking if we could talk. I immediately wondered if he was intoxicated or something, as this nocturnal visit was definitely outside the norm. I didn't smell alcohol or pot on him, but I did sense urgency about his need to talk, so I flipped on the light and sat up in bed. Matt proceeded to sit on the end of my bed and then began to cry.

"Dad has never even called me since I left for school, not once. Today I saw him at Grandma's and he still didn't ask one question about how I was doing, about my classes, nothing. You know who he did ask about? Michelson!" Michelson, whose first name I never had known, was a ball player from an opposing team in their high school league who ended up playing baseball there at SLO. To Matt, his dad seemed more interested in asking about that stranger than his own son.

My heart broke for him. Knowing about past issues he'd had with his dad, and how much he craved his approval, it was evident that Matt was deeply hurt. At the same time, seeing his pain also ripped the scab off the wound of my own suffering from the marriage, triggering feelings of intense anger toward my ex. However, this was not the whole story.

Matt sat there crying for about fifteen minutes, telling me how sad he feels all the time. He told me he had been struggling with insomnia, and how some nights he would go out to the baseball field there on campus and hit balls by himself in the middle of the night because he missed baseball so much. He had gone to the health center to get some relief for the insomnia, and was prescribed trazodone. He said the drug caused him to have terrible nightmares; vivid, scary dreams that only made matters worse. He told me he had contracted mononucleosis along with several other students, and had no energy to go to class for two weeks, setting him behind in his engineering class. He seemed very unhappy.

All I could do while he shared his struggles was to offer encouragement. I tried to explain away his dad's insensitivity, and also offer him some motivating words about catching up at school and overcoming the difficult transition to living away at college. I remembered how that first semester, even the first year, could be rife with challenges as students become acquainted with the new college lifestyle. But deep inside, I was troubled by this scene that was unfolding in the middle of the night. Matt was unusually down and seemed a bit hopeless. It was odd, because his usual nature was so positive and upbeat all the time. I gave him a hug and went back to sleep, hoping in my heart that this was just a blip that would resolve with time.

When Coach Johnson sent out the email to former players announcing his plans for an alumni game that April of 2007, Matt was pumped. He had been missing the sport deeply and looked forward to seeing all his friends once again in the high school dugout where so many great memories had been made. His teammates were scattered across the country now, so he was excited about reconnecting with them and playing at the alumni game.

During the week before the game, a couple of the guys who had initially said they were coming bowed out. Matt was disappointed, but knew that about half a dozen of them would still be present at the game. But when game day came, only Matt and one other player from his graduation year showed up. He couldn't mask the feelings of sadness on his face. He had been so excited to see everybody, but apparently no one else placed much importance on the alumni game. I could even see in the photos I took at the game how disappointed he was.

Towards the end of the second freshman semester, Matthew informed me that he honestly hated engineering and wanted to switch to a different career path. When he was a kid he always wanted to be a firefighter, and I had encouraged that aspiration. I remember thinking how perfectly suited to that occupation he was, with a compassionate, caring nature and a strong physical build. So when he announced his intent to leave SLO and enroll in a fire science program I didn't put up any resistance at all. It was his calling, and I wouldn't stand in the way.

There was an excellent fire science program and academy at a community college in Santa Rosa, so we decided it would be financially prudent for him to live at home and commute to his classes. He agreed, so after finishing that second semester at SLO he packed up and moved back home. This proved to be a bit of an adjustment for me, as he brought with him some new behaviors.

As is widely known, the college environment is more about partying than academics these days. College is often seen as one big four-year long party, with abundant alcohol, prescription drugs, and recreational drugs proliferating on campuses. This is not a new development, but seems to have taken on a deeper dimension in defining the college experience of today.

One day, soon after Matt moved home, I returned from work to find him and some friends playing beer pong in our garage, all of them underage. I swiftly shut it down and gave Matt the lecture that he had to respect my rules and not take risks that could involve liability issues for me. He understood, and said it wouldn't happen again.

Over the course of the ensuing weeks that summer, I became aware that something was different about my now nineteen-year-old son. He was coming home late at night intoxicated after hanging out with local friends and partying. His mood was perpetually low. He seemed very depressed and was sleeping a lot. I told him he needed to get a part-time job, which he did, a sales associate position at a local sporting goods store. He hated the job, found it boring and uninspiring, but I assured him he needed to work so if not there, somewhere.

On the Fourth of July he had made plans with some of his old high school baseball friends, which was great. I thought that it would have a positive effect on his mood to see his friends who were home for summer break. At about 5 p.m. on the Fourth I received a call from Matt. I could barely understand him, his voice so thick from an obviously high level of alcohol consumption. He had gotten cited for underage drinking in public and possession of alcohol, and needed me to pick him up and drive him to the local police station for some paperwork. I was infuriated.

When I arrived to pick him up on the west side of town he staggered over to my car, belligerent expression on his face, holding the paperwork he needed signed off. When he got in the car I asked what he was thinking, drinking in public on the Fourth of July. Sheer stupidity. He was in such a foul, drunken mindset he sassed back at me, completely ungrateful that I had come to help him out.

MY 13th STATION

We arrived at the police station and I accompanied him inside where he would be released to me officially, and we were then instructed as to how to set up a mandated court appearance. It was all so foreign to me, standing in a police station with my intoxicated son planning a court date. Mentally I was already wondering how to get the misdemeanor charge expunged from his record.

Six days later on July 10, Matthew came home from work and asked if we could chat. I described this talk in an email to his dad.

> **7/10/07:** ... He immediately broke down in tears. He is extremely depressed, where I think he needs to see someone. He feels despondent—very depressed over the legal problems and his future being in jeopardy. I talked to him for over an hour, trying to give him perspective and hope and encouragement. I told him to see the bigger picture, to imagine his goal and then take one step at a time to get to it.

Aside from his obvious abuse of alcohol, in this email to John it was clear I had concerns about his state of mind.

On July 26th, two of his close friends, one who was his roommate at SLO, and both baseball friends, stopped by the house. I decided to ask them point blank if Matt was doing drugs. I explained my concerns about his change in demeanor, the event on the Fourth of July, and his general lack of responsibility. He had always been very dependable and had suddenly become a complete flake. Lately, he was racking up parking tickets and missing shifts at work, things that Matt would have formerly not been so careless about. Mostly, it was a change in his mood that made me think there was something serious going on.

When both friends adamantly stated that Matt was no different than them or their other friends in his use of alcohol and occasional weed, I decided to schedule a physical exam at our primary care provider. Matt signed a release so that the lab results could be made available to me, a necessary HIPAA compliance procedure. When the results came back I asked the doctor to review them with me. Apparently his liver enzymes were significantly outside the normal range, indicative of liver damage. I told him about the change in my son's demeanor and mood and he suggested a consult with a mental health provider to have a psychological evaluation conducted.

Meanwhile, his relationship with his dad continued to be very strained. One day in late July, a situation evolved between him and his dad that quickly escalated to a very disturbing event. I heard a loud bang from down the hall, finding a hole punched in Matt's bedroom door. He burst through his door and pushed past me in the hall, carrying three framed photos of the All-Star teams he'd played on, each including his dad standing alongside the players. He marched down the hall and into my bedroom where there was a deck. I ran to catch him just as he was attempting to throw the framed photos off the deck and grabbed them from him.

A few minutes later, thinking that he had settled down, I heard a loud thumping sound in the backyard. Peering through my bedroom window I spotted Matt crushing his dad's wooden baseball bat over the concrete steps, obliterating it. This bat was a remnant from John's short baseball career in the minors, which he'd left in our garage when he moved out back in 2004. Matt looked completely crazed as he held up the splintered stump of the bat.

Soon after, when his dad drove up to drop off Emma, Matt met him out on the driveway holding what was left of the bat in a threatening manner. What ensued was very upsetting. Matt confronted his dad, loudly. He assailed his dad with vehement accusations, cursing at him at the top of his lungs, and then he spit on him. I won't defend his dad, as the issues being railed against him were accurate.

However, observing Matt's rage, it truly seemed as if something had snapped mentally. All the anger he felt toward his dad had hit a boiling point and literally caused a switch to flip in his mind.

The next day I contacted the psychiatrist's office that the doctor had referred me to and scheduled an evaluation for Matt. When I informed Matt about my concerns and the upcoming appointment, he responded in anger, leaving me a note on the stairs as he stormed out of the house. I still have that note. It read: "If you love me as much as you say, then trust me. I am not an addict to anything. If you want me back you need to trust me more. Bye."

When he didn't come home that night I was worried. It wasn't like him to just not come home without telling me his plans. Over the next two days there was no word from Matt. I tried not to panic, and continued to pray for him to return home. I contacted the parents of his closest friends to ask them if they had any information about my son that could shed light on his recent mood and conduct, or his whereabouts. A couple of the moms got back to me later, after discussing Matt with their sons, and revealed that Matt had told the boys some crazy lies about our home life. This completely floored me because I could not figure out what would motivate him to tell such tall tales. This lying was yet another sign of mental instability.

Finally, on the third day of his absence, Matt called. I picked up the phone and tears immediately began to flow when I heard his voice. I walked out to the hallway to get Sarah's attention, to let her know I had Matt on the line. She joined me there while Matt stayed on the line, crying.

He was in Colorado staying with some friends from high school. He told me he "couldn't live this way any more." He said he wanted to die. I sat down on the floor, Sarah, age twenty-one, following suit. She could tell by my expression that something very wrong was going on, and before I knew it she had tears streaming down her face, too.

Over the next ten minutes I tried to calm my son down, basically walking him off the proverbial ledge over the phone. My heart broke hearing my son speak that way, in so much pain he wanted to end his life. I told him to stay with his friends and that I would fly out to Colorado and together we could drive his car home to California the next day. As he settled down, he promised not to hurt himself, and that he would journey home over the next few days, which he proceeded to do.

This disturbing phone conversation confirmed my fears that Matt was struggling with mental problems in addition to the alcohol abuse. How and why this could possibly happen are questions that will dog me for the rest of my life. How could this levelheaded, responsible, beautiful, *normal* young man be suddenly beset with a mood disorder? It made no sense to me at all. The mental health issue helped explain why he was drinking so much recently. He was evidently self-medicating the emotional pain away using alcohol, and the marijuana helped him with his ongoing struggle with insomnia.

Later that afternoon, after our emotional phone conversation, I emailed Matt what I hoped to be an inspiring little pep talk:

> Blue,
> Please try to get to a place where you see God's hand at work all around you. Look at the gorgeous scenery in Colorado, especially the mountains, and see that God created it all for us to enjoy. Look at the face of a little kid, the sheer innocent joy in their face, and see that God created that child. Look at the way a mother holds her precious baby, and see that God created that baby just for her to love and adore. There is so much beauty around you, so much to be thankful for.

MY 13th STATION

    Most importantly, see that *you* are worthy of love. The unbelievable outpouring of love I have seen, from your friends and their moms, is absolutely incredible. To see your sisters so upset about you, and dad calling me regularly to see if I have heard from you, shows how loved you are. Everyone is so upset and worried about you. There is so much love out there for you, my boy, please accept it as yours. You deserve love.
    Matt, you have always been a class act, a great kid with a loving heart. Right now you are in distress and not yourself at all. This is not who you are. Now is the time to face your issues and take care of the life God gave you. Let God lead you out of the lies and confusion and help you get back to a healthy, truthful life once again. He created you to love and be loved. No matter what, I love you and will do whatever it takes to help you get back to a healthy place. You are so very special to me.
I love you,
Mom.

When Matt returned to California he did agree to meet with a psychotherapist to help process whatever issues were tormenting him. He only went once, though, stating flatly that he got absolutely nothing out of the session. Soon after, he announced he would be delaying the start of the fire science program until January, instead taking a semester off to live in Hawaii with his high school friend. The friend and his roommates were Mormons, so I figured at least they wouldn't be sitting around drinking.
    I didn't try to talk him out of it, sensing in my gut that this would be a good respite for him and might help renew his mental state. He

was still not willing to talk to or see his dad, so maybe this short break would help him process his feelings and get to a place of forgiveness.

Those four months in Hawaii turned out to be very beneficial to him, and he came back tan, trim, and full of funny stories about the adventure. He and his buddy had bought a car for like fifty bucks, so there were lots of hilarious mishaps involving that pile of junk. He related the story about the day before Thanksgiving when some locals jumped out of a truck and beat him up while he was walking along the highway with a girl, cutting his lip so bad he couldn't eat Thanksgiving dinner. Beaming, he talked about snorkeling, spearfishing, surfing, and about his antics at a job at the local hardware store that he took to pay his living expenses. This chapter of his life, his Hawaii adventure, would be one of the happiest periods of his lifetime.

CHAPTER 13

The Enabler

MATT FOLLOWED THROUGH IN JANUARY 2008 on his promise to begin the classes at the fire science program in Santa Rosa. Following his stint in Hawaii and the holiday season, he seemed relaxed and happy, ready to start a new chapter in his life. I was ecstatic, knowing my son would someday be out there rescuing people and doing good deeds in the community. He had such a giving heart and so much to offer.

In addition to his classes, he signed up to volunteer at a local firehouse on Thursday afternoons. These programs allow young people interested in the profession to get hands-on experience with equipment and procedures while they are in the fire science program. He seemed to enjoy hanging out at Station #7, getting along well with the firefighters there. Matt also got hired at a local golf course, so of course he enjoyed the free rounds of golf and tips that came with that gig. All in all, I felt confident that my son had turned the corner and would only continue to progress towards achieving his life's goals.

One night in the spring, after his shift at the station, he joined a couple of the guys at a local bar for a beer or two. At this point Matt was twenty years old and most likely had a fake I.D. Later, as he and the firefighters exited the bar, Matt was still holding a beer bottle in his hand. He suddenly spotted a police car in the parking lot and quickly pitched the bottle into a nearby bush. Unfortunately for him, an officer witnessed this and wrote him a citation for underage drinking, carrying an alcoholic drink out of the establishment, and littering.

When he told me about the citation I was angry. The vetting process for getting hired as a firefighter or police officer is extremely thorough and extensive. Each time Matt racked up another citation, his chances of ever getting hired diminished. Any little infraction could torpedo someone's hopes of working as a first responder. Because of this misdemeanor, he had to satisfy certain court-ordered sanctions, such as attending classes about drug and alcohol addiction among other activities, before they would expunge this offense.

Meanwhile, he was beginning to struggle in his classes, barely passing the weekly tests that had a pass threshold of eighty percent and above. He just barely missed on one and had to retake the test, setting him behind by a week. In addition to the struggles in school, unpaid parking tickets were coming to my attention via mail notifications. Matt would receive a parking violation and then ignorantly throw the citation away. This blatant disregard for the law resulted in huge fines, and I was mystified why he was reverting back to his irresponsible behaviors of last year.

In my panic to attempt to keep him out of legal trouble that could hobble his quest to become a firefighter, I reluctantly continued to pay these exorbitant parking fines. I was frustrated that he was causing me financial hardship and didn't seem to care. Matt was not right, not himself at all. He seemed emotionally absent and apathetic. But I found myself sweeping up the messes as they occurred, feeling frustrated and exasperated that he had such blatant disregard for my diminishing financial resources.

By the summer of 2008, Matt was once again engaging in heavy drinking, and was deep into the death metal music scene, attending live concerts regularly. A local kid, Andrew, who had not gone off to college, became a drinking buddy, and they would stay out late getting wasted. By now, it was evident that my son was actively abusing alcohol, but I, feeling hamstrung, did not know what to do about it. He was still working at the golf course, volunteering at the firehouse, and was plodding along in his classes, so I tried not to become too alarmed. But he seemed depressed again, which seemed to correlate with the increased alcohol use.

As his worried mother, I continued to stamp out any fires that erupted threatening to sideline his career goals, a classic co-dependent enabler. Mothers are hardwired to be enablers. It is painful to sit back and watch a child's life implode; how can we not jump in and try to help them? Well, the hard truth is that by enabling someone with a substance use disorder, usually a result of being firmly in denial of its existence or severity, parents do far more damage, usually only exacerbating the problem. Driven by love for my son and concern for his future, I consistently doled out money to manage the tangible and destructive effects of his increasing alcohol abuse and persistent state of depression. He seemed to no longer care about the negative repercussions. Meanwhile, I just stood by stupefied, watching any opportunity for Matt to get hired, much less succeed at his chosen profession, go right down the tubes.

Because I was so emotionally invested in Matt's psychological state, I ignored danger signs left and right. Even when his selfish behaviors and declining mental state demanded my attention, I would make excuses for them or explain them away as unusual departures from the norm. I hadn't yet allowed the increasing body of glaring red flags to penetrate my consciousness, preferring to exist in a state of stubborn denial instead.

One day, I went to the grocery store to pick up a few items for that night's dinner. When I attempted to pay with my debit card, the cashier discreetly informed me that my card had been declined. Embarrassed, I wondered how could that be? Back then I didn't have a direct link to my savings account for overdraft protection, and would instead just transfer funds as needed. After paying with a credit card, I went home feeling totally bewildered.

The next morning I stopped by the bank to have them investigate why my card was declined at the store the day before. She reviewed my account and told me that I must have forgotten to record an ATM withdrawal I had made a couple of days prior. I adamantly stated that I had not made an ATM withdrawal, that there must be some mistake on the bank's behalf. She stood her ground, giving me the exact time of day that the money had been withdrawn at the ATM.

I asked both Matt and Sarah if they may have used my debit card to get money from my account. They both flatly denied doing such a thing. It was so unbelievably out of character for any of my kids to outright steal from me that I didn't hesitate to believe them, and called the bank to ask for a supervisor. The bank representative suggested they retrieve the video from that day and time when the ATM was accessed to see who exactly was using my debit card. She did, however, suggest in a very diplomatic way that I inform my two oldest kids that the bank has access to video documentation.

Sure enough, when I presented them with that information, Matt immediately confessed to taking my debit card and stealing money out of my checking account. I was astonished to learn this, as he had never, ever stolen from me in the past. This was not who he was. He apologized profusely and promised to repay me out of his upcoming paycheck, but from that point forward the trust bond was ruptured.

Matt had been spending far too much time partying with Andrew. With the increased alcohol consumption and Matt's recent lies and irresponsible behaviors, I could no longer deny that my son had a serious problem.

I decided one Thursday to act on a hunch. Matt was still volunteering at the station on Thursday evenings, or so I assumed. I would periodically ask him about what he was learning from the men and whether there was ever any drama during his stints, but realized I hadn't asked him in a while. Each Thursday at 5:45 p.m. off he'd go to work at the station. On this particular Thursday I had a sneaking suspicion about his claim to still be doing the volunteer work, although I can't remember what provoked my suspicion.

Matt left for the station that day at the usual time, so I waited for about a half hour before driving to the fire station myself. I searched the parking lot and the adjacent curbs for his car, but didn't see it. A sick, sinking feeling set in. I decided to call his bluff, so I took out my phone and called him. He picked up right away. I asked if he was busy at the moment, and he said no, they were all just hanging out and watching the Angels game on TV. So I said, "Great! I am just now approaching the firehouse and would love to say hi and meet the guys you work with." He abruptly stated that he wouldn't be able to just leave and meet me outside.

To that I responded, "No worry, I will just ring the front desk."

After two or three seconds of silence, Matt admitted he wasn't really there at the firehouse at all, that he was at Andrew's house. I felt nauseous. Was this even my son anymore? This person was not the same son I had raised. He lied, stole my money, didn't pay his debts, didn't follow through on important things—who was this young man impersonating my son?

About a week later, Matt walked off his job at the local golf course after a disagreement with his boss.

I felt ashamed of myself. I had allowed my son to play me, offering all that financial and emotional support while he treated me with utter disrespect. I had fallen into the trap of codependency, making excuses for his selfish, thoughtless behavior, continuing to fork over money to keep him out of trouble, and ignoring the obvious signs of addiction taking root. I was an enabler in utter denial. I was a mother.

CHAPTER 14

Enter Amanda

ONE MORNING IN EARLY JANUARY 2009 Matt was in an especially sunny mood. He wanted to chat about the party he had attended the night before where he had met a girl. He was completely giddy as he described her. He liked that she was not like the East Bay types, who he considered superficial and vacuous. He disdained the overly made up faces and empty heads that he claimed dominated the chick scene in our neck of the woods. This girl, Amanda, was different. He described her as a natural blonde who wore virtually no make-up and loved camping and surfing. In fact, he said she was a bit of a tomboy type, not at all like the girlie girl types from our area.

Matt had had a couple of fairly serious relationships during high school, but nothing really steady since then. But that morning I could see he was infatuated. He said he and Amanda had been up all night talking after the party. In fact, they were already making plans for their next meeting later in the week. Over the next few days, every time I walked down the hall I heard him talking on the phone with Amanda.

The following week I got to meet Amanda myself, seeing immediately the charm that attracted my son's attention. She had a broad, friendly smile and beautiful blue eyes, and came across as a kind, warm person. The two of them were obviously enamored and quickly became attached at the hip, seeing each other nearly every day. While I was supportive of his new relationship, I was also bearing the financial brunt of his lack of employment and feared his efforts to find work would be sidetracked. Just feeding a big guy like Matt was taking a huge chunk of my humble little paycheck. I was already struggling financially post-divorce, running up debt and having difficulty keeping up with what seemed like a constant barrage of household repairs.

I couldn't help but notice that when he and Amanda were together they were usually drinking. I became concerned, and annoyed, as they appeared to be living in their own little fantasy world, neither of them holding down jobs at the time. Occasional bouts of drama would flare up when they had been drinking, usually when an emotional Amanda would share her family issues and cry. I had come to notice that Amanda was somewhat moody, which concerned me. They were becoming so close, and Matt was such a trusting person, I worried a bit about his increasing vulnerability.

One spring day Matt and I were chatting about Amanda, so I decided to share my concern about her struggling with a possible mood disorder. I also mentioned that their drinking habits were troubling to me. He shared with me that Amanda had been diagnosed in high school with a mood disorder, but he implored me not to hold it against her, saying emphatically, "It's not her fault." He wanted me to understand how much he cared for her and not to form a negative opinion based on her mental health issue. How could I? My own son was also suffering from mental health issues.

One late afternoon in April 2009 when returning home from work, I turned up our street looking forward to throwing on my sweats and putting my tired feet up. As I drove along toward our end of the street I spotted several squad cars, a coroner's van, and yellow crime scene tape cordoning off the lower end of the street from through traffic. Just the sight of the coroner's van triggered a racing heartbeat and memories from 1994 when Linda Nichols had shockingly committed suicide.

How horrible it was to later learn that a fourteen-year-old boy had, just a few hours earlier, stood out on the sidewalk about ten houses down from our house on Meadow Lane, put his father's gun to his head, and killed himself. How could this be—a second violent and tragic suicide in the space of sixteen homes? I didn't know his family so it took a few days for the details to emerge. Sadly, he was apparently suffering from depression due to bullying at school, and felt he simply couldn't go on.

In early June, as she did every year, Emma prepared to head out with her dad for their annual trip to Sequoia National Park. In years past, for about six consecutive summers, our family went together to Sequoia and thoroughly loved it. Since the divorce in 2005, the kids, some or all depending on schedules, would go with their dad as he continued the tradition.

These yearly trips to Sequoia actually began in 1991 when I was pregnant with Emma. I remember being utterly exhausted and snippy that trip, irritated that the bears roaming around in the National Park were out of control, destroying anything in their path to get to yummy camper food. Each time I needed to get any little snack, even toothpaste, for Sarah or Matt I had to clomp up the path to the giant bear box and wrestle with its super heavy steel door. No wonder I was annoyed, I was unknowingly expecting a baby and totally fatigued *all the time*. Regardless, the natural beauty of this place hooked us, and for several years we made a point to spend at least five days annually in the park.

This year, Emma had invited a girlfriend, Sophia, to join her. The girls were besties and had just completed their junior year of high school. Sequoia would provide a fun and adventurous jumpstart to the summer. Since Emma's dad would be picking the girls up at the crack of dawn, it made sense for Sophia to spend the night at our house.

The next morning, Emma noticed that Sophia seemed off, just not herself. When she asked Sophia if she was okay, she told Emma that for some strange reason during the night she had awakened with an intense desire to kill herself. She literally got out of bed, rummaged through her purse for her prescription medication and swallowed a handful of pills. Emma was extremely shaken when Sophia told her this, and upset that her best friend hadn't woken her up to tell her she was feeling so despairing. Thanks be to God, Sophia was shaken but unscathed by the medication and they proceeded to go camping as planned. This unnerving event happened just three months after the young teen had committed suicide on the sidewalk down the street from us. Emma kept their secret for years, finally sharing this incident with me just two years ago.

Matt and Amanda continued to spend copious amounts of time together, both still unemployed. The country was deep in the grip of the Great Recession and older adults were given priority over teens and young adults if there was a job to be had. More trouble ensued, as the two managed to get in a car accident on the freeway, of course claiming in unison that it was the other driver's fault. After the adjuster investigated the accident it was determined that Matthew was at fault. Of course, they had no ability to pay the $1,000 deductible to get the car repaired, so as usual I ended up putting yet another unplanned expense on my credit card. Money was increasingly becoming a source of resentment for me toward Matthew. It seemed the costs associated with his irresponsible behaviors kept mounting while his efforts to gain employment seemed half-hearted at best.

In June Matt informed me that he didn't pass the emergency medical technicians (EMT) course and would have to take it over. He was very ashamed about failing to get his EMT certification. I was upset with him for not passing, knowing full well his partying and time spent with his girlfriend had taken priority to studying for the exams. Passing that part of the program would have allowed him to begin working as an EMT and earning income while also gaining critical work experience. This development was very disappointing and had me gravely worried about his future career prospects.

By July, it was evident that Matt's depression was worsening. He seemed to have absolutely no motivation to go find a job or to be productive in any real way. His drinking escalated. I was so emotionally connected with my son I could literally feel his despair. I became so worried that I decided to set up another appointment with a different psychologist. This time his sister Emma took him.

As Emma related it, "I stood against the doctor's office door so he could not leave."

Both his sisters had become increasing worried about his dark mood and heavy drinking, and I was really impressed at Emma's determination to get him help.

Just as he'd said after the appointment in 2007, he told me that this shrink hadn't helped him at all, so he would not be returning. My heart sank. I felt frustrated, angry, and hopeless. I decided it was time to get tough, so I gave him a two-week timeline to make plans to move out. He exclaimed that he had nowhere to go, and I told him to go sleep in a campground then. I had simply had it. I felt I could no longer afford to have him living at home and contributing nothing, only causing me emotional and financial distress. He seemed selfish and completely oblivious to how much his life choices were negatively impacting his sisters and me.

A few days later, just as I had summoned the guts to kick my son out of the house, he and Amanda called me downstairs to announce they were expecting a baby. They said they were going to keep the baby and that Matt had proposed to her. They would get married as soon as possible.

My immediate reaction was red-hot anger. How could they allow this to happen? Neither of them had jobs, they were twenty-one years old, and what had looked like difficult financial challenges now suddenly seemed dire. I envisioned all his dreams going right down the drain. It was a very devastating blow to an already problematic situation.

After I stormed up the stairs to my room for a good cry, I started processing the news. I was going to be a grandmother! And my son and his fiancé made the wonderful choice to have this baby. Neither of them batted an eye, knowing instantly that they would keep the baby and get married. They chose life. I began to turn around.

Over the next eight weeks, Matt and Amanda worked on making their wedding plans. It would be a small backyard ceremony at Amanda's aunt's house in Oakland, presided over by a Christian minister. Amanda's mom and aunts, who all lived within blocks of each other in the Rockridge area, busied themselves with the wedding preparations, and I took my son shopping at Macy's for a suit. I was operating in a fog during those weeks, not really sure what was actually happening. I was very supportive of the kids, as were all the family members on both sides. Yes, we all knew they had a tough road ahead, but somehow God orders things in crazy ways and it's not always easy to understand while you are in the middle of it.

Thankfully, Matt found a job in October, although it was a graveyard shift. This was pretty much the nail in the coffin to the fire science program, as it was evident he couldn't go to school all day and then work all night. He had to step up and provide for his new little family, so the job took priority. In hopes of keeping his dream alive, he planned to switch to a day shift at the beginning of the year when something opened up, and then enroll in evening EMT classes.

So on October 21, 2009, Matthew and Amanda were wed. It was a very festive wedding and everyone was upbeat and hopeful for them. I loved the way all the family and their closest friends rallied around them to make the day very special. One of my favorite photos ever taken was the one my daughter Emma took that day. Prior to Matt and Amanda joining hands for the ceremony they each delivered a red rose to their mothers. Emma snapped the most beautiful picture of Matthew giving me a big hug after handing me that rose. It has been on my refrigerator door ever since.

In looking at the photos from the wedding I thought that Matt looked good, although I did notice a slight softening around his jawline. Barely noticeable, but I detected just a bit of puffiness that I knew was due to the excessive drinking. Thankfully, though, even though he was indeed anxious about becoming a husband and father, his mood had improved dramatically since the summer.

Amanda was also able to find a job that November, so they got a nice apartment not far from her side of the family, and about forty minutes from us. From that point through the end of 2009 we all just awaited the arrival of this beautiful little grandchild. I felt grateful to God for this gift, and now that the two of them had jobs, felt a renewed sense of hope.

CHAPTER 15

Hope and Heartache

AFTER THE HOLIDAYS PASSED I decided to start the New Year, 2010, with an ambitious project—converting Matt's old room to a guest room. This way, when they would come home for visits, I would have a presentable room for the little family. Knowing full well that tackling this project would be tantamount to tackling a haz-mat scene, I dragged all the cleaning supplies and hefty bags I would need to convert the bedroom inhabited first by a little boy, then a teen, and, eventually, a young adult, into something respectable for guests.

Digging through the years of nostalgia stuffed in my son's closet, I discovered several empty vodka bottles. Not those little pint bottles, but half gallon bottles that he had stealthily consumed. I sat there dumbfounded as I discovered them in the closet, under his bed, and fifth-size bottles stuffed under clothes in his dresser drawers. Having had no idea of the severity of son's drinking problem, I was confronted that day with the physical proof of it. His problems with depression, and now anxiety too, were layered with alcoholism. How could I not have known it was this bad? My heart sank considering that he would be a father soon, and how his alcohol abuse could cause real pain to the people he loved. This little child deserved fully present and healthy parents. That day a sense of deep foreboding set in.

On March 12, 2010 Matt and Amanda welcomed Grace Elizabeth into to this world. I was honored to be present, along with Matthew, Amanda's mother, and her grandmother, to witness the awe-inspiring event, the arrival of my first grandchild. I maintained a background presence while Matt stood at the bedside speaking quiet, consoling affirmations and mother Liz gently stroked her daughter's forehead. Seeing my son managing this intense scene with such calm made me feel proud. There he was, barely twenty-two years old, coaching his new wife as she birthed their child.

Matt never had gotten a tattoo before, and I was not a fan of tattoos. But how could I object to the tattoo he later had placed over his heart—his daughter's newborn footprints with her name etched below. His tattoo was an outward symbol of the love he felt in his heart for this beautiful baby daughter.

As happy and excited as we all were to welcome this delightful baby girl into the family, my strong emotional connection with Matt told me things were getting worse with him. I knew his graveyard job was wearing on him, and he had become pale due to lack of sun exposure. He and Amanda barely crossed paths because they worked opposite schedules, and working graveyard only added to the feelings of isolation and loneliness so common with depression.

Amanda and Matt were both doting parents to Gracie, taking very good care of her and responsive to all her needs. It was obvious that they were completely besotted with this little child. Meanwhile, I continued to pray for my son, praying also for the intercession of Saint Monica on his behalf. Saint Monica was the mother who prayed for her wayward son, for years on end, having the eventual result of not only bringing her son back into the fold of his faith but to go on to become the Doctor of the Church known as St. Augustine.

MY 13th STATION

I continued to hope and pray that, with the added responsibility and focus of fatherhood, Matthew would step up and assume the role without the need to self-medicate any more. At the time, this seemed logical, that he would just stop. But in hindsight, I can see how naïve I was. I had literally zero understanding of the forces at work.

One day in August, Amanda brought Gracie for a short visit. Sarah and her fiancé, Danny, had just moved into a cute little apartment downtown, so we all met there. While we were visiting and enjoying Gracie, Amanda blurted out that she felt marrying Matthew was a mistake. Apparently, his drinking problem had already become a serious issue in their marriage, something that I had seen coming. Even so, it hurt to hear her describe him with so much disgust in her voice, and it was painful to hear my daughter-in-law state that marrying him was a mistake. Yes, Matt had problems, but so did Amanda, after all.

After Amanda and Gracie left, Sarah and I discussed the situation, trying to come up with a plan to help her brother. All we knew about addiction was that, until the person was interested in getting help, it was fruitless to attempt to force them into treatment. We both recalled reading that the person with the addiction must hit bottom, whatever their personal bottom is, before they will finally be ready to get help. Well, if Matt loses his wife that would definitely be a serious bottom. I was very concerned about the depression. If she left him it could really set fire to that disorder. Needless to say, after that visit with Amanda Sarah and I were deeply concerned about Matthew.

About a week later, Matthew stopped by for a visit. Because it was the dead of summer, he was wearing shorts that day. I could not believe what I was looking at. Engulfing his right calf was an enormous tattoo, taken from the gothic artwork of Iron Maiden. The image featured a particularly grotesque version of the band's demonic-looking icon, "Eddie," from the *Fear of the Dark* album cover. So there on my son's flesh was a permanent image of a tree monster (Eddy), the creature embedded into a bare, leafless tree, with horrible long spiked teeth, red eyes, an ominous, menacing expression, and hideous branchlike limbs and ears, with a full moon in the background. I was utterly exasperated that he would put something so demonic-looking on his body, not to mention the gross waste of money at a time when he had mounting financial responsibilities.

It wasn't until all these years later, while beginning the preparation process for writing this book, that I decided to finally look up the lyrics to the song, "Fear of the Dark." Hindsight continued to be enlightening as I sought clues to help explain what may have contributed to Matt's demise. I pulled up the lyrics online and read the words to the song behind the image he had chosen to tattoo onto his body, and felt sick.

Fear of the Dark
By Iron Maiden
I am a man who walks alone
And when I'm walking a dark road
At night or strolling through the park

When the light begins to change
I sometimes feel a little strange
A little anxious when it's dark
Fear of the dark
Fear of the dark
I have a constant fear that something's always near

MY 13th STATION

Fear of the dark
Fear of the dark

I have a phobia that someone's always there
Have you run your fingers down the wall
And have you felt your neck skin crawl
When you're searching for the light?
Sometimes when you're scared to take a look
At the corner of the room
You've sensed that something's watching you
Fear of the dark
Fear of the dark
I have a constant fear that something's always near
Fear of the dark
Fear of the dark

I have a phobia that someone's always there
Have you ever been alone at night
Thought you heard footsteps behind
And turned around and no one's there?
And as you quicken up your pace
You find it hard to look again
Because you're sure there's someone there
Watching horror films the night before
Debating witches and folklore
The unknown troubles on your mind
Maybe your mind is playing tricks
You sense and suddenly eyes fix
On dancing shadows from behind
Fear of the dark
Fear of the dark

One day in the early fall of 2010, I was determined to get through a bunch of housework and laundry that I had put off all week. These days, it was just Emma and me and our two dogs that occupied the house on Meadow Lane, so chores could be ignored a bit longer than back when the house was full. I was home alone with no distractions, so I plowed through the house cleaning with a vengeance. After completing the final load of laundry, which was mostly Emma's, I headed upstairs to place her clean clothes on her dresser so she could put them away later.

I approached her room with a large stack of laundry in my arms. The two bedroom doors that intersect there at the end of the hall, hers and the guest room that was once Matt's bedroom, were both closed. In the couple of seconds it took for me to balance the laundry in one arm so I could grab her doorknob, a thick, dark, heavy, incredibly chilling sense of evil seemed to surround me, to penetrate me. I sensed it as a column from the ceiling to the floor, with me in the center of it. It was so powerful, so strong a sense of pure evil, that I immediately dropped the laundry on the floor and raced to my bedroom at the other end of the hall and slammed my door shut, heart pounding as I leaned against the door.

I realized later, of course, that a door is obviously not a barrier to an evil presence or demonic spirit. But in that moment, my instinct was to run away from the source of the darkness that I so clearly felt in the hallway, to protect myself. I didn't tell Emma about this. I tried to convince myself that I had probably imagined it—a fool's errand. I knew what I had experienced.

In October 2010, when Gracie was just six months old, Amanda asked Matthew to move out. Part of me was heartbroken for him, while another part of me understood how his alcoholism, depression, and anxiety must have been overwhelming for her. His addictive behavior was escalating. He had stolen some of my sleeping pills out of my medicine cabinet and snorted the drug. He also tried to get high using inhalants a few times, nearly passing out one time and scaring Amanda to death. She needed stability for her own sake, and his instability was not healthy for her. Still, I was sad that neither one of them had dealt head-on with the elephant in the room. He desperately needed help for his substance abuse and his mood disorders.

During this period, Matt stayed at our house in his old room, he and Amanda shuttling the baby back and forth between them. Matt was very withdrawn and depressed, for obvious reasons; as his mother, it killed me to see him so despondent. One evening in particular just broke my heart. Amanda had come to retrieve Gracie and I was upstairs in my bedroom. After Amanda and Gracie left, Matt ascended the stairs to return to the dark solitude of his room, I heard him crying. I immediately started crying, too, feeling his pain so vividly as if it was my own. I waited a few minutes to compose myself and to give him some privacy, and then tapped on his door. I asked if he wanted to talk and he replied firmly, "Not now!"

I noticed that many evenings he sat in one spot on the couch staring at the television, not talking or moving, just staring like a zombie. He always had a Gatorade beverage at his side. I knew that the contents of the bottle contained mostly vodka even without seeing him pour it. He would sit there like that with a steady supply of "Gatorade" until about 9:00 p.m., and then go pass out in his room.

One day, while I was out in the garage, Matt came out of the house to leave. Just the night before, I had decided, after watching his usual drinking routine, to confront him about the alcoholism, so I did. I told him that it was clear he had an alcohol problem, and he needed to get help. He was very defensive and irritated at me for mentioning it, commanding me to not, "even go there right now." I knew enough to back off because of his emotionally battered state. Something told me I would only drive him away if I pushed too hard at this raw, sensitive time while he and Amanda were separated. In Matt's mind, he needed the alcohol to survive the pain.

Around Thanksgiving, Amanda surprisingly invited him to join her, Gracie, and her family on a trip to Disneyland in Orange County. They planned on making a road trip out of it, stopping in Santa Barbara for a day before ending up in Anaheim. I could sense his entire demeanor had improved overnight. He set off with the family and had a very good time being with them all.

Within a week, Matt and Amanda were making plans to reconcile and try to work things out. I was ecstatic, so hopeful for their little family. He still needed to address his problems and get treatment, and I assumed, prayed, that had been part of the discussion when they were reuniting. Then, shortly after Christmas, Matt announced that he had received a job offer to work for the Vail Resort in Summit County, Colorado, and that Amanda had agreed to relocate with him. They were excited to start fresh with new surroundings and opportunities in that beautiful place.

The families were both shocked by the announcement, and we grandmas were a particular mess knowing how hard it would be to no longer have our precious granddaughter nearby. There were many, many tears. I felt I was grieving a terrible loss as the day of their departure approached. I had gotten so attached to Gracie in the past nine months and would miss her terribly.

By this time, late 2010, Matthew's appearance began to change, revealing the damage the drinking was doing to him physically. We gathered on the living room couch for a group photo at our going away party, and later I looked at the pictures in dismay. In the photos Matt look unhealthy, with a bloated face, bloodshot eyes, and a growing belly. I tried to conceal my deep-seated worry about him going off to live in the mountains, far from his family, where the mental health and drinking problems could worsen and I, ever codependent, would not be able to really know the scope of the situation or to help him. Regardless, I had to be happy for them and just shelve my concerns while ramping up my daily prayers. I kept reminding myself that God was in control.

CHAPTER 16

Escalation

THE NEW YEAR STARTED OUT WELL. All reports from Colorado were positive, with both Matt and Amanda working hard and little Gracie thriving. They kept us all informed on special moments, like when Gracie finally got her first tooth. They really loved living in the mountains even though 2011 brought record snowfall and ridiculously low temperatures. They sent over lots of photos of their apartment and the beautiful surroundings, and videos of the baby all bundled up and playing in the snow. Even though it was hard not having them local anymore, both sides of their family were happy that they were working things out and enjoying their new life in the Rockies.

These pleasant feelings ended abruptly in early March when Matthew called to tell me that the marriage was on the rocks again, this time for a different reason. He was very hurt and angry over what he'd discovered, and was choked up on the phone. A first birthday party was already planned in California at Amanda's aunt's residence, so it was important that we all just make the best of the situation and celebrate Gracie.

It seemed like forever since they had been back home, even though it had only been a few months. All the family members came, as well as some close friends of both Amanda and Matt. Only close family members were aware of the latest turn of events, but I know that everyone noticed the change in my son's appearance, and his sad demeanor.

Matt was now looking like an alcoholic. Even a young person, no matter how attractive, will suffer changes in appearance due to alcohol abuse. There is a glassy sheen in the bloodshot eyes. There is a red, ruddiness to the complexion. There is facial bloating, and, usually, the telltale distended gut. Matt exhibited all of the above, much to my dismay. He forced himself to smile and chat with everyone, but I detected the pain in his eyes. My fear, and his, due to the recent turn of events, was that Amanda would leave Colorado and return home, with Matt left behind in Vail. He absolutely loved his job and it offered career growth and opportunity. But if she decided to leave him and go back home to California, taking Gracie, he knew he would have no option but to follow them. It was a terrible quandary and this turmoil was exacerbating his mental health and drinking problems.

Thankfully, they eventually made a decision to stay together and continue to try to work things out in Colorado. I was relieved that they had gotten past yet another hurdle. These two absolutely loved each other to the core. That was never the issue. They were, however, only twenty-three years old, both struggling with mental health issues, alcohol abuse, financial pressures, and the unrelenting stress of raising a child. They each developed maladaptive coping mechanisms to manage the increasing stress they were simply unprepared to face at such a young age.

That Mother's Day I received a delivery of a dozen gorgeous long-stem roses—all different colors—from Matt. His note read: Happy Mother's Day, Mom! You are the best mother anyone could ever ask for. I love you, Blue. What a wonderful surprise. This upbeat and thoughtful gesture gave me hope that he was doing better.

MY 13th STATION

In June 2011, Matt and Gracie came home for a three-day visit. He was able to arrange time to spend with all the family members, sharing his beautiful baby girl with everyone. For all the upheaval in that little girl's life, she was an amazingly secure and confident child, an absolute delight to be around. By now Sarah was a mommy, too, having a beautiful little boy to add to the mix of grandchildren and to become the perfect cousin and playmate for Gracie. The two of them were immediately compatible. Nine-month-old Jake was not yet walking so we would place them side-by-side in those rolling walkers and watch them play bumper cars with them on the kitchen tile. Matt was a doting daddy, obviously deeply devoted to his daughter. While he was staying at the house, he uploaded onto my hard drive about a dozen short videos from his phone, little mini-movies of him and Gracie in the mountains. How blessed I am to still have those to this day.

Later that month I made plans to take a road trip to Colorado for my birthday in July. Even though I had just recently seen Matt and Gracie, I felt a growing sense of urgency to discuss his drinking problem and try to motivate him to get help. Not to mention, I was dying to see the beautiful place where they now lived. Based on the photos they were posting on Facebook, the natural beauty was so spectacular I just had to go and witness it for myself. Things had seemed calm for a couple of months now, so I looked forward to spending time with the little family in their new digs.

The day before I was to depart I received a call from Matthew. He was emotionally distraught, and obviously intoxicated. He told me not to bother coming out, as it would only ruin my birthday because Amanda had left him and he was a mess. I told him that was an even better reason for me to come out, so that together we could come up with a plan to get him the help he so desperately needed. Despite his objections, I headed out as planned for the two-day road trip that would take me across California, Nevada, Utah, and into Colorado.

Two days later, as I was approaching the destination, I tried to gear up for what could be a difficult visit. I braced myself when I drove into the parking lot near their apartment complex where I had planned to meet them. As I drove up I saw Amanda handing off Gracie to Matt. She waved at me, and then quickly got in her car and drove off. She apparently knew I was upset with her, so she avoided any conversation.

He and Gracie walked over to me and I couldn't believe how much she had grown in just the past month. What a little doll! I hugged my boy and when I did I could literally *feel* his deep pain. I struggled to retain my composure, knowing I had to keep it together for the baby. I had hoped we could go out for dinner at one of their favorite local restaurants, but Matt told me he was too sad to sit in a public place. Instead we drove around so he could show me some of the breathtaking sights as he attempted to keep up a strong front for Gracie.

I looked over at my son at one point and noticed his hand tremors. This was a new symptom. Later, back at the apartment, he told me he had such bad tremors at work, trying to get through his shifts without alcohol, that he was now afraid to drive the work truck. Matt said he now asks a coworker to drive, out of fear of possibly having a seizure and crashing the vehicle. He shared how he had gone to a picnic the past Sunday with fellow security personnel and local EMTs and paramedics, and wouldn't eat or drink any of the refreshments because he knew that they would notice how badly his hands shook. My heart just broke hearing this. I felt completely helpless as his mother, seeing how much emotional pain he was in and realizing he had lost all control over the disease of alcoholism.

After we put Grace to bed we began making a plan to get him some help. I had asked him, prior to my arrival, to set up an appointment with a mental health practitioner so he could be evaluated. He had found a psychologist who was in-network on his insurance plan and an appointment was set for the next day. I was anxious for him to be assessed and given some kind of game plan. It broke my heart to see him so sick.

Later that night, when I returned to my hotel room at the resort, I literally got down on my knees at the window and, looking out at the dark mountain sky covered with what seemed like a million stars, prayed to God that He not allow my son to die there, alone in the mountains. I had such a profound, ominous fear of losing him. I knelt there sobbing and pleading with God to save him. I was so afraid for my son.

The next day Gracie and I dropped Matt off at the behavioral health center they have there in Summit County where he would undergo a two-hour evaluation. Meanwhile, Gracie and I went into town and tooled around the shops, enjoying a frozen yogurt, hers topped with jellybeans and sprinkles, of course. We passed the time walking around and enjoying the scenery until his appointment with the doctor was completed.

He seemed relieved after the appointment, partly because he had been anxious about going and partly because he had been given some proactive steps to take. In 2011, I was still very ignorant about the disease of alcoholism, clueless really, so it didn't dawn on me until the following year, when I began to really study addiction, just how inadequate this plan was. Matt was told he needed two outpatient therapy sessions per week and should join a local Alcoholics Anonymous group, and left it at that. Since neither of us knew much better, Matt attempted to follow this directive.

That night he was feeling better, so we had dinner at a restaurant on the lake, which was so great. I felt happy when he didn't order an alcoholic drink with dinner and seemed to be enjoying himself with Gracie and me. I snapped the cutest photo of him at the table next to her, smiling broadly while she reached her hand to gently touch his face. It is one of my favorite pictures of them together. He was beaming.

Later that evening I handed him a blessed Miraculous Medal (Our Lady of Grace) to put in his wallet, which he did. When the kids all lived at home, I had placed these blessed medals under each of their mattresses, unbeknownst to them. Knowing he would be carrying this medal around with him gave me a sense of peace: "O Mary, conceived without sin, pray for us who have recourse to thee."

On our last day together he took me down the hill to a cool little mountain town called Georgetown, knowing that I would love to take photos of the old buildings. My kid knew me. One of the wonderful blessings of homeschooling is the opportunity for your children to really get to know you as not only their mom, but as a person. Matt knew all my kooky childhood stories, all about the mischief I got into, who my favorite musicians were, how much I adored my grandfather, and pretty much everything about me. He also knew I had a passion for photography, and in particular my love of photographing old buildings.

That day we spent a few hours tooling around Georgetown so I could take photos at a leisurely pace. He was so patient as I kept stopping the car over and over to jump out and capture a special shot. We found a little park and he and Gracie played on the equipment and slid down the slide together like a choo-choo train. At one point, he changed her diaper inside my trunk, and we got a chuckle out of that.

The following morning I left Vail feeling much better than the day I had arrived. I had high hopes, in my ignorance, that these steps laid out by the addiction counselor would take care of the problem and put him on the road to a healthy life free from alcohol. The two-day trip home to California gave me lots of time to process all that we experienced together on this short visit, and also gave me an opportunity to take even more cool photos along the way.

A day or two after I had returned home, Emma said she wanted to share something with me that had recently happened. I honestly had no idea what to expect, but she had a serious expression so I stopped what I was doing to give her my full attention. She said that this had happened twice, once in June and then again in July when I was in Colorado, both times in the evening when she was alone at home. She then proceeded to tell me that she had been hearing strange sounds coming from upstairs in my bedroom when she was sitting directly below in the family room on one occasion, and in the adjacent kitchen nook on the other. I asked her to describe the sounds.

"The first time I heard the noise I assumed it was the dogs until I realized they were downstairs with me. You were out to dinner that night, so it was just me down in the kitchen eating at the table." Emma continued, "I was watching TV. I heard some sounds coming from above that sounded like something was in your room, so I muted the TV to listen. I thought maybe the wind was blowing a tree branch against the side window or something, but then saw there was no wind blowing. I heard a shuffling sound, not exactly footsteps. Then the next time (in July), I was sitting on the couch watching TV. I heard the same sounds again, and both dogs were right there with me. I muted the TV to see if I could figure it out. It actually sounded like something shuffling between the floors. It was creepy, Mom."

"Do you think it was just a mouse or a rat somehow stuck between the floors?" I asked.

Emma replied, "No, it was a heavy shuffling sound that moved in intervals, not like steps. At first I thought it might be a pipe making noise, but then realized there is no plumbing there."

This was a new event in the house, and the first one since 2009 when her friend had experienced a compulsion to kill herself. In 2018, while preparing to write this book, I asked Emma to recount the things she remembered, and these sounds above the family room were again described in detail. Also, she noted it was only the beginning of these strange sounds back in 2011, that she would hear those sounds on multiple occasions until she moved out in 2013.

In August things took a serious turn for the worst. Matt called me one afternoon very sad and upset. I reached out to my mom via email on August 11th to share with her this latest development:

> Mom,
> Things have gotten so scary with Matt that I was not able to even sleep on Monday night. He called me Monday afternoon and I could tell he'd been drinking, and he admitted it. He told me he had just left the therapist appointment and all it does is make him want to drink, that all the guy talks about is alcohol and it makes him start craving it. He said the same thing happens after the A.A. meetings, and he can't control himself. He admitted that he can't do it alone, so his therapist told him he needs to be hospitalized.
>
> Matt and I talked three more times that night, each time lots of tears. He said all he needs is his dad, that he feels like he doesn't have a dad, prompting me to call his dad and leave a voice mail for him to call Matt as soon as possible. I asked if he had food and he said he only has Top Ramen to eat. So, I called the local grocery store up there, City Market, and ordered him a $50 gift card to buy

groceries. They don't sell alcohol in their grocery stores in Colorado.

Mom, Matt said he goes to sleep every night thinking that he won't wake up the next morning. He said he feels like his body is failing, that there was some blood in his urine. I told him to contact his therapist in the morning to help arrange for the detox.

He cried so much, saying how sad he is about the person he used to be and what he has done to himself because he couldn't control his drinking. Uncle Jim called him yesterday and talked to him for thirty minutes, and Matt was really grateful to hear his own recovery story. He said it gave him hope. Amanda's uncle, also in recovery, called him offering support and trying to motivate him.

This has been horrible, Mom. I was so hopeful because he had been going to the therapist and A.A. for the last three weeks, but he evidently just can't do it on his own. He is too far gone. My son may not make it, Mom.

I drove to the little Catholic bookstore as if on a mission. I needed something tangible to help me increase my prayers for Matt. Too often, my intentions to pray for him are lost in the commotion of daily life and all its distractions. I decided to purchase five medals: St. Matthew, St. Anthony, St. Monica, St. John the Baptist, and a Miraculous Medal (Our Lady of Grace). As Catholics, we use intercessory prayers to amplify our direct prayers to God. There is power in imploring the Blessed Virgin Mary and the saints for their divine assistance, to plead for us to Our Lord, lovingly interceding on our behalf. I very purposefully selected these specific medals. Saint Matthew, his namesake, Saint John the Baptist, his patron saint, Saint Monica, the mother who never gave up praying for her wayward son, Augustine, Saint Anthony, my favorite saint, and the Miraculous Medal for the powerful intercession of the Blessed Mother.

I strung the medals onto a ball chain and snapped it around my lampstand on the night table next to my bed. There I would see it every single morning and night and remember to say extra prayers for my beloved son. Praying for my boy seemed like my only hope of helping him at that juncture, feeling otherwise utterly powerless.

Matt came to town for a quick visit in early October. I know that the girls noticed how bloated his face looked, as well as his attempt to hide it by growing an unattractive goatee. My fear ramped up another notch upon seeing the deterioration in the three short months after visiting him in Vail. I was grateful for the short time we all spent together that October, and just continued to pray fervently for him.

While they were in town Gracie and I spent a day in the city, crossing the bridge into the wonderland that is San Francisco. We took random rides on the trolleys, landing in various parts of town that each seem like their own small country, unique in culture and vibe. We spent time at Golden Gate Park at the exhibits and playgrounds, and watching her play I felt so incredibly blessed to have such a vivacious and energetic little granddaughter. After a nice lunch at a local café we headed back home.

This year the holidays would not include Matt and Amanda because they could not get away from work, but at least Gracie was able to fly home via her other grandma for a visit the week before Christmas. I found myself growing closer and closer to this sweet little girl, and was sad to have to say goodbye after the Christmas Eve celebration was over.

During the holidays Matt hurt himself snowboarding, ending up in the ER with a broken rib and punctured lung, only adding to my worries. Amanda now had a new boyfriend and Matt was riddled with loneliness and sadness over the situation. Even so, they both loved their daughter dearly and somehow managed to make things work as well as can be expected under the circumstances.

By this point, the end of 2011, I realized that I was completely unprepared for the daunting challenges that lie ahead so I ordered four books to educate myself on the disease of alcoholism. They were *Addict in the Family* by Beverly Conyers, *How to Help the One You Love* by Brad Lamm, *Beautiful Boy* by David Sheff, and *Alcoholics Anonymous* (aka the Big Book). Merry Christmas to me.

CHAPTER 17

Crescendo

IT WAS JANUARY 2012. I settled into my book-reading spot on the living room couch and cracked open the first book to begin learning in earnest about addiction. Immediately, I realized how much I did not know about the unrelenting disease that had a death grip on my son. After just one chapter, I could see I was virtually ignorant about the topic. No matter, I had a two-fold mission, to first learn about the nemesis that threatened to steal my son, and then to help him conquer it.

Yes, I am a fixer, the classic overachieving and somewhat controlling mom who mistakenly thinks that by my sheer will I can overcome any and all obstacles I face and just mow them right down. No way would I succumb to inertia when my son's life depended on action. On the contrary, as I read and learned about the disease of addiction, and its power to utterly destroy the person held in its clutches, I entered full-blown mom enabling mode.

Beverly Conyers' book, *Addict in the Family*, devotes an entire chapter to this conundrum . . . how mothers, genetically predisposed to being caregivers, problem-solvers, and bandagers of wounds, should relinquish all instinctive efforts to control the outcome through whatever means necessary, and somehow, mysteriously, detach with love.[2] As all parents of addicts experience, the overwhelming desire to want to help their child survive, or at the very least minimize the life-altering consequences of addiction, leads to such actions as paying their bills, paying their rent, putting food in their refrigerator, and so on. In an effort to be able to live with ourselves as parents, we have a compulsive need to know our child isn't on the streets, starving.

But Conyers, and umpteen other addiction specialists I have read to date, define such efforts as only contributing to the problem by doing for the addict what they should be, and could be, doing for themselves. Our charitable actions, while done with the most genuine of intentions, make it easier for them to continue in their addiction. As hard as it is to gut out, parents need to retract from showering the life preservers upon them and just let them sink. Easier said than done, unfortunately.

Along those same lines, parents of addicts go all out to help them right their lives. As I sit here now, five to six years later, reading through emails and text messages between my son and me over that incredibly difficult two-year period, 2011-2013, I cringe at the level of my enabling behaviors and my pitiful efforts to control the outcome. Again, as a perennial doer, I saw that my purpose in life during that period was heavily influenced by a fear-fueled need to offer guidance, advice, and financial assistance as Matthew's illness raged on.

Email after email reeked of enabling. "Here are some interesting job listings (a list of links to the listings) to look at," "Don't forget to mail your car registration. Do you need the money?" "Contact the county DA's office to find out how to get that charge expunged," "Don't forget to pay that parking ticket. Do you have the money?" "Do you have any food in the house?" On and on, my valiant efforts to somehow reduce the pain he was in only served to make him feel inadequate as a man. His mommy had to help him.

I start this chapter relaying these wise nuggets about the pitfalls of good intentions because it was this year, 2012, that the gravity of the situation became undeniable. In hindsight, I don't regret my efforts to help my son, though; I only regret how those efforts may have made him feel emasculated, or if I had aided his addiction in any way. Although I was definitely queen of the enablers, my heartfelt desire to be there for my kid sprang directly from my deep love for him. I knew who he was underneath the dark cloak of alcoholism. I still saw that good guy, the kind, sensitive, thoughtful person who had so much to give. I had tried to rescue *that* Matthew.

In the spring of 2012, Matthew called me often, more than usual. I remember one disturbing conversation when I could tell he had been drinking. He usually didn't act inebriated, but his tongue had a thick sound that gave him away. I asked him with sincerity why he continued to drink when it was so destructive. He told me that it helped him, saying, "You have no idea what is going on inside my head." I remember being afraid to ask for clarification.

He was lonely, that was obvious. When Gracie was with her mother, Matthew would sit alone at home and drink, watch heavy metal concert DVDs, and not much else. He had become slothful, his apartment a disgusting dump. He had lost interest in exercise and had grown soft and pudgy. Photos he had posted from December, when he and Amanda had taken Gracie for her first attempt at skiing, depicted, sadly, a very bloated version of my once handsome son.

Many of our conversations that spring revolved around issues with Amanda. She was between boyfriends and whenever that was the case she would ask Matt if she could again stay at the apartment. Any opportunity for him to have both his wife and his child with him was always welcomed. He had unceasing hope that they would someday be together again as a real family, but they were both so unstable that there was no foundation upon which to build a normal, healthy family unit.

Sometimes, he would express anger and resentment at her antics, and other times he would cry, missing her love so much. This time, as before, he slept on the couch and she and Gracie took the bedroom. Matt earned the money for their expenses while Amanda took classes to become an EMT. He fully supported her in these efforts, believing in her abilities and wanting to help her realize her goal.

The next few months, though, brought more chaos when Amanda found her next boyfriend, crushing his hopes of reconciliation yet again. Meanwhile, Matt's alcoholism became severe, rising on the same trajectory as his depression. Like a vicious cycle, one disorder fed the other, making each disorder increasingly worse, all being fueled by a lonely, sorrowful heart and very low self-esteem.

During this period, I myself began to suffer from anxiety. That's the thing about having an addicted family member; you are not spared in their battle. The scourge of addiction oozes out and infects anyone within the person's immediate orbit, even from twelve hundred miles away. I was having a very hard time suppressing the effects of my constant worrying about Matt—his health, his child, his job, his finances—so the symptoms of anxiety began creeping in.

I visited the doctor for help, and was given a prescription for Ativan to help with insomnia and anxiety as needed. He referred me to a psychologist who I saw several times during the spring. The most beneficial thing I got from those sessions was learning how to practice deep breathing to help control the stress, a technique I still access when needed to this day.

One day at a gathering of Amanda's family, I was sharing with her uncle and his wife about how worried I was, and how the constant worry was impacting my own mental health. The wife, Cara, took me aside and asked if I'd like for her to join me at an Al-anon meeting. Well, I didn't even know what Al-anon was, so she schooled me. She, herself, had accessed Al-anon several years prior and shared how it really helped her feel like she was not alone with her experience as the wife of someone in active alcoholism. Her husband was about six years sober at that point, offering another source of hope for Matthew.

Cara explained how the meetings at Al-anon work, what I could expect, and the purpose of the organization, which was to provide emotional support for people closely associated with an addict. I figured it couldn't hurt to try a meeting, so I set up a plan to attend my first Al-anon meeting with Cara at my side.

The group of about a dozen people met in an empty schoolroom at a private school, not too far from both our residences. I just kept mostly to myself, like a fly on the wall, observing how the meeting was structured and listening carefully to the topics being discussed. I learned that night that cross-talk, or discussion among the members, was not permitted, which made me a bit confused. How can you get support if you can't discuss your own situation and gather suggestions and advice? But I eventually learned that the mingling that takes place before and after meetings is when sharing and discussing specifics takes place. The librarian of the group kindly handed me some free pamphlets and sold me a little book called *One Day at a Time in Al-anon*. Her suggestion to me, as she handed me the materials, was to read the section on detaching with love. She said doing that saved her own life.

I did feel better after the meeting. There is something about that old saying, "Misery loves company." In my regular life, around friends, family members, and coworkers, I felt totally alone in the pain of having an alcoholic, depressed son. But spending just an hour with these kind folks who readily shared intimate details of their own "qualifier," an Al-anon term for the addict that makes you eligible or qualified to be a member, I learned some helpful tips, found a little hope, and realized I was in good company.

It was in August that I saw concrete evidence at just how bad things had gotten for Matt. I hadn't seen my son since the prior October, about ten months. I arrived at San Francisco airport to pick up Matt and Gracie who were coming in for a four-day visit. As I stood there at the terminal awaiting their arrival, I felt so excited, gleeful even, to finally see them both after so long. Suddenly, a beautiful cinnamon-haired little girl came running toward me. Instinctively, I squatted down to wrap my arms around my little granddaughter in a big hug. My eyes then glanced upward to see a tall man standing behind her. It was my son, now barely recognizable.

His face had become so bloated that he no longer had a visible jawline, just swollen all the way around to the neck. His scruffy goatee did nothing to hide the bloat. His once big, beautiful brown eyes were now red, puffy, bloodshot, and squinty. His belly was largely distended. His hands shook noticeably. I wanted to sit on the floor of the airport and sob. Who was this stranger?

I managed to hide my shock pretty well, mostly for the child's sake, and I sure didn't want to make him feel even worse about himself. So, off we went to have lunch at his favorite burger place, In-N-Out. While I was in line waiting to place our order I glanced over at the two of them seated at a booth. My heart just broke. Seeing how sick he was, I knew the situation was dire. How much longer could he be able to function at his job, or as a parent even?

Over those four days, I made a decision to focus on the family party I had planned, the baseball game we were going to attend, and a concert we had tickets to on his last night in town. I decided to preemptively warn my mother about the dramatic change in her grandson's appearance, as she and my stepdad would be attending the family party the next day. In an email dated August 10, 2012 I wrote:

> Hi Mom,
> I just wanted to prepare you for when you see Matt tomorrow. It is so heartbreaking to see him deteriorating right before my eyes, and there is nothing I can do. He is very bloated. His eyes are watery and look weird. His hands shake. His mood is depressed, as if there is no joy in him. I can tell he feels like crap due to the alcohol.
> So, I thought I should warn you. All I can do is pray for him that he will decide soon to do the hard work to tackle this horrible demon and get healthy for his little girl. Mom, she is the sweetest child! It just breaks my heart.
> Ok, see you tomorrow. Just love him, that's all we can do.
> Love,
> T.

I had been recently reading *How to Help the One You Love* by Brad Lamm, which had a passage that spoke to me in this moment. Lamm wrote, "The idea that we really are powerless, that we should just watch and wait until someone hits bottom, is dangerous. You watch and wait and pray and hope and you end up with a dead spouse..."[3] This gripping passage went against everything else I had been told by well-meaning individuals. Thinking we had to just sit there and wait until Matthew found his "bottom" suddenly seemed ludicrous, and even, as Lamm had written, dangerous.

But I was torn, unsure of what to do. Between reading Conyers' book and Lamm's book, I was confused about how to proceed. I had devoured *Beautiful Boy* by David Sheff, a mercilessly honest and poignant memoir about his son's ongoing battle with addiction, namely methamphetamine. Reading about the multiple attempts David Sheff made to help his boy, rehab after rehab, each account taking the reader from the peaks of hope to the depths of despair as relapse dogged the boy, gave me pause. Do we wait it out, hoping that the next setback will result in his commitment to get treatment, or do we intervene now?

Gracie would stay behind with family for a few more days, so one day I took her downtown for lunch and shopping. Yes, this little thing loved wandering in and out of boutiques, oohing and aahing at whatever caught her eye. Gracie spotted some pretty seashells in the front window of a gift shop and wanted to get a closer look.

Just when we walked up to the window, one of my fellow baseball moms—both our sons played baseball together from Little League through senior year in high school—happened to be exiting the store. I introduced Christine to Grace, Matt's little girl. She had heard that he had gotten married and had a child and was delighted to meet her. After catching up with some small talk, she told me she had started a small Bible study group in her home. I asked what the group meetings consisted of, and she said, "We pray for our kids." I instantly got tears in my eyes and asked if they could please pray for Matt. She said, "Sure . . . what's going on?" I told her that he had developed a serious addiction to alcohol. She grabbed my hand and asked if we could pray for him right there and then.

She held my hands and we each said a prayer for Matt, then Christine said, "Lord, you are the God of Miracles, and this is what we pray for, that you will perform a miracle and cure Matt from his alcoholism. Look at all the miracle cures you have done, with so many witnessing them. Please Lord, grant this miracle for Matt."

Those words, 'Lord you are the God of miracles,' would ring in my head for the next few days. Over and over my mind chanted, Lord, you are the God of miracles.

MY 13th STATION

I spent time in prayer, listening to my heart and searching for some direction from God. I felt strongly that I needed to act, a gut-level, God-inspired call to action. The next evening on August 15th, after he had arrived back in Colorado, I sent Matthew a text:

Me: Matt, I have been thinking about you a lot. I am worried sick about your health. Your addiction is taking a toll on you and I don't know what to do to help you, except pray for you every single day. But the day you call and tell me you are ready to commit to getting free of this demon and get sober I will be there for you. I will take a leave of absence and stay in Colorado for as long as it takes. But you have to be ready to do the hard work and my hope is that it's sooner rather than later. You look very unhealthy and it scares me. I cry almost daily because I am so afraid you will die from alcoholism. Gracie needs you, she loves you so much. So when you are ready, I will be there for you. But if there's one thing I've learned from the reading I've done this year is that no one can make an addict seek sobriety. It has to come from you, and it will be a long, hard road. But in the end, you will be alive and healthy and clear-headed and not feel terrible every day. You will be the daddy that she deserves to have and the son that I deserve to have. I have faith that that day will come. I love you will all my heart.

Matt: Thank you, Mom. I know I need to take a turn. I know you feel helpless being so far away and I am so sorry for making u cry. Victor (his friend and supervisor in Colorado) sat me down before I left and we had a really good talk about it. I want to be accountable for it now. He told me he is worried that I won't be there to see Grace grow up and that really killed me. I am holed up in this place alone with no one to relate to while I have to constantly work out deals with housing to keep my place. Amanda won't help me, Denise (the babysitter) threatens me with quitting weekly if I can't pay her the whole amount. It's just too much for me. Everyone is asking me for something I don't have.

Me: I understand your stress and feeling powerless to all the demands. You've made some mistakes and taken some wrong turns, but so has everyone else on the planet. But until you get healthy, which you cannot do alone, you will never feel any sense of control over your life.

Matt: I don't know where to start

Me: You need to get to a point where you make a conscious decision, a choice, to admit yourself into a treatment program. The treatment may be difficult and even painful, but in the end you will be Matt again. You will also need counseling after the program, there is so much pain inside you. Your eyes are so sad.

Matt: I know this, but I don't know how to do it. I have no place to go.

Me: I believe you can do it if you decide to take the first step. The rest will reveal itself to you. I may have to come to CO and live in your apartment while you're going thru it so I can help out with Gracie. When you get out I will stay for as long as it takes while you do outpatient/meetings. But this is a big step and you can't be reckless about it. I would be leaving my job and my life so you have to be committed to stay the course.

Matt: Who will bring me in when I'm broke?

Me: Well, you will need to ask for a medical leave so your job is still there when you're done. They can't fire you for going to treatment.

Matt: But I'll lose G

Me: No you won't! Are you kidding me? If anything, it will strengthen your position with her as a father who will do what it takes to live.

Matt: Ok, well I need help. I'll do anything it takes. I want to Be Grace's dad. I just need help.

Me: Matt, I will help you

Matt: Thank you.

Me: You need to get with your boss and ask for a medical leave. H.R. will work it out. Then you need to call that shrink you saw last summer who knows your case and ask him to get you admitted to a treatment center. Those are the first steps. When you get that dialed in let me know the plan and I will start planning how to get there to help you.

Matt: Ok

Me: I love you

Matt: I love you too. Thank you.

Me: I only want you to love life again, and to forgive yourself. Please give this some serious thought because if you aren't 100% committed it won't work.

Matt: I am, I don't have any other option. I love G too much to disappoint her. She needs me. The real me.

Me: A year from now she will be amazed at what an incredible daddy she has, an amazing, loving, sensitive, fun, handsome, strong man. That is the real you.

After we ended our text conversation I immediately got down on my knees and thanked God for intervening and putting all this in motion. He *is* the God of miracles and I needed to become like a child, to step aside and allow Him to be God and work His miracle on my boy.

I then went about making plans to go off to Colorado for a month. I had very little money, having gone through serious financial difficulties since the divorce. I paid my bills in advance for the month, but otherwise was moving forward on a wing and a prayer. I was going to have to trust in Jesus to provide.

Two weeks later, I got the call that Matt was ready. He had arranged with his H.R. representative to obtain a medical leave of absence. He seemed to have a sense of urgency about getting in to treatment, even sounded a bit frantic. So, I asked my manager if it was okay to go ahead and take the extended leave of absence that I had forewarned her about a couple of weeks prior. Thankfully, she was kind enough to give me the green light.

Poor Emma, who was a full-time commuter college student and also held down a job working twenty-five hours a week, would now be in charge of our house and two dogs on top of her own responsibilities. She took it like a champ, just so relieved that her brother had finally decided to get the help he needed. Even so, I realized how much work there would be keeping up with everything all by herself during my long absence. I appreciated how gracious she was as I packed to leave.

MY 13th STATION

The September weather in the Rockies at 8,000 feet would be all over the map, according to Matt. Daytime temperatures could be in the 80s or the 50s. Sudden thunderstorms would pop up unannounced. Snow was even a remote possibility, and not unheard of in September. So, I shoved a variety of clothing into two large suitcases hoping to be prepared for anything. By 1:00 p.m. I was packed and ready to go off on this important mission.

The first leg of the journey took over eight hours, driving through California and Nevada and landing in Utah. Along the way I chatted with my close friend Francesca, who had been so supportive over the past two years as Matt's problems worsened. We had been friends since the late 1970s and I cherished our long friendship; a reciprocal relationship that we had both nurtured over the years. I chatted with Sarah while on the road that first day as well, so she would be up to speed on her brother's upcoming plans. Otherwise, most of that day I drove in silence, processing the momentous task ahead.

On the second day of travel, about half way to Vail, I suddenly got the notion to record my thoughts and feelings by dictating them on my phone. Somehow I must have known these reflections would mean something to me in the future. I knew I never wanted to forget how much love I had in my heart for Matt, even at the lowest point of his life. I wanted to document the hope I felt, that he would return to the happy, stable, productive person he once was.

Painstakingly, I transcribed the recordings to include in this memoir. As I listened, it brought that day back into sharp focus, as if I'd recorded those words only yesterday. I noticed that my voice was measured and calm in the first half of the recording, as I recounted the purpose for my trip and the basic information about Matt's struggles over the past few years. Since I have covered this already, I will include just the last three, very emotional, minutes of that thirteen-minute recording made on September 7, 2012:

Yesterday was my first half of the drive. I drove for 8½ hours and ended up in an old historic town called Ely near the border of Nevada and Utah where I spent the night. During that drive I didn't really listen to the radio or anything, I just drove in silence and spent a lot of time praying. Praying for my son . . . praying, praying, praying for my son that he doesn't die, that he will follow through, and that he will have the courage to do this because it is going to be *so* hard . . . so difficult for him every single day for the rest of his life. I prayed that he would persevere. I prayed for him to find God again, to embrace God. I prayed for God to take him in His arms and protect him and love him as His child, and I prayed for our Blessed Mother to love him as a mother loves her child. I prayed for the intercession of St. Monica. I prayed for the intercession of St. Matthew and St. John the Baptist, and for Matt's guardian angel to protect him and keep him safe. I prayed for God to give him peace in his heart. And then for myself, I prayed that I could let go of the anxiety and let God work His miracles. I prayed—I commanded—for Satan to leave Matt, to get away from him in the name of Jesus Christ! Jesus has control of him now.

My friend Francesca and my daughters have been calling and texting. This has been very emotional, very, very emotional. I think, okay, I am giving up my income and putting my life on hold. Taking this much time off work will impact all of my coworkers because my duties will have to be distributed among them. I feel badly that my being gone will cause added work for them. I don't have money for this at all. I don't know what else to do though, other than answer God's call to do *this* job right now. Right now, this is what I am to be doing. I am his mother. I have to come out here and help him with his little girl so he can get help. I must believe that everything else will work out—and that this is actually a gift. A huge grace and gift that I am able to help my son find his life once again and become the man he should be; the man I know he is, and that I know he wants to be again. So, I will continue to chronicle this journey. I will make it in to Vail by about 6:00 (p.m.) and then will call Matt and see where we are.

As I got closer to my destination, I began to feel a bit stressed. I was exhausted from the seventeen hours of travel over two days, and not quite sure what shape I would find him in. He told me the day I left California that he would admit himself into a detox place so he wouldn't be allowed to drink anymore. He was seriously worried about how bad his condition was and actually went to there just to impose control over his own behavior. When we chatted earlier this morning, he had just come home and described it as a smelly, filthy drunk tank where low life types were vomiting all around him. I was hopeful that he was, now eight hours later, still not drinking, but was preparing myself nonetheless.

I summarized the rest of this day, Friday September 7th, on my voice recorder the following day, Saturday the 8th:

I am driving back up Vail now and want to recap the rest of Friday's events. So, I got to Vail and the first thing out of Matt's mouth was, "I've been drinking." He was discharged from the drunk-tank in the morning, but was only able to stay sober for four hours. He admitted right away that he had been drinking. I was prepared for that. I also was prepared to not be judgmental, to not say anything other than, "It's okay."

We went into his apartment and sat down. We were going to make dinner, but I had a terrible sense of urgency about getting him into a rehab as soon as possible. So he took his phone and I took mine and we divided a list of rehabs between us. He had already been calling rehabs and hadn't had any luck so far. We were both calling all the different rehab facilities in the Denver area. I was hitting one brick wall after another. They all wanted either a huge amount of cash up front, even with PPO insurance (he was on his dad's insurance policy now), or they didn't have a bed, or the state facilities had a ninety-day wait.

Well, he won't make it ninety days. I was getting discouraged when suddenly Matt had a breakthrough. He held his hand up to signal that he found a rehab with a bed. I heard him giving them his insurance information and his name and address—I couldn't believe what I was hearing after forty-five minutes of pure failure. They were actually going to admit him—*if* we could get to Denver in time because two other people also wanted that bed.

There we were in this hugely rushed situation. We had no time for dinner. We just threw some pants, t-shirts, and a toothbrush into his backpack. I wrote down our phone numbers for him, since they take cell phones away in rehab. Instead, he'd be using their house phone. We grabbed some trail mix, cheese and crackers and two bottles of water, and that was our dinner.

Before we left Vail Matt asked me to stop at the babysitter's house so he could say goodbye to Grace, who would soon be picked up by Amanda. So we called the sitter, Denise, to set it up and drove to her house. When we got there, the first thing Grace did was run over to me saying, "Nana!!!" because she wasn't expecting to see me. Then she walked over to her daddy, smiling when he picked her up. He started crying—sobbing, sobbing—he couldn't stop. He just kept saying, "Grace, Daddy's gonna get healthy, Daddy's gonna be healthy." He even said, "Daddy's not gonna be fat anymore." She just hugged him tight and didn't understand why he wasn't taking her home like usual. But oh, gosh, seeing how much that young man loves his little girl, and how much she loves him back, just melted me.

Then while Matt and Gracie were still standing together, Denise approached me. She said to me, "Your son is a fantastic human being. He is such a responsible guy and so thoughtful, and I think the world of him. I am so proud of him for taking this step." It was a beautiful moment and I was very grateful that Grace had such a kind person as her babysitter.

About half way to Denver, as we drove along in the dark, Matt was looking out his passenger window. I could see tears on his face. I asked him what was wrong. He said, "Nothing is wrong. I just look forward to the day when I can look in the mirror again and not be disgusted by what I have become." It crushed me. I had to fight back my own tears.

And so we drove down the mountain to Parker, which is just outside Denver, and it was the most awesome two hours with my son. As we drove along the alcohol effects were wearing off, but he was not agitated or anything, he was very calm. He did seem a bit anxious because he knew he was going to be doing something big and scary, but he was resigned to it. Just had this tone of resolution in his voice. And I was sitting next to him thinking that this was so much like our little road trips we used to take to Nevada when I had the business. Matt and I really enjoyed those trips together, when we'd listen to music and talk, or just ride in silence.

When we got into the Denver area he found a classic rock station on the radio and he seemed really together and lucid while we chatted . . . just like his old self. We were having the most honest, awesome conversation, and then we got kind of lost in the Parker area. So Matt called the rehab and spoke to the person with such kindness, just such a pleasant guy. And I thought to myself that this is one life that can't be wasted. No. This is a man that has so much good in him to give to the world, to his daughter—this life must be saved.

So we find the place. It's in a beautiful area, a nice suburban area and the facility itself was very nice. Not high end or anything, but very clean and nice. You walk in and there were guys playing Ping-pong, there's a pool table, and a small group session starting up. The two intake gals were so nice. They were warm and compassionate and respectful. We had to wait about two hours to finally get him admitted, so by this time it's 11:15 p.m. and the thought of driving back up the mountain—no way could I do it. I was shaking from being so tired, sleep deprived, and hungry. So, I found a hotel close by and spent the night.

Now it's Saturday, September 8th. I just got off the phone with my Uncle Jim who is a recovering addict. He gave me some good advice and words of hope, and said he is praying for Matt. Everybody is.

Now I get to enjoy the fun part of my stay here. I'm gonna drive back up the hill and about noonish Amanda will bring Gracie to stay with me in Matt's apartment. I will have her all day, all night, and maybe tomorrow, too. And this is how it will go. Whenever Matt would usually be taking care of Gracie I will be taking care of her. We're giving Denise some much deserved paid time off. She has been such a godsend over the past year and a half. Okay, going up the mountain now . . . time to have some fun with my beautiful granddaughter!

At that, I made the exhilarating journey up the mountain, marveling at the stunning beauty in every direction. The rich patchwork of lush green pines, spruce and fir served as a perfect contrast to the sparkling cerulean sky. Even though the temperature was in the mid-50s, I couldn't resist the temptation to roll down the window and lean my head out a little, enjoying a blast of brisk clean air on my face. The sheer relief after the long slog to get here and successfully getting my son into treatment was filling me with the most amazing sense of purpose as I climbed the mountain toward that beautiful resort town. Soon I would be on the floor playing Legos and reading books with beautiful Gracie.

CHAPTER 18

Saffron September

OVER THE NEXT FOUR WEEKS I experienced things I could have never anticipated when I started my journey from California on September 7th. By "experiences," I refer to deep and lasting moments of fresh spiritual insights, intense love, joy, inspiration, and, especially, hope. Although this spiritually rich experience is permanently etched in my memory, rather than write about it now through the perspective of a rearview mirror I would rather use my actual journal entries, the meticulously written notes that captured my real-time emotions over that period of time. In fact, at the end of my sojourn in Colorado, having clocked about 13,000 words on my laptop, I drove away thinking I had the makings of a little book on that hard drive. Today, now finally writing the book, I see that those words I so judiciously typed serve as just one chapter of a much bigger story that I could have never predicted.

September 8, 2012
Like little candles placed among the mountain landscape, the various hues of saffron, red, and yellow aspen leaves decorate the majestic scenery. I am thrilled to witness the changing of the seasons here, with the array of stunning color that these trees showcase. What a blessing! Depending on the time of day and the

lighting, these small round leaves alternately sparkle like sequins or emit a soft inner glow.

There is something so magical about the month of September. Suddenly, one day, it seems the light is just somehow different, bringing with it the promise of change, of leaving behind the summer and embracing a new season of productivity. As kids, this pattern was hardwired into us over the years of adhering to the school calendar, which is why the end of summer always feels bittersweet.

Now to the job at hand . . . First I made a Target run to buy the essentials, cleaning products, food, fresh sheets, and of course a cute outfit for Gracie. Amanda brought her over at about 1:00, and the two of us played and played. Later on, a local little girl named Jessica knocked on the door. Jessica is eleven years old and is the daughter of the apartment complex superintendent, who also happens to be a pastor at a local church. Apparently, Jessica often stops by to play with Gracie, and today's visit was perfect timing, allowing me clean the pigsty of an apartment that belongs to my son. I started in the kitchen, scrubbing it from top to bottom.

Gracie is clearly a sweet and well-adjusted little girl, regardless of what challenges her parents faced. She was so delighted that I brought the box of Legos that I had bought for her back in August on her last visit to California. So, today much of my time was devoted to just sitting on the floor playing toys with her.

I called the rehab to see how Matt was doing with the medical detox process and was told he was doing great. He had signed a HIPAA release form that allowed the staff to share any updates or medical test results with me, thankfully. I just needed to know he was okay. I feel so relieved to know that he is in a good place, working toward sustained sobriety, and no longer poisoning himself.

I just gave Gracie her bath and we have our first sleepover tonight. Being with her, I feel like I have an important purpose at the moment, to care for this sweet girl as a stand in for her daddy.

September 9, 2012
I had the day to myself, so decided to clean the bathroom and finish vacuuming the place. It was hard work and, with the high altitude, I was exhausted by the end of the day. All I wanted was a good night's sleep, but, alas, that was not to be. As I was drifting off to sleep, I heard what sounded like a mouse under the bed chewing away on something! I jumped out of bed with my heart pounding and switched the light on. I stood there straining to hear if it was really under the bed. Eventually, I went back to bed hoping I had imagined it. Nope. The chewing continued throughout the night. I finally got up and took an Ambien and covered my head with a pillow, eventually managing to drift off. Ah, life in the mountains.

September 10, 2012
Today I drove with Gracie down to Parker to visit Matt at the rehab and to bring him some toiletries and petty cash. Matt seemed good, having completed the worst of the detox period, but his mood was still down and he seemed a little edgy and impatient. These are normal alcohol withdrawal symptoms. Gracie loved watching her daddy shoot some pool, and then we all went outside to the volleyball court and just hung out there for a while. It was mutually beneficial for Matt and Grace to see each other. We stayed about two hours, and then headed home. Matt was really appreciative that we had come to visit him, although I could tell he was a little unsettled having his daughter in the rehab environment. I think he felt ashamed of himself.

Tonight I fished out of my purse the chain with all the medals on it and snapped it to the lamp base on Matt's nightstand. Just as at home, this daily physical reminder will prompt me to reach out to the Blessed Mother and the saints for their intercessory prayers, pleading with Jesus on my son's behalf. I knew I must practice extra prayer power for my son. I honestly don't know what I would do without my strong Christian beliefs. I can't imagine floundering around through such an intense and emotional time in life without knowing that the loving arms of God were firmly wrapped around me.

September 11, 2012
Today was very emotional. Well, every day has been emotional since this month began, but today something beautiful caused tears of gratitude. I was on the phone with my mom, catching her up on events, when the UPS guy appeared at the door with a package from Amanda's aunts. I opened it while still on the phone with mom. There was a toy for Gracie and a card for me. The card read: "Theresa, our thoughts and prayers are with both you and Matt. We heard from Liz (Amanda's mom, their sister) what you were doing for Matt and Grace—we know how difficult it is. We just wanted to send a little something to help out. Love, Patti, Lisa, and Grandpa Brower, their dad). Enclosed was $250 in cash to help out with groceries and gas!! I was simply overcome with emotion. I cried and cried, so moved by their thoughtfulness and generosity. I immediately called each one of them to thank them, and bawled tears of gratitude through every call. This act of generosity was absolutely heaven sent.

I have been praying daily for God to find a way to provide for us. I needed to mail in my auto insurance payment and had to literally hunt through my car and Matt's Jeep to scrape together forty-four cents to buy a stamp! The other day I was at the market with my short list of items to feed Gracie and me this week. I had written next to each one the estimated cost, and added it up. I had barely enough money to make it happen. When the actual costs were tallied up at the cash register, I was off by a dollar and had to take the cookies out of the order. Dang. So, this gift today was a prayer answered.

September 12, 2012
I am utterly amazed every day at the breathtaking beauty of this place in the Rockies. The aspens are approaching peak colors, so all around us are bold splashes of bright yellows, gold, and orange sprinkled among the evergreens. The air is cool and fresh, and it is absolutely gorgeous here. Each day I discover new things to admire in Vail.

Also, the neighbors at the apartment complex who know Matt have been so welcoming and supportive. They all have the nicest things to say about him. It is heartwarming to know that my son has made such a positive impression on the people he has befriended here. I like to sit outside on the front porch and have my morning tea, relishing the solitude and the crisp mountain air. Sometimes a neighbor will be on their way to work and stop and chat for a bit, making me feel right at home.

Francesca has been such a wonderful friend, calling me every day to check on me. She knows how isolated I must feel in a town I don't know, located high in the mountains. She has become a constant connection to my real life, giving me an opportunity every day to share my emotions, the daily highlights, and to brag about Gracie. Someday I will look back on this and be in awe of the guts it took to up and leave my life and head to the middle of the country to live for a month in the mountains. Each day I await what wonders God will reveal to me here, and He never disappoints.

September 14, 2012
Today I drove down the mountain to attend a counseling session at the rehab with a therapist named Christa. She was really nice and it was a good hour-long session with her. She was able to get me three counseling sessions free through scholarship funds, and I was very grateful for this support. Addiction is a family disease, and has definitely taken its toll on me.

I only saw Matt for a few minutes today. The clinical staff has put him on Lexapro to help with his anxiety and depression, but to me he looked and acted drugged out. It really bothered me, but hopefully as he adjusts to the medication these effects will subside.

While I was there I asked to review the lab report for Matthew's blood work. The results had come back today and I wanted to know if there were any medical issues revealed in the results. A physician's assistant was nice enough to sit down with me and go through the report.

My eyes immediately spotted the letter "H" in multiple places, indicating lab results that are high, or out of range. I held my breath as he explained the significance of each while managing to maintain my composure. In a nutshell I received quick schooling about just how toxic alcohol is to the human body. One of the liver markers was four times the top end of the range. There was blood detected in the urine, high bilirubin, high liver enzymes, and more. It was too much for a mother to take. I thanked him, made a hasty exit, got into the safety of my car and wept. My son was very sick.

September 15, 2012
It has now been a full week since Matthew went into treatment. I can't begin to describe the sense of relief I feel, just knowing he is in a supportive environment and no longer drinking. The tension

in my neck and shoulders that has been with me for over a year was beginning to finally relax a little.

Today Amanda, Gracie, and I drove to Frisco, a quaint little western town near Breckenridge. We went on a hike to Rainbow Lake, and little Gracie was such a trooper, a natural hiker. The scenery out there was spectacular, and the color of the changing leaves was much more enhanced in this much-higher elevation, about a half hour drive from Vail. The aspens literally look like explosions of gold fire on the mountainside.

My daughter-in-law and I have been getting along well lately, and I really enjoyed spending this time with both her and Gracie together. While we were taking time to enjoy the beauty of Rainbow Lake, Amanda snapped a photo of Gracie and me from behind while we were both sitting in the dirt gazing out at the lake. The image shows grandmother and granddaughter, side by side in awe of the wonder before our eyes. Her little round head with its puffs of crazy hair—oh, my gosh *so* adorable. I loved the pic so much I asked Amanda to send it over to me.

September 16, 2012
Today was so much fun. I took Gracie "exploring" out and about not far from the apartment. The weather was absolutely perfect, about seventy-five degrees and sunny. I took my new digital camera along to capture any special moments we might share on our little hike. We found a small creek that had gorgeous flowers dotting its borders. So we stopped and threw rocks, something I told her that her daddy loved to do when he was little. Whether we were at the beach, in Sequoia, at a lake, or in the mountains, young Matthew was obsessed with throwing rocks.

Along the way we came upon a small resort that had a large sloping front lawn. I couldn't resist the temptation, so I demonstrated how, as a kid, Nana used to roll down grassy slopes. She evidently liked what she saw, so we began to roll down the slope together, laughing as our bodies would roll off in the wrong directions. Those big belly laughs will stick in my memory forever.

September 17, 2012
Today I had a free day, so I walked to the local Starbucks to plant myself at an outdoor table and write. I want to describe the wicked thunderstorm we had last evening, not long after Gracie and I returned from our hike. I have experienced many, many thunderstorms in my day, but this one was so loud and so spectacular, with buckets of rain seeming to come out of nowhere. I have always loved thunderstorms—I find them exhilarating and sensuous. The earth takes on a distinct, musky scent, and the air is charged with amazing energy that propels my spirit.

I want to carefully document this experience in Colorado by disciplining myself to write just a little bit each day, or as often as time permits. Why document something like this, the month my son spent in rehab? Because I never want to forget how it felt to have hope like this, how energizing it feels to wake up each day in a state of gratitude and joy, looking forward to God's plan for the day. For several years now, I have been afraid for my son's life.

These past ten days have been buoyed by the hope that he will get his life back on track. He is only 24 years old, a young adult just finding his way in life. He now has the opportunity to reinvent himself, to set new goals and take the steps to get there. With the alcoholism and depression managed, he has an excellent chance to live a long, fulfilling life.

How can I ever thank God enough for putting all this in motion? Through the generosity of my manager and my employer, I was able to just up and leave my job and get to my son. God's hand led us to find a rehab with a available bed. By His grace, we beat the other two people who also wanted that bed. I hope and pray that they, too, were able to locate a rehab. For nine days Matt has not had a drop of alcohol, something he hasn't been able to do in several years.

I am beginning to feel very attached to Summit County. I have been out exploring Breckenridge, Keystone, Silverstone, and Frisco, and have just fallen in love with this amazing paradise in the mountains. I notice that I go for days without make-up, and have even been ignoring the gray roots that are becoming noticeable. So not me! But here, it just didn't matter to me. People here are outdoorsy, natural, and completely opposite of the California scene. There is very little obesity here, as people spend their free time hiking, cycling, and golfing, always outdoors and on the move. I have felt the stress drain out of my body since I got here, with a sense of deep peace replacing it. Everywhere you look is a postcard snapshot of sheer natural beauty. The muscular mountains, beautiful lakes, brilliant aspens dotting the evergreens, it is truly a spectacular site.

So sitting here at Starbucks, with people milling about and the beautiful scenery distracting me I didn't get much accomplished. At least I was able to thank God and express my gratitude for every single blessing. Through this experience, God has given my life special meaning and I won't ever forget to be thankful.

September 18, 2012
Today I drove down to Parker and attended a group session with about thirteen other parents. There was active participation among the group and I found Christa a very effective therapist. She gave us an assignment for tomorrow's family therapy session.

I saw Matt for just a brief moment as I was starting to leave the center. He looked better! His eyes are starting to look normal again, which makes me very happy. I have always told him that he had Sean Connery eyes.

September 19, 2012

Today was very powerful and emotional! I admit I was anxious driving down the mountain, not really knowing what to expect in family therapy today. The therapist led these scripted interactions between us parents and our adult kids, asking us to each share our honest feelings—good and bad—about the topics she introduced.

I found it a bit uncomfortable to witness other parents with their kids while these issues were confronted. It seemed a bit voyeuristic to me. But apparently the idea is that, since the disease of addiction produces some very predictable issues within the family dynamic, that we can learn a bit from each parent-child as they related their own particular stuff.

Matt and I were very calm and kind in our answers to each other as we responded to the prompts. I bawled my eyes out when I was asked to tell my son what I like about him. I told him I love what a great father he is, how he puts Gracie's needs above all else. I told him I like the way he shares with me all the things in his life, like he does in our long chats on the phone and weekly text conversations. I told him I like seeing the man he has become, a sensitive, sentimental guy who is caring and loving.

Matt told me he likes how much I love his daughter, telling me how much that means to him. He also told me he appreciates how supportive I am, and how I jumped in my car and drove out to Colorado to help him.

We each shared a couple of things that we do not particularly like, which is tough to say and to hear but a necessary part of this exercise. After we were done with our turn, the next pair began. In all there were six pairs of parents and kids. One pair of a mom and son made me feel sad, they seemed so distant from each other. And then one pair was a middle-aged woman and her elderly mother. The mother, even though looking at her daughter, would not use the pronoun, "you," but instead spoke in the "she" pronoun. One pair was a married couple, versus a parent-child, and I literally cried through their turn. They had so much genuine love for each other, so much respect. It was sad to see how much damage alcohol had inflicted on this couple.

After the family therapy session I returned to Vail and Amanda dropped Gracie off for the evening. That night we had to barricade ourselves in the bedroom because the mouse was now under the couch out in the living room. So, we hid away from the varmint and I vowed to get some help from the superintendent tomorrow.

September 20, 2012
I have decided it is time to start a fitness routine while I'm here. It's been two weeks since I have taken a real walk, other than the hike to Rainbow Lake last week, so I really feel the need to start a regular walking routine again. I miss the pups!

This evening I was on my own, so I grabbed my tennies and set out into the brisk September air, marching up the hill that runs adjacent to the apartment complex. But about half way up, only about ten minutes in, I had to stop and catch my breath! The altitude still gets to me, plus I have been so sedentary for the last two weeks. But I continued up the hill for another ten minutes until I reached the top. Good enough for day one. It felt really great to huff and puff and push my body a bit. It also helped me restart my usual prayer routine that I do each evening when I walk the dogs back home. I felt invigorated and alive, soaking in the beauty that surrounded me and paying careful attention to the crunching sounds of the pine needles beneath my feet.

There was a small, local gym that was advertising a free nine-day trial, so I figured, why not? I so missed my usual gym workouts. The gal at the gym gave me the tour and demonstrated how to use the equipment, which, thankfully, was very similar to my gym's equipment back home. It felt really good to be working out again. Fitness is very important to my state-of-mind.

I cannot say enough about how much I appreciate hearing from my friends. Francesca continues to call and text me daily, and other friends have been checking in with me, too. It warms my heart to know that I have so much support for what I am doing.

I went down the hill to the rehab to participate in another family therapy session. The therapist spent some time just with me alone, reviewing a list of enabling behaviors that she wanted to educate me about in advance of Matt being released. I must say, it was hard to accept that these are all considered negative, but what do I know. For example, my gut feeling is to stay as long with him as possible after discharge, just to watch over him and be a physical deterrent to drinking. Well apparently, that is considered enabling. To me it makes no sense to just leave the person who is so new in recovery and so vulnerable, but I am a student and have to admit I don't know that much about addiction. I am also not to check in with him to ask if he has attended A.A. meetings or counseling appointments, per the advice given me today. This so goes against my mom instincts! And then there were the basic enabling warnings, not to do for them what they can and should do for themselves. The list also told me not to obsess about the addict and to not lose sleep by worrying about them relapsing. Okay, well . . . this may be much easier said than done.

Emma called saying she had a dog emergency. Apparently, Bailey somehow hurt her back, probably jumping on or off a bed. She is nearing ten years of age and has always been attached to

Matt. In fact, everyone just accepts that Bailey is Matt's dog. So, when Emma described how much pain she was in, I feared the worst. Losing the dog at this time would be just horrible, for all of us, but especially for Matt. He has such a strong emotional attachment to her.

My wonderful and very thoughtful boyfriend, Mike, graciously offered to take Bailey to the vet and also paid the $300 vet bill. Thankfully, the doctor was able to remedy her issues with a cortisone shot and some pain medication. But poor Emma, I could sense how much strain she was under trying to manage everything in my absence.

September 21, 2012
I picked up Gracie at about noon, and we headed down the hill to visit her daddy. We went together every Friday, meaning that I drove that long drive up and down the mountain three times every week. But our support was so important to Matthew's recovery process, so these drives were not drudgery at all. Instead, each time I headed out to Parker I felt so happy and excited, knowing that every time I saw him he looked and acted more like himself.

Whenever we went through the tunnels, Gracie and I would attempt to hold our breath. Sometimes we would stop and pick flowers to take him, or hit a mini-mart to grab his favorite candy. So that day at the rehab I just sat back and read a book in the rec room and observed Matt and Gracie playing together, and just hanging out. It is always heartwarming to witness this relationship between father and daughter.

September 22, 2012
This morning I decided to deal with the bad tire on Matt's Jeep. Although I have been very consciously trying to avoid any enabling

behaviors, some things just need to be done for safety reasons. He would have no paycheck for a couple weeks after he returns to work, and the thought of him driving an unsafe vehicle would just make me anxious. He needed to have a car to get to his A.A. meetings and his therapy sessions after rehab, but the tire had a slow leak. I had been filling it with air about every other day.

So, I headed over to the Big O Tires in nearby Avon to get it patched. While driving there, I also noticed it shimmied when I applied the brakes, so I asked them to check those while they were at it. They quoted me $11 to patch the tire, and would call me about the status of the brakes later. So I walked over to Target to buy some warm clothes for Gracie, since the weather would soon be changing radically.

Of course, wouldn't you know it, the Big O guy called and informed me that there isn't enough tread on the tire to patch it, and the other front tire is bad too, so he recommended I replace those two at minimum. The rear tires I would leave for Matt to take care of. Also, the brakes were metal on metal, so that initial $11 quote grew into a $600 car repair bill. But what could I do? Matt and Gracie in a car with bald tires and no brakes, with snow coming soon? No way could I ignore this, so I just pulled out my almost maxed out credit card and drove home to the apartment feeling incredibly stressed about finances.

September 24, 2012
I didn't have Grace today so I took advantage of my free day and went to the gym for a good workout. It felt so good to be taking care of myself again. Later, when I got back to the apartment I decided to take a walk. I am gradually becoming more accustomed to the altitude, and feeling stronger. It is hard to describe how it feels to walk in this setting. It takes me straight to prayer and

feelings of deep gratitude. In fact, my iPod was dead tonight so I prayed the Joyful Mysteries. I seem to be much more in touch with my spiritual self here in Colorado. It is probably because I don't have the distraction of going to work at the moment. Most likely, though, it has to do with my sense of purpose here in Vail, to take care of my granddaughter and to be a strong support for my son. Whatever the reason, I am finding myself in some form of prayer and thanksgiving throughout the days.

I also took myself to a matinee. I have always enjoyed sneaking in a movie whenever I can, so I stopped at the market for some candy and headed out to see *Lawless*. I am beginning to feel right at home here. Later, I worked on my mom's party. My sister and I had made plans earlier this year to throw her an 80th birthday party, and it is a month away. So, we split up the tasks between us in making the preparations. It has been logistically difficult for me, being out of state, but I have located a venue online and my sis and I have agreed on the menu and color scheme, so at least that is accomplished. Some of the details will just have to wait until I get back to California.

Earlier today I decided to look online for a local Al-anon meeting. I really felt the need to connect with others and share about this experience. I knew instinctively that once Matt was done with rehab I would be facing new challenges in his sobriety and wanted to be as prepared as possible. I found a group in Eagle at a Methodist church and decided to give it a whirl. It turned out to be exactly what I needed, a group of kind, compassionate people who could relate to me. In fact, this group was the most comforting Al-anon group I had found to date, after experimenting with three or four different groups back home.

When it was my turn to introduce myself I stated my name and said I was in town for a month to help out with my little granddaughter while my son was down in Denver in rehab. Oh, my gosh, the warm support these folks gave me was just amazing. At the end of the meeting, one fellow gifted me with a book, *How Al-anon Works, For Families and Friends of Alcoholics*. How sweet—and I'm sure I will find great solace in those pages! I stayed about thirty minutes after the meeting chatting with people and gathering helpful hints and support. For sure I will incorporate these meetings into my weeks here.

September 25, 2012
Today was one amazing blessing after another. The last time I visited Matt I asked him if he was ok with me picking up a regular twin bed for Grace, since it appears she has outgrown her little plastic Disney princess toddler bed. I didn't want to overstep; Matt may have already planned to get her a bed. He was actually very appreciative and gave me the green light to find her a bed. I think he must have realized how happy it would make me to do this for her.

I had contacted a woman in Eagle about a twin bed she had up for sale on Craigslist. It was a sturdy solid wood bed, perfect for Gracie. The gal, Trina, wrote me back saying the bed and mattress were in excellent condition and that she would only be home until 1:00. So, I immediately wrote her back saying we would be there by 11:00 a.m., but we just needed directions to her place.

We didn't hear back from her so Gracie and I decided to go to McDonald's for an early lunch while we waited for her response. Imagine sitting in a McDonalds with a spectacular view of the slopes! In fact, all of their interior artwork depicts Swiss alpine vistas and people wearing lederhosen and dirndl skirts. So cute! Somehow the food even tasted better. Finally, my phone rang and it was Trina, giving me the directions to come get the bed.

We took the Jeep because my Honda wouldn't be able to handle such heavy cargo. Trina and I lugged all the various pieces of the bed and the mattress down two flights of stairs and fastened the mattress to the roof of the Jeep. Because of the drag of the mattress, and my fear on the mountain road, we drove about 45 mph the whole way, looking like the Beverly Hillbillies.

When we got back to the apartment I suddenly realized that no way could I get all this up to the apartment by myself. Frantic, I went out to the parking lot and began scanning it for a would-be helper. Seeing no one, I decided I could do it. But the bungee cords were fastened so tight I could not budge the hook to free the mattress, and it was starting to drizzle! Just when I was about to cry, a sturdy young fellow was walking towards us in the parking lot. I asked if he could help and he said, "Sure." So, this nice guy schlepped all of these parts up to the apartment.

Now that all the components were in the place, how the heck would I assemble the bed? This wood was solid and super heavy, not like the IKEA furniture I had assembled countless times by myself. Just then Jessica, the superintendent's eleven-year-old daughter, appeared at the door to play with Grace. Heaven sent! I asked her if she could see if her dad was free to assemble Grace's new bed, and that I would pay him for his efforts. Soon, there was Juan at our doorstep to come to my aid. About twenty minutes later, Gracie's big girl bed was put together!

I had already bought some horse-themed sheets at Target in anticipation of this momentous occasion, horses being Gracie's favorite animal. I had so much fun putting all the "horsey" bedding on and surprising her with the finished product. She was so amped up, jumping from her bed to her daddy's bed and back with all the energy a 2½-year-old could muster.

This day was important on a personal growth level. I am finally learning how to ask for help, something I have never been comfortable doing. I am finding that people are more than happy to lend a hand, and by swallowing my stubborn pride and allowing them to help me, I am growing as a person.

September 26, 2012
Today I didn't have Gracie so I started the day by taking an invigorating walk. I had discovered a really pretty pathway the other day, so I grabbed my camera to take along. I found a spot along the curving path with a wood cabin off to the side, and set the self-timer on the camera. I captured the perfect shot of myself, expressing an abundance of joy with a colorful backdrop of saffron aspens and rich green pines. The muted light of the morning, through clouds, gave the aspens a slightly subdued hue. The shot captured the essence of my spirit, with outstretched arms and a huge smile. Over the past nearly three weeks I had grown so fond of this place, and this photo will forever represent the joy I had felt in my heart while in Colorado.

Later, I went to the gym for a workout. The treadmill, which faces a picture window looking onto the gorgeous mountainside, prompted a thought. I decided the next time (didn't have my phone with me) I come I am going to take a picture of what beauty I get to look at while I am on the treadmill at the gym. This is *so* not California!

On the way home, I stopped to check out a little antique store. I have always loved poking through antique stores, allowing the vintage items to evoke soothing memories of my grandparent's home, my childhood toys, albums I loved, and just cool old stuff. I rarely have time to just mosey through an antique store, so this was a nice treat. Just as I was leaving it started to rain, so I decided to take in another matinee, this time *Trouble With the Curve*. It was just a really great day in the mountains.

September 27, 2012
Today was chilly and rainy, but incredibly beautiful. Crisp autumn weather. I had gotten a notice from the post office that a package awaited me, so I stopped there on my way to pick up Gracie. I opened the package, which was from Judi, my dear friend from work. She had collected my favorite candies (York Peppermint Patties and Heath bars), some stickers for Grace, and some bath salts and body lotions for some self-pampering. The enclosed card read, "Dear Theresa, When times are tough it's always good to know someone is thinking of you. Be the strong woman you are, and soon this will be a distant memory. I love you to pieces. XX Judi" This just made my day!

I picked up Gracie and we headed down the mountain to visit her daddy. She is always so excited to see him and chats about him as we drive. "I wuv daddy," I miss my daddy," Where is daddy?" She munched on a smorgasbord of fishy crackers, yogurt-covered raisins, Cheerios, and grapes, and just chatted away. The road was wet, so it made me a little nervous, but we got to Parker in one piece.

Matthew was waiting for us in the parking lot when we drove up. He looks like Matt again! Twenty days sober today! He gathered his darling daughter into in his arms and took us inside to meet his counselor, Tom. Tom is about 6'5" and balding, a gentle giant. He has kind eyes. Matt was very proud to introduce us to Tom, you could tell. It was obvious that they were a good counselor/patient fit.

Then, Matt and Gracie went outside to hang out and I sat in an oversized leather chair by the fire reading a two-week old People magazine. After about twenty minutes, I stood by the big window that looks out on the grounds and watched Matt and Gracie together . . . and I got choked up. It is just so touching. Matt spotted me at the window and pointed at me so Grace could see her Nana. She got a big smile on her face when she saw me standing there.

Later, Matt and I chatted while Gracie was working with the "big girl" felt markers creating a masterpiece at a nearby table. He shared that he is becoming weary of the daily routine and some of the redundancy of rehab. It is actually a healthy development, that he's showing signs of preparing to re-enter his real life. We discussed the timetable for the next week. I will come and get him on Friday, October 5th at noon. He said he wanted enough time that afternoon to get to the bank and pay his rent. This made me happy, that he is already showing signs of the responsible person I know he really is, not to mention that his rent would be a tad late.

I told him I would stay the weekend so the transition for Grace is not abrupt. Originally I had planned to stay at least a week following his discharge, but Emma was struggling and the dogs were misbehaving, so I will need to leave by Monday. I honestly don't know how I am going to leave that little girl. I have grown so attached to her these past three weeks, and she to me. At one point today, she stated from the back seat, "I don't want you to go, Nana."

So, after about two hours with Matt we said our goodbyes and headed home. I had texted Amanda earlier asking her what the plan was for the rest of the day, and she texted back that she was in Silverthorne shopping for some new clothes for Grace. There is a Chipotle right there, so I suggested we have dinner together at Chipotle. This is a positive development, my relationship with Amanda. I like that we have had honest interactions while I have been here, and, for the most part, have gotten along very well. So, dinner with Amanda was fun, as we chatted about Matt's progress, Grace, and her new career goal to become a nurse.

MY 13th STATION

I drove from Chipotle straight to Eagle for the Al-anon meeting, about a forty-five-minute drive in all. Some of the familiar faces were there, in addition to some new members. I am really beginning to enjoy my time with the group. The people are very kind and welcoming, and honestly seem to care. I am always struck by how each one, in their own way, conveys their inner most feelings so eloquently. I take away a nugget from each and every person. Tonight, I couldn't help looking around the circle at these faces and think how sad I will be to no longer attend the meetings after next Thursday. After each meeting, I have had the pleasure of chatting with such nice people and always leave there with a smile. Tonight, Deb, the Director of Health and Human Services for Summit County, handed me a book called *Courage to Change*, telling me it was a gift from her. Again, I am in awe of the outpouring of goodness in the people here. I got to my car, opened the book to today's date, September 27th, and read:

If only I had infinite wisdom, I secretly think. If only I could see everything before me, a clear path, the knowledge of how I must spend each moment of life! But in meeting after meeting in Al-anon I am reminded that I can only work with what I have today. I don't know what tomorrow will bring. What's more, I am better off not knowing. If I knew what was coming, I suspect that I would spend all of my time trying to run from painful experiences instead of living. I would miss out on so much great stuff.[4]

By the time I left the parking lot I was overcome with emotion. The thought of leaving here was so painful. I told God that I am willing to land where He wants to plant me, and if it is here then so be it.

September 28, 2012
Today I finally got to meet up with Gracie's babysitter, Denise, for lunch. We met at a darling little café downtown called Pepi's that specializes in Austrian comfort food. Denise and I had a really nice chat, and I got her all updated on Matt's progress in treatment. Because she hadn't known him before the alcoholism, I shared with her about what a stud he was in baseball and what a truly wonderful son he had always been. I explained how the depression and addiction seemed to come out of nowhere five years prior, and how baffling it was when it appeared. I told her she would notice a big change in his appearance when she sees him next. Since we both love Gracie so much, it was like we were in a contest to see who could give the most compliments about her! When we parted, I paid her for her first two weeks when Gracie returns to her, knowing that Matt won't have any means to pay her until mid-month. It was the right thing to do, and she was very appreciative.

Emma texted me today, really worried about Bailey. Apparently Bailey had been standing on the side yard of the house barking her fool head off at nothing but the closed gate for an hour. The only things that are on that side yard are the three trash bins and a couple of old, empty plant pots. That's it. Emma said she kept looking out the window to see what the dog was barking at and there was just nothing there. Later that day, someone had left a note on our front door complaining about the barking. Emma was also freaking out because yesterday she found a dead rat on the family room floor, and then today a huge dead crow on the steps to the deck out back. She had to enlist the help of a neighbor to get rid of the corpses. I definitely felt the tug to get back to the life I left behind. My daughter had too much on her plate to be dealing with the dog issues and dead animals, too.

Later this evening, Amanda texted me with a request; she asked me if I would go to Mass with her on Sunday, that she has wanted to go but feels awkward going alone. I immediately agreed to go. This could be yet another God thing. Maybe there will be something said, in a reading or the sermon, that will speak to her, to bring her back to the sacraments. Plus, it is time for Gracie to get a taste of worship. I cannot wait until Sunday.

September 29, 2012
Today is Saturday and I have Gracie all day and night. We started our day by going outside to play ball on the basketball court. We took her purple ball and her little plastic golf set. She didn't really get the hang of the golf thing, but she like passing the purple ball back and forth to me, and then kicking it all over the place. She is such an exuberant little girl. It was fun being outside on a brisk morning with the sun shining.

Next we went exploring. This time I chose the trail that runs along the golf course. I brought along my camera, and a bag for her to collect some "treasures." By the end of the walk she had pinecones, a rock, various flowers, leaves, and sticks. I took photos along the way, including some of us together using the self-timer. I paid close attention to how I felt while on the adventure. I was singing, smiling, dancing along the trail, HAPPY. I love it here. I have even been listening to country music in the car! I know, me? Country music? But, hey, it just fits.

Later, we went to the village to just hang out, and, of course, ended up at the ice cream shop. I ordered a large sundae made with homemade ice cream, and we sat out on the patio to devour it. Down the way there was music playing, and near us were families and dogs—just a wholesome, beautiful scene. I sat there with my cute granddaughter who had chocolate all over her pants, her face, and her hands, and just grinned, reveling in the moment there with the stunning mountains as a backdrop.

September 30, 2012
The last day of September was very memorable. I got Gracie all dressed up really cute to go meet her mommy at church. Amanda had generously given me some money last week to help with food and other expenses related to Grace, so I used some of it to buy the cute black patent leather boots she wore to Mass. I grabbed her little prayer book so she could thumb through the pictures, and some snacks, then off we went.

Amanda was waiting for us in the parking lot, so we all walked in together and took our seats. The sermon was germane to what is going on here with Amanda, Matt, and me because it was about putting aside divisive behavior and pride and doing what is right for all. I was emotional throughout the Mass. I felt some spiritual healing was at work during that hour. Amanda wiggled around like any two-year-old, but was never disruptive.

At the sign of peace Amanda and I hugged each other tightly, saying we loved each other. After church she said she, too, was very touched and emotional at the power of this Mass and how the sermon had touched her. She felt as if the priest was talking directly to us. Just as this whole month has been spiritually driven, this last day of September punctuated that fact.

After church, I changed and went to the gym. Only two more workouts before my free coupon expires. I had a good workout and felt really strong. Conditioning at 8,000 feet is making me stronger. I was alone in the little gym so I talked out loud to God as I moved from machine to machine, processing the power of the morning mass. It is honestly overwhelming, this strong sense of God's presence in every moment here.

Then I took my usual walk and found it much easier now to march up that big hill next to the housing complex. I prayed the whole way. I prayed every prayer I know by heart and, with tears running down my face, thanked God for every blessing he has bestowed on me. I literally felt a vertical energy from above, like His love was just boring right through me from Heaven. I told Him I hoped He could see how grateful I am. I vowed to regain my devotional life and return to Adoration at least once a month for starters. After this experience, this blessed month, I am beholden to God—He saved my son. He *is* the God of miracles.

October 1, 2012
Matt called early this morning to tell me that he would be released on Thursday, a day early. I plan to leave the mountains at 9:00 a.m. to pick him up at about 11:00, with little Gracie in tow. I cannot believe we are finally closing in on the end of this chapter in our lives. I have mixed feelings, of course. I tear up the minute I think about driving away from them and this gorgeous place that has been my home for almost a month. I am so grateful for this opportunity to serve. But on the other hand, my life in California beckons me. My job, my daughter, my man, my dogs . . . they need me, too, and I miss them.

I went shopping later to pick out some gifts for my mom for her eightieth birthday, and something for Emma, Sarah, and little Jake. I also got myself a cute set of salt-and-pepper shakers with rustic horses, perfect for my décor theme back home. After shopping I stopped at Starbucks to get Internet and got caught up on my emails and Facebook. I chatted with Francesca, too—our often emotional and always honest conversations have been woven throughout this past month. I thank God for our friendship and how she has been there for me through the whole ordeal.

I took my daily walk in the pines, feeling so utterly close to God. I figured that the reason I feel so close to Him here is because I am physically so high up—over eight thousand feet in elevation—like I can just reach my hand upward and touch Him. As I approach the day when Matt leaves treatment I find myself praying extra hard, very targeted prayers for angels to cover him and for God to fortify him.

I really felt alone tonight. So utterly *alone*. I began to process the gravity of this period in my life, to really take stock and consider the role that God placed me in. I also had to face returning to my real life, the financial uncertainty that the expenses here have only added to, and dealing with various deferred maintenance projects in the house that now demand my attention. So, tonight I began to prepare myself emotionally for leaving the place I have fallen totally in love with.

October 4, 2012
Gracie and I jumped in the car and booked it down the mountain. When we got to the rehab my feelings were, surprisingly, a little bittersweet. The nice lady who had admitted Matt that sad night about four weeks ago happened to be there. I thanked her for all she had done to help my son.

Picking him up today, with his cute little daughter at my side, was both joyful and poignant. Matt was handed his discharge papers and was ready to more forward in his new life. While he was glad to be done with rehab, he chatted animatedly on the way back up the mountain about the various people he had met there, all the inside stories and drama that took place during those weeks, and also sharing his feelings about being in recovery.

We got back to Vail by 3:00 p.m. The first thing I did after we got out of the car was to snap a photo of him holding his daughter in front of the apartment. The picture says it all. He is grinning from ear to ear and Grace looks like she is in Heaven up there in his arms. Now, they are off to rent a movie and I will take my daily gratitude walk. All is good with the world.

October 5, 2012
I had slept on the sofa bed in the living room so Gracie and Matt could enjoy the room to themselves. The mattress is pretty lumpy, and that mouse never was caught, but oh well. This morning was quiet and mellow. I can't describe the sense of peace I have just watching Matt with his beautiful little girl.

We drove to the lake and found a good spot to feed the fish (huge trout!) and "duckies." After that, we went to a little arcade and the two of them played a bunch of games together. It was just a lovely afternoon hanging out with Blue and Grace.

Matt attended a local A.A. meeting but didn't feel it was a fit, so tomorrow he will try a different meeting. Eventually he will find one that works for him. We had a really nice talk tonight about God and miracles and how things happen that sometimes can't be explained any other way. It was an emotional chat, but really good.

Now I am in the process of detaching, getting ready to leave Colorado. I am very sad to leave them, and this mountain. Every time I imaging leaving I get choked up. But it is now time for me to return to my real life. I need to get back to work and earn some money again.

The trees are dropping their leaves now and beginning to look sad and haggard. The saffron colored leaves lie scattered on the ground beneath them like an afterthought. Soon it will be winter and everything will be coated in frosty white. I won't get to see that, but I can imagine it will be beautiful in its own way.

October 6, 2012

I went about the sad task of packing up for my return trip home. I tried not to let Gracie see my tears. It was a stressful morning because leaving a day early was a last minute decision and I had to be on the road no later than 1:00 p.m. I kept Gracie distracted with toys and would sneak a suitcase at a time out the door to take to my car. I summoned all I had learned from the wonderful group at the Al-anon meetings to garner the strength to trust God to watch over my son and give him the strength he will need. Just thinking about the Al-anon group made me sad—I will really miss them.

While I packed the car, Matt was attending an A.A. meeting, which gave me peace. The recovery meetings, plus the twice-weekly outpatient sessions and just getting back to work, will hopefully provide the support system he will so badly need. When he returned from the meeting it was time for me to go. I could feel that he was sad to see me leave, too. I didn't want an emotional scene, so I tried to keep an upbeat tone and demeanor. In other words, I faked it.

We walked down to my car and hugged. He told me how much he loved me and appreciated all that I had done for him. I told him I already knew it, that he didn't have to say anything. I could feel the tears threatening to fall so I quickly hugged little Gracie, got into my car, and drove away.

As I travelled toward Eagle on the I-70 I began to process my emotions about leaving Colorado. I looked at the scenery, which was now taking on a different appearance, less crisp and more indicative of the upcoming winter. Some of the aspens had morphed into grayish stick trees, their once lovely leaves now lying at their feet. All of the little "candle lights" were slowly going out, one by one, a natural end to this chapter in Colorado, this saffron September.

MY 13th STATION

All along the route towards the Utah border I was in awe of God's creation. The beauty that He has graced us with is a sight to behold. Rivers and colorful trees, thick pines and rugged mountains all filled my senses with such profound gratitude. How lucky I am to have been born in such a beautiful, diverse country.

As the hours passed, I was able to access my survivor instincts and cycle from feelings of loss toward embracing the life that lay ahead for me back in California.

CHAPTER 19

Devastation

THE DRIVE HOME FROM COLORADO had felt extremely long. After two long and boring days of travel I finally made it home at about 5:00 p.m. I just sat there on the floor with my dogs, so happy to be home. As I started to unpack, I could tell the pups were glad to know their mommy was finally home to stay. Later that evening, I sat at the computer and uploaded about 275 photos I had taken while on this journey. Seeing the images fill the screen, one gorgeous postcard-worthy photo after another, filled me with feelings of melancholy. My month in Colorado was over. I got a lump in my throat as the images of Gracie intermingled with the scenic shots. I will never forget the impact of this experience on my life, my spirituality, and my priorities.

I spent the weekend getting caught up with laundry and errands as I settled back in to life on Meadow Lane. It felt like I had been gone a year. I contacted my manager and set up my return to work for the next Saturday, October 13th. This was perfect, giving me time to see the dentist, work on my mom's birthday party planning, touch up my roots, and take in an Al-anon meeting.

On Sunday afternoon, Matt texted, saying he was in a really bad place. My heart sank. Early recovery is very difficult. It is hard to adjust to life back home after leaving the structured rehab environment, and I knew Matt was lonely. His struggle with depression continued, but now was to be endured without the alcohol to mask the painful emotions. I asked him to call me so we could talk about it, but he said he couldn't, that he was too sad and upset. So we continued to text.

When I asked him what was going on he said that earlier that day he had texted Amanda and asked her, if he proves himself and stays sober, would she ever consider reconciling so they could be a family again. She was very kind about it, but gently told him no, that it was not a possibility. She had moved on to a new relationship and was happy. In fact, she had actually mentioned to me her intent to begin the divorce proceedings, so this development came as no shock to me. I was grateful that she was kind in her response to him, but my heart just broke for my son.

On Monday, I called Francesca and invited her for dinner at my house on Wednesday. I wanted to make her a nice dinner as thanks for being such a devoted friend to me during a challenging time. I had a full week planned ahead, and felt encouraged that I was slowly adjusting to California life again. I'd begun to accept that my time in Colorado was now complete, and knew I needed to focus on my own life and relationships.

Tuesday morning when I woke up I saw that Matt had texted me at 1:35 a.m. Included in the text was a photo he'd taken of the little wooden cross I had hung on the wall next to his front door now resting in the palm of his hand. His message stated, "For some reason I woke up and felt like I needed to pray, so I am sitting here praying Our Fathers." Hmmm. Okay, well, I figured, that is a good thing; God had tapped him on the shoulder and he'd responded nicely. I was happy that the cross was still up on the wall, half expecting him to take it down after I left. I thought, wow, he got out of bed and traipsed to the other end of the apartment to grab the cross and say prayers in the middle of the night. Powerful.

That day, Tuesday, I felt a strong urge to go to the Adoration chapel. I acted on this prompt, wanting to make good on a promise to God made under the Colorado sky. I walked to my bookcase to peruse my collection of spiritual reading options, as I enjoy spending that time both journaling and reading. I decided to go with my little book on Saint Anthony, as it had been a few years since I'd last read it. I grabbed the book and headed over to the church to spend a quiet hour with Jesus where I could personally thank Him for all his provisions and love while I was in Colorado. When I came home from the church, I tossed the book on my dresser, took a nice warm bath, and hit the sack.

The next day, Wednesday, October 10th, I texted Matthew just to say "hello." Surprisingly, he immediately called me back. He wanted to tell me about a disturbing event that had happened during the night. He had been alone in his apartment, sleeping with his bedroom door open as usual. Grace was with Amanda. Matt said the feeling that someone was watching him had awakened him. He glanced over at the doorway and saw a large black shadowy figure standing there. He said he thought for sure he was dreaming it. Then, just as he was trying to convince himself it was a dream, the thing, in a split second, was sitting on top of him. He said he could barely breathe, like it was squeezing the air out of his lungs. He said he literally thought he was going to die of suffocation. Then just as suddenly, it left. He said it completely freaked him out, knowing that he had not imagined it.

Hearing this triggered my own disturbing memory from about seven years prior when a demon was in my bedroom, sitting on me and pressing my chest. I also recalled Ashley Peterson witnessing a large black demonic figure following her dad up the stairs in the late nineties. There was also Jo's nineteen-year-old daughter, who'd had a demon sitting on her during the night and choking her. In addition, a woman at work shared that she had the exact same experience a few years back, happening on three consecutive nights. She had responded by purchasing a collection of decorative crosses to hang on the wall behind the headboard, and hadn't had any demonic visitors since.

I didn't question for a minute that what Matt had experienced was real, I knew in my gut it was absolutely authentic, and absolutely evil. So, I just told him to continue to pray and to seriously consider going to church. I would double up on my prayers for him, my chain of prayer medals now once again fastened to the lamp on my own nightstand.

Wednesday was busy. I had a dentist appointment at 2:00 p.m. and then went grocery shopping for the spaghetti dinner I would make for Francesca. I couldn't wait to see her! We had grown very close in recent months and had so much to catch up on.

As expected, the visit with my friend was just great. We feasted on spaghetti and meatballs, a nice green salad, and enjoyed a glass of Chianti with dinner. After dinner, as I was loading the dishwasher, Francesca and I continued to chat while she wandered around my kitchen looking at my knick-knacks and artwork. Suddenly, she turned to me and said she needed to stop the conversation so she could tell me something. I thought it a bit abrupt, and her tone of voice was oddly serious. I remained quiet so she could say what she wanted to tell me.

Francesca then turned to my little art shrine hanging on the narrow wall by the refrigerator that I had bought on my pilgrimage to Fatima, Portugal. She said, "I believe that this is protecting you."

I was a bit mystified by this and replied, "What do you mean, Franny?"

She said, "I believe that this, and also that," pointing to the standing Crucifix that was behind my kitchen sink area, "are protecting you; because right now, to my left, toward the front entry area, I feel something very dark and evil is there. I don't see it, but I feel it. And I am sorry if this sounds rude, but I feel sick and I need to get out of your house immediately."

I said, "Oh my gosh, Franny, there have been strange things happening in my house for years!"

Francesca stated forcefully, "Do not tell me, just let me get out of this house now!"

With that, we quickly exited through the garage and stood out on my driveway. She wanted to wait for Emma to get home from work so I wouldn't be alone, and she was due home any minute. It was about 10:00 p.m. and beginning to drizzle. I realized that I was shivering, even though it was a warm, humid evening.

Francesca said, "Just do not tell me about the things in the house when it's dark out. You will have to wait until we have a sunny day and then you can tell me about it, okay?"

Within minutes, I spotted the old Honda that my daughter drove cruising up the street. I hugged Franny goodbye and she headed home. As close as our friendship was, and continues to be, she never again stepped foot inside my house.

I had been living in the home for over two decades at that point. Whatever spirits lurked in the house, and around our neighborhood, had been there for a long time. There would often be no supernatural activity for long periods, like a year or two. However, now it seemed we were in a renewed period of attack. This event with Francesca, Emma's recent comments about the shuffling sounds coming from between the floors above the family room, and even the dog's bizarre barking behavior in the side-yard last week, at something not visible, were all deeply concerning. I didn't tell Emma about what happened in the house with Francesca that night, fearing it would just scare her unnecessarily. So, into the house we went, me silently praying the prayer to St. Michael the Archangel.

The next day was Thursday, October 11th—10/11/12, a cool date. Matt and I had been texting during the late morning, he joyfully sharing that he was at Target with Gracie picking out her Halloween costume. I had left them some cute Halloween stickers to decorate with, and he told me they'd put them up on the front window that morning. He seemed very upbeat, much better than the sad guy from Sunday's text conversation.

In the late afternoon Matt sent me a silly text—something about Joan Jett that I couldn't really follow. For a brief moment I wondered, is he drinking? I pushed the uncomfortable thought aside, unable to even fathom the possibility.

That evening my sister, Elaine, called to discuss our mom's party plans. We had a nice long conversation allowing me to share some of the highlights of the month in Colorado and to give her the current status of her nephew, who also happens to be her godson.

Later during our conversation, I heard the beeping that indicates someone is calling. I have a habit of ignoring those interruptions, assuming that whoever wants to chat will leave a voicemail and I can get back to them later. When it happened a second time, I told Elaine that it appeared Matt was trying to reach me, so we hung up.

Unfortunately, I missed his call anyway and he didn't leave a message, so I called him back. When Matt answered it was clear that he had been drinking. I tried to rein in my feelings of anger and avoided condemning him. I asked him why he didn't call his sponsor, since he had claimed on Monday to have one now.

He answered, "Because Mom, my mind is playing tricks on me." As angry as I felt at the moment, knowing he had already relapsed, I just suggested he attend a meeting in the morning, and we said goodnight." As soon as we hung up, however, I felt compelled to have someone go check on him.

I reached Amanda and she said she, too, had received calls from Matt and that he sounded "off." I asked if she could go over there and check on him. Amanda felt uncomfortable going to his place alone, saying he just seemed really strange tonight. Matt was a mellow drunk, a quiet, lonely alcoholic who usually just drank in solitude until he passed out. He was never violent or mean, so for her to feel a visceral sense of concern about going there alone spoke volumes about his apparent state of mind. Amanda said she would try to get her friend Molly to go with her, or maybe her boyfriend. I was hoping they could just make sure that he's okay and maybe even get him to a meeting.

Meanwhile, since I'd befriended two of his neighbors, Trina next door, and Victor on the second floor, I had their contact information in my phone, so I sent them each a text. Neither responded, so I called and left voicemails asking if they could go check on Matt.

Meanwhile, Amanda called me back saying Molly wasn't home and that her boyfriend was stuck at work. We were discussing whether we should contact Vail security and have them stop by Matt's apartment when suddenly I had an incoming call—from Matt! Oh, what a relief! I told Amanda, no worries, that Matt was calling me, and we hung up.

When I picked up the call I said, "Hi Blue. What's going on?"

A stranger's voice asked, "Are you Matthew's mother?"

My heart plummeted like a rock. I timidly asked, "Who *is* this?"

The male voice said, "This is Deputy Lewis from the Summit County P.D. I am sorry to have to tell you some bad news. It seems your son, Matthew, attempted to take his life tonight by jumping off the fourth floor of his apartment building. It is amazing that he survived the fall. He landed on concrete steps and hit a steel handrail, too. It is a miracle he is alive."

My whole universe became frozen in an instant. I suddenly felt nauseous. I began shaking uncontrollably. My mouth became dry as dirt as I chirped out, "Where is he now?"

The officer responded by informing me that my son was being life-flighted down the hill to a Level One trauma hospital. He said that Child Protective Services had been called in because "his daughter was left sleeping in her bed alone." He told me, "The mother, Amanda, is being contacted to come and get the child. I am so very sorry to give you this bad news."

I could feel myself going into shock. I managed to utter, "What hospital? What is the name of the hospital?"

The deputy replied, "St. Anthony's, in Lakeside."

I thanked him, got off the phone, and my eyes immediately shifted toward the spot on my dresser where I had placed the St. Anthony book two days prior. Amazing.

I slumped to the floor next to my bed. My whole body was trembling. I had no strength to get up and walk, so I crawled, scooting a little bit at a time, toward the bedroom door. I needed to tell Emma, who was in her room at the opposite end of the hallway, what had happened. I attempted to call out her name, "Emma!" but only silent breaths manage to come from my mouth, no sound. I crawled a little further until I was just inside my bedroom doorway. This time when I called her name I tried my best to make sound, to get her attention. She heard me.

When my twenty-year-old daughter saw me sitting on the floor sobbing and shaking she knew instantly something had happened to her brother. I had to tell her the horrible news that Matt had tried to kill himself; that he was in serious condition and being flown to a top trauma hospital outside Denver.

My youngest then picked me up off the floor and sat me on the end of my bed. She instructed me, "Breathe . . . breathe . . . Mom, take a breath!" Suddenly, the reality of the news hit her and she burst into tears. But then she looked back at me, sitting there shivering, and told me to calm down, to breathe. Together on the bed we sobbed. Emma vacillated between offering comforting words of hope to me, expressing sheer anger toward her brother, and then heartfelt compassion for him.

Eventually Emma gathered her wits and called Sarah, who lived only ten minutes away with her family. At about 10:30 p.m. Sarah arrived, finding me once again seated on the floor between my dresser and the bedroom door, immobile . . . catatonic. The three of us, distraught and crying, struggled to process this awful development. Soon, Sarah's attention shifted toward my needs. Down to the kitchen she went to make me a smoothie, encouraging me, against my will, to try and drink it.

After about an hour, just after midnight, Sarah returned to her family and Emma tried to get some sleep. I called Amanda and we both just cried our eyes out, half in shock while trying to offer each other some solace. Amanda felt traumatized by the scene she encountered when she arrived at the apartment to retrieve little Gracie, who, thankfully, had slept through it all. There were half a dozen first responders and paramedics still there, as well as four police officers, and the C.P.S. official who needed to interview Amanda for the report. Residents at the apartments were outside, trying to ascertain what had happened in their sleepy little hamlet. Amanda was very, very shaken, and was feeling bad for not going over to check on Matt. He had left her a suicide note, only adding to the burden of guilt she was feeling. But I reminded her that I had supported her reticence about going to his apartment, understanding how his unusual behaviors made her so uneasy about going alone.

After we got off the phone, Amanda and I continued texting back and forth until 4:00 a.m. Through our text conversation we attempted to process this shocking turn of events, struggling to comprehend what had happened that night with Matt. We had no idea what might have triggered the relapse, much less a suicide attempt. It was very obvious he was not in his right mind at all; Matt would never, ever purposely put his daughter in danger. Amanda knew that, too. We agreed that something we could not grasp had triggered this event.

Through the commotion of the night I was able to speak with the trauma center spokesperson at St. Anthony's. He said that Matt was in "T-10," which is the emergency operating room for the worst-case trauma injuries. The man said that when a patient is admitted to T-10, all available surgeons are beckoned to the room to attempt to save the patient's life. He told me they initially believed Matt had suffered a broken femur, and said they would confirm that during the course of the medical interventions. He said that Matt was severely injured but that it was believed he would survive his injuries. He made a point to tell me that most people would not have survived that fall.

I called John, who was very, very distraught at hearing this shocking news. He said he would make plans to fly out to Denver in the morning. Just hearing that, how he would immediately drop everything to be there for his son, caused layers and layers of resentment and anger to suddenly evaporate. I was so grateful that he was putting Matt first above all else. He needs his dad.

Around midnight, I texted Francesca about Matt's suicide attempt. After receiving my overwrought text she immediately got back to me, attempting to soothe my broken spirit and calm me down. Just knowing she was there for me was comforting.

I also received a phone call from Amanda's mom, Liz, who cried right along with me. She and all of Amanda's family adore Matt, and were crushed by the news of his relapse and subsequent suicide attempt. She was so gracious and kind, only saying the nicest things about my poor son. I also received calls from both of Matt's neighbor friends that I had attempted to contact earlier, each feeling horrible about what happened and apologizing for not being available when I'd reached out. They described to me what the scene there at the apartment complex had been like, with all the pandemonium.

Victor, who is also his supervisor at work, broke the news to me that, sadly, little eleven-year-old Jessica, the super's daughter who loved to play with Grace, had witnessed Matt jump. Apparently, she was out in front of her apartment on the fourth floor. She told the officers that Matt had climbed the stairs, and that when he got to where she was standing he was talking crazy gibberish, making no sense. Then he marched past her, climbed up on the railing, and jumped. She was terribly traumatized, screaming until her parents came out to see what had happened. My heart was utterly broken by this news along with strong feelings of anger toward my son for the emotional pain he had caused this innocent child.

All of this communication transpired between 8:30 p.m. Thursday and 4:00 a.m. Friday.

The next morning, I woke up hoping that it had all been a terrible nightmare. My eyes were swollen like slits. I was completely blown out emotionally and felt physically ill. The gravity of what had happened, and the devastating consequences it would have on not only Matt's life, but also his daughter's, began to sink in. Amanda had told me that C.P.S. had filed a child endangerment charge against Matthew, and that he had lost all parental rights. He lay in a psychiatric I.C.U. bed at the top trauma hospital in Colorado, completely unaware of this.

I stayed in bed attempting to process this unthinkable new reality; that my son had actually tried to jump to his death last night. Because I had spent so much time at his apartment I knew exactly where he had positioned himself before jumping, aiming for the narrow concrete steps set amidst a wide expanse of lawn. I just couldn't believe he had done this, especially with Gracie right there sleeping in her little "horsey" bed. It just didn't make any sense at all.

My mind returned to the dark music that he still listened to. Those despairing lyrics, words of doom and death that are woven throughout the songs that he listened to daily in his car or on his iPod; they were penetrating his mind and darkening his soul.

Relentless Reckless Forever, by Children of Bodom
Relentless, no way I'm giving up
I dare you make me stop
Reckless—shattered dreams and broken ribs
Annihilated into bits
Forever I'll stay on the run
You like to cling to my back like a monkey
Not even a chance you'd let me go

While pondering the events I suddenly realized that the reason Matt didn't die last night was because his guardian angel had intervened to soften his landing. There is no way that a six-foot three-inch tall, two hundred-fifteen-pound male, jumping from that height, gathering that kind of velocity and landing on concrete and steel, could have survived otherwise. I saw this as Matt's wake-up call to get back to church, to rekindle his relationship with God. Suddenly, I remembered my voice recording traveling out to Colorado on September 7th, how I had specifically prayed to God, the saints, and his *guardian angel* to protect him and keep him safe. Wow.

I texted my manager; I just couldn't bring myself to call her and have to utter the words. I told her in my frantic message that my son had tried to kill himself by jumping off the fourth floor of his apartment building. I would have to return to Colorado. Here I was supposed to finally go back to work the next day, Saturday, but obviously I was an emotional wreck and needed to get back to my son. Work would have to be put on hold.

I could not talk to anyone except my mom. I felt so bad telling her about Matt's suicide attempt knowing how much pain this would cause. I also had to tell her the birthday party we'd been planning for her would have to be postponed, and she was very gracious in her response. But other than my mother, I could not bear to speak to anyone. No one. I was traumatized. Not Amanda, not my sister, not my friends, no one. I simply could not form coherent sentences. I was barely able to put a text together, and those were riddled with multiple typos. Through text or email I notified my close friends and family members, as did John for his side of the family. Everyone was beyond shocked and sad to hear this news about Matt. There had been so much hope for him.

I was broken-hearted, ashamed, and guilt-ridden for not staying with him longer. Yes, after a month in Colorado I had felt a strong need to return home to help Emma, and to get back to my job and earn some income. But had the rehab clinicians at discharge just told me how incredibly vulnerable Matt would be in early recovery, especially living alone, I would have figured out some way to stay. But in fact, they didn't warn me or prepare me, they simply handed Matt the paperwork that listed the meds they'd put him on (Lexapro and trazodone), and sent us on our way.

No doubt, during his weeks of therapy, relapse prevention was thoroughly discussed and guidance had been provided. But I wasn't in on those sessions and had no clue what the dangers to recovery were. Matt knew the risks, but I didn't. Rehabs should inform the family members or spouses of these risks to sobriety so we are adequately prepared to offer ongoing and needed support while they adjust to sobriety back in their home environment, *especially* if they live alone. Enabling? Hogwash!

Late that afternoon, as I struggled to make sense out of what had happened, I thought to check Matt's Facebook account. He posted on Facebook regularly, usually just short one or two sentence musings revolving around his daughter's antics. His posts were always easy-going and humorous.

There on his timeline, standing out among all the light chatter of his other Facebook posts, was a post from early evening last night, just an hour or two before he jumped. He had written, "The coming curse got me," followed by a sad emoji. A comment from a friend noted these words as lyrics from a band called Iced Earth. Immediately, in search of clues, I Googled the lyrics to the song.

The Coming Curse
By Iced Earth:
I walk the Earth just as they planned
Baptized in fire for my ancient land
The coming curse, your anti-Christ, I am the Watcher's eye
I vindicate and cleanse the Earth of all mankind
For many years, I've walked among you
Through the folds of time and space
Kingdoms fall, leaders die, as I see fit
I devour souls of those that pose a threat
I walk the Earth another day
The wicked one that comes this way
Savior to my own, devil to some
Mankind falls, something wicked comes
I bide my time planning your fate
With bated breath, The Elder wait
The coming curse, your anti-Christ, I am the Watcher's eye
For your crimes on our kind you all will die
Forged in the sacred flames

MY 13th STATION

On the sixth day
Of the sixth month
In the sixth hour
I am your anti-Christ, I will destroy mankind
Born of the beast and flames
I will devour, I will divide
Hellfire rages in my eyes
Blood will fall like rain this night
The coming curse, the anti-Christ, I am the Watcher's eye
I vindicate and cleanse the Earth of all mankind

My son's Facebook post sent a signal to his friends and family, before he was compelled to jump off that building, that the demon, *the coming curse*, got him. I recalled the events that preceded the suicide attempt, the obvious spiritual warfare going on there in his apartment—waking up feeling compelled to pray on Monday, and then being crushed by a large black demon on Tuesday. It appeared there were multiple demons in our home and one of them had attached to Matt, accompanying him to Colorado. On Wednesday, Franny had sensed demonic energy in my house, and then on Thursday Matt jumped off the apartment building.

Later that day the full emotional impact of his suicide attempt began to hit me hard, and by nighttime I found myself inside my walk-in closet digging through a tub of mementos I kept in there. I was frantically searching for some clue, some sign that would help me to reconcile the man who jumped off a building with my beautiful son. Rifling through photos of smiling, happy, handsome Matthew at various ages suddenly overwhelmed me, triggering deep feelings of grief. I stood there in my closet howling at the top of my lungs, "WHAT HAPPENED TO MY SON?" yelling this over and over. Then, slumping to the floor, I sobbed—deep, guttural, inhuman sounding sobs, like the wailing tones of a dying animal.

Although it was very late on Friday night, I texted Francesca, asking her how could God have allowed this to happen. Where was He when my boy needed Him? Why didn't God stop Matt somehow? Didn't my daily, heartfelt prayers matter? Wasn't anyone listening to my pleas?

I will always be beholden to my dear friend for getting me through that night. She was actually on a date with her boyfriend, and was driving, as my frantic texts came rolling in. Later, she shared with me how she had initially asked him to read to her what I was texting, and even dictated her first text response for him to type to me. But as the intensity of my emotional state became evident, she pulled over and texted me for the next sixty minutes.

Her texts to me over that hour were hand-delivered from God. In fact, she told me that the words she typed were straight from the Bible, that the Scriptural references just popped into her head and traveled to her fingers as she typed, shocking even her. She just allowed God to guide her responses to me, and in those profoundly spiritual texts was so much compassion and love that I was able to eventually settle down and go to bed.

John had arrived at the hospital, located outside Denver, by early Friday afternoon. He called soon after to update me on Matt's status. I am forever grateful that it was he and not me who had to witness our son's condition at that early juncture. John told me that I would have come undone had I seen our son that way. Matt was completely out of his head, delirious, and on multiple pain medications. He was required to have a sitter with him in the room 24/7, and his I.C.U. room was outfitted with an "eye in the sky," a camera that allowed the nurses station to keep an eye on him as well.

MY 13th STATION

I was relieved that John was there with Matt. He sat there with him for twelve hours a day until I could get back to Colorado five days later. I had to find some financial aid in that period, as I was tapped out. My credit card limit had been reached and my bank account was empty. I was broke. Thanks be to God, my co-workers in their loving generosity, came through to help me. One of them offered me her miles so I could purchase airfare, and several of them contributed to a collection for my hotel stay, covering five nights at a nearby Marriott. My ex already had a room there and suggested I contact the nun associated with St. Anthony's who could offer me a bargain rate through a scholarship agreement they had with the Marriott. This was a huge blessing, as this gracious nun arranged for my room rate to be just $50 per night. In addition to these gifts, my sweet boyfriend, Mike, generously handed me a sentimental card with $1,000 cash tucked inside.

On Tuesday, October 16th I received a short, loving email from my friend, Jo, my fellow homeschooling friend who had been guiding me on the matters of spiritual battle. Here is what she wrote:

> Dear, dear Theresa,
> My heart is breaking with this news of Matthew's situation in ICU. I have been sobbing all morning. Please, tell him we are praying for him. If you can, put a green scapular under his pillow for Our Lady's powerful intercession. I am closing now to pray my rosary for Matthew's recovery. May you find peace under Our Lady's mantle.
>   Blessings for a safe journey to CO.
> Love,
> Jo

Jo and I were close friends and shared a deep love for the faith. This valued friend also happens to be an extremely intelligent, well-read woman and has taught me so much about Catholicism over the years. She introduced me to Catholic traditions and devotions that I had never learned as a child. I was quite touched by her note that day and wrote her back at about midnight. Today, as I re-read these old emails, one particular paragraph jumps off the page confirming that back in 2012 I had connected the dots. On that day I had written to Jo:

> " . . . But the addiction is just an effect of being touched by the demon that latched onto him about five years ago. I still believe we have a demonic presence in this house. Still, on occasion, I get chills up my spine because I can feel the presence. Whenever I do, I state loudly and clearly, "Be gone in the name of Jesus Christ, you have no power here."

CHAPTER 20

Colorado Redux

I ARRIVED BACK IN COLORADO on Wednesday morning, October 17th. Determined not to have to check a bag, which would only delay my arrival at the hospital, I managed to literally stuff all clothing and supplies into one carry-on bag and a backpack. Travelling that day I moved through the airports like a zombie, not like that fired up mission-inspired mother I was on my first journey to Colorado less than six weeks prior. Had it really only been mere weeks since my heart soared with newfound purpose? Seated on the plane I thought how unaware my fellow passengers were of the mother's shattered heart seated in 17C.

I took a cab to St. Anthony's Hospital knowing I would have no need for a car on this trip, as the hospital provides shuttle service to the Marriott. I arrived at the hospital at about noon, immediately impressed by the modern, cutting edge facility that housed my boy. Riding up the elevator to the I.C.U., I could feel my heart pounding out of my chest as anxiety spiked. John had kept me updated over the past five days, and said Matt had come a long way. Although relieved to hear that, I found myself struggling for composure in the moments before entering his room.

As I took a deep breath and opened the door to Matt's room, I had to force my face into a neutral mask, hiding my shock as I gazed at my precious son. Only with God's grace do we find the strength to confront such disturbing sights without crumbling.

Matt had six broken ribs, five on the right and one on the left. His right clavicle was broken. He had a huge gash in his head, held together with twenty-five staples. There was a tube in his lungs draining bloody fluid to help prevent pneumonia from setting in. I knew that, by far, the most serious injuries were to his left leg, although a sheet covered him from the waist down.

I somehow managed a smile as I approached my son to give him a delicate hug. He seemed out of it, high on a cocktail of pain medications, but was coherent. His demeanor seemed very guarded, even a bit hostile. I tried to not let that hurt my feelings, assuming he likely felt ashamed to have me see him like this, and for his actions last week that brought him here. The metal staples embedded in his scalp were startling to see. Just imaging the massive bleeding that a laceration that huge would have caused was beyond what I could have ever handled.

John was seated on one side of the bed, looking extremely drawn. No doubt the strain of these past five days, borne by him alone, had taken its toll. He witnessed his son's condition at the very worst phase of the injuries, and had described how unsettling it was to see the horrible physical injuries, as well as Matt's semi-delusional psychological condition.

In the corner sat one of what would become a long parade of sitters during my son's stay at St. Anthony's. In fact, I made a point to write each name down in my journal entries during this second trip to Colorado. I noted their names because during my time there with Matt, I always struck up conversations with them. They had to be incredibly bored, sitting there in that chair. These individuals were interns, volunteers, or low-paid employees, and each one struck me as having a kind, compassionate soul. After all, they were entrusted with looking out for my boy.

As the afternoon hours passed that day, Matt's disdain for me became more apparent, and hurtful. He seemed to now prefer the company of his dad to me, a complete turnaround. At one point I left the room in tears. I just couldn't understand why he was so angry with me. I noticed a distinct darkness in his demeanor that I had never seen in him before. I wondered if it was due to the pain medications he was on. Or maybe, as he was processing what had happened, the fallout and fears about what lay ahead for him were sinking in. Maybe he was angry that he had survived. Whatever the cause of this disturbing change, it troubled me. He was not at all himself, not at all.

Later that day, when he returned to his bed from the bathroom, I asked if he would show me his injuries, and he agreed. He lifted his hospital gown so reveal the huge black and purple bruises up and down his right side and his right arm. The tube inserted into his lungs was collecting a blood-tinged fluid, which was hard to look at.

I braced myself for the leg already knowing it was very badly injured. He revealed his calf first, with an enormous wound that resembled a shark attack. The injury to the upper thigh, into the lower left buttock took my breath away, a deep gash about fifteen inches in length topped with an enormous hematoma on the left hip, deep purple in color and swollen with fluid. The hematoma was the size of a kid's Nerf football sliced horizontally, about six inches in size.

The rudimentary sutures used on these injuries were huge and dramatic. When someone is seriously injured, the trauma team is focused on just one thing, the patient's survival. That being said, they do not place emphasis on cosmetic outcomes, rather the trauma team simply acts swiftly to treat any life-threatening injuries.

Seeing the injuries for myself, although in a more healed state than my ex had witnessed five days ago, made me curious about that T-10 room the hospital representative had told me about. I found a photo online of this exact room at St. Anthony's hospital and gasped. It looked like a set from a science fiction movie! A lone bed sat situated in the center of an enormous, cavernous operating room with gigantic lights, the lamps looking to be two or three feet in diameter, encircling the bed. Several computer monitors and emergency medical equipment completed the scene. I shuddered when envisioning my son, bleeding and broken, lying on that table.

This day, Wednesday, presented John and I with a dilemma. He had made plane reservations for Thursday morning, so needed to stay at the hotel tonight. I, too, needed a place to stay, so we agreed, unbelievably, to have a sleepover. So the handy sleeper sofa became my bed for the night.

It was so refreshing to no longer feel anger toward my ex, ever since he had sprung into action the prior Friday. We stayed up until midnight reminiscing about past family vacations, our kids, and, of course, discussed Matt and his future. We even found ourselves laughing over memories of silly events from our married life together. Regardless of how difficult the marriage was, we did have some fun times and had made cherished memories raising our children. I guess this is what forgiveness looks like.

John left for California the next morning, Thursday, meaning that this part of the sad journey would be left up to me to manage. I admit I felt anxious about what may lie ahead here at St. Anthony's. Matt clearly didn't want me around. His negative attitude was hard to be around for extended periods, so every few hours I would venture downstairs for some fresh air.

On my way back up to his room I spotted a little chapel, a tiny Catholic church, on the lower level. I stepped inside, just as a man was exiting, and found myself alone in the church. I walked up to the altar and dropped like a rock to my knees. Stooped over, tears gushing, I begged Jesus to help my son. I slowly picked myself up off the floor and plopped my weary body with its battered soul into a nearby pew. I have a habit of recording significant points in time, so I decided to capture this sad moment, me in that little church a few floors below where my son lay broken, with a selfie.

In the image is a grief-stricken woman with puffy bags and dark circles under her eyes. Her brow is creased. Her mouth is closed, serious, resigned, the jaw set. In the eyes you see a blank stare, almost lifeless, like the eyes of a dead fish. Just over my right shoulder, in the background, is a statue of the Blessed Virgin Mary. My Mother was right there with me, to soothe my broken heart. I texted the sad selfie to Francesca. She said seeing my sorrowful face made her weep. This little chapel would become my refuge over the course of Matt's stay at St. Anthony's.

While I was on my way back to Matt's room, I received a text from Victor. He asked me to call him when I got a minute, so I went ahead and called him right back. He wanted first to get an update on Matt's progress, but the purpose of the call was to prepare me for what was to happen next. Being Matt's immediate supervisor, he was informed by H.R. that Matt would have to be terminated due to his suicide attempt, and, additionally, would have to vacate the apartment, which was employee housing. They would give him one week.

While he was talking, I had detoured into a waiting room area for visitors. Even though I was not surprised that his employer would take this action, tears filled my eyes upon hearing this from Victor. Matt absolutely loved his job and his apartment, and losing both will be devastating. He has already lost his parental rights, the biggest blow of all. Adding these to the list of losses put fear into my heart. I feared my sensitive, broken son would be destroyed.

Victor expressed his sincere regret, but stated there was nothing he could do, that it was out of his hands. He told me to expect a phone call in Matt's hospital room between 11:30 a.m. and noon, at which time a representative from H.R. would notify him of the termination.

I walked into the room with a sense of dread, finding Matt awake and watching some silly cable show called Storage Wars. I did my best to keep my facial expression from revealing what I knew was about to happen, and sat down in the adjacent chair pretending to watch the show with him.

At 11:35 a.m., the phone on his bedside rang and he picked up. I tried to keep my eyes fixed on the TV while he was on the phone; I couldn't bear to witness it. But out of my peripheral vision I could observe his demeanor, which said it all. He had his head down, replying to the caller in a calm, quiet voice. There was a pause while he was being told the procedural stuff about the termination process and for vacating the apartment. I saw him wipe tears from his face. He was very kind and respectful in his responses, and never became defensive.

When he got off the phone he said, "I guess I expected this to happen."

I turned to look at him and saw tears on his face. My own heart was breaking just knowing how much this hurt him. I asked if he wanted to talk about it. He shook his head and told me he had just lost his job. I said, "I am so sorry, honey, so sorry," and started to weep, too. For the next several minutes, we both sat there staring silently at the TV, reaching alternately for the box of tissues on the hospital tray between us. I was so sad for him. Everything he cared about was gone. He'd lost it all.

Later, when he felt ready to discuss it, he told me they gave him until next Wednesday to get his apartment packed up. Upon hearing this, I knew immediately that this difficult task would fall to me, since Matt was hospitalized and John was back in California. So, I told him I would rent a car and take care of packing up his apartment next Monday or Tuesday.

He became very, very angry, firmly stating, "No! I want to handle this."

I told him I completely understood his feelings but that, under his present circumstances, he was not physically able to drive or to do the job. He became extremely agitated and cursed at me, stating that he will call mountain security and forbid me to enter his apartment.

He had become so wound up I knew it was best if I just left him alone for a while. It suddenly became clear why suicide risks needed to have a 24-hour sitter. Just look at the issues that can arise as the fallout from a suicide attempt begins to mount. Had the sitter not been there, who knows if Matt would have yanked out his IV and attempted to walk out of there, even though he could barely shuffle to the bathroom at that point in his recovery. I walked back to the visitor lounge and called my ex, telling him the latest round of bad news. I told him that I had to pack the place up within a few days but that Matt was enraged about it. He promised to call Matt to try to talk some sense into him.

I went downstairs to the cafeteria to get some lunch, allowing plenty of time for them to have that conversation. When I returned to the room, Matt looked grim. I sat down in the chair and asked if he wanted to talk yet. He said no, not really, but that dad had called and made him understand why he wasn't able to pack up the apartment. I was grateful.

He then said, "I just wanted to say goodbye to the place I love," and we both sat there in silent sorrow. Oh, how deeply we feel our child's pain.

On Friday, I was there with Matt when the psychiatrist came for their session, so I decided to take a walk around the hospital grounds. It was a sunny, beautiful day and I was feeling a little better after getting a good night's sleep. I was grateful that Matt had someone with whom he could discuss his emotions about losing both his job and apartment. He needed someone objective to talk with about all the losses.

I ventured down the street and found a large, bustling deli, and to my pleasant surprise, saw they offered gluten-free deli sandwiches. I hadn't had a deli-sandwich since I was diagnosed with celiac disease in early 2008, so this was quite a treat. I decided to get Matt a sandwich too, knowing how sick he now was of the hospital fare. I sat outside on the patio and enjoyed people watching as folks passed by. The clientele appeared to be predominately professional types, so I figured I must be close to a commerce hub.

Without a car I just had no clue about what existed in my surroundings there in Lakeside. When I'd leave the hospital each night around 8:30, I would grab a shuttle and cruise to the hotel in darkness. I was fortunate to have some really nice drivers to and from the hotel and some fun conversations. I noticed that, in general, the people in Colorado are really friendly. In the elevator they actually look right at you and say "Good morning." This is unheard of in California, at least in our neck of the woods. People in California pretty much keep to themselves, safely ensconced in their little invisible shells, navigating around their fellow humans without even acknowledging their presence.

When I returned to the hospital, Matt was snoozing, so I just sat and read. Later, he enjoyed the sandwich and told me the session with the shrink had helped a little. These baby steps meant progress. I spent some time updating my family on his condition via emails and texts, not really wanting to engage in conversation. My energy was extremely limited and I needed to preserve it for this very trying chapter of my son's difficult journey.

Later, the doctor came to examine him and informed us that Matt would be moved to a regular hospital room the next morning. After eight days in I.C.U. he was happy to become a regular patient in a regular room. This was an excellent sign that he was healing and getting close to being released.

Just as I got back to the hotel that night I received a call from Sarah, wanting to share something she had put off telling me for a couple days because she knew it would be upsetting. Apparently, on Wednesday night, when my ex and I were both here in Colorado and she was dog sitting at my house (Emma was doing the same at her dad's house) something strange had occurred.

She told me that she and my two-year-old grandson, Jake, were sleeping in the guest room, Matt's old bedroom. During the night, Jake woke up screaming. Sarah tried in vain to quiet him down, but the child screamed and cried for ten solid minutes before he finally fell back to sleep. He had never had a nightmare or night terrors before, so Sarah thought it was very odd.

The next night, now back at their house, Sarah went to get Jake ready for bed. She told him it was time for "night-night" and to put on his pajamas. While she was attempting to change him, he started freaking out. She said he was crazed, crying and saying loudly, "No Granny's house, no Granny's house" (my grandson calls me Granny). She assured Jake that they were home, not at Granny's house, but he continued on, "No Granny's house! Big, scary man Granny's house. Big scary man!" The hair on the back of my neck rose up as she recounted this disturbing event. Had a demon taunted little Jake while they slept in Matt's old room? Had he seen a dark figure, too?

I immediately pulled up the website of my parish in Walnut Creek and found the email address for Fr. Matthew, whom I have known for about ten years. In this lengthy email I attempted to summarize the events in the house and the neighborhood, ending with my son's recent suicide attempt and now my grandson's terror while sleeping in Matt's old bed. I asked Fr. Matthew to get back to me as soon as possible because I was in serious need of a spiritual cleansing of my home. This latest event was the last straw.

On Sunday morning, I texted Matt to tell him I wouldn't be arriving at the hospital until about 1:00 p.m. that day, as I was going to walk to Our Lady of Fatima Catholic Church for Mass. I was so thrilled to find that church—of all the patrons I found a church called Our Lady of Fatima. Heaven sent! I just needed to sit in church and sing and pray. My soul needed that. The past several days had left me feeling depleted . . . and dejected. My son continued to take his frustrations out on me. On top of that, now I was worried about my grandson, too. I just needed Jesus in the Eucharist. Badly. So I made the half-hour trek on foot to church. It was another spectacular day and the walk did me good.

By the time I got to the hospital, after Mass and grabbing some lunch, I was in much better spirits. I was gearing up to face the next day, Monday, October 22nd, which I knew would be very trying on all fronts. I will be making the trip up the mountain to face the scene of Matt's suicide attempt, something I deeply dreaded. And then there is the physical task at hand, to pack up his life there and put his belongings into storage.

While sitting in Matt's room a hospital representative showed up to notify him that he would be discharged from the hospital on Monday, but would be transported directly to a psychiatric hospital. I sat there in utter shock. A mental hospital? What? The representative then explained that Colorado state law mandates that individuals who attempt suicide must have a thorough psychological evaluation prior to being released from the hospital. I couldn't believe this! He had been seen numerous times by the psychiatrist here at St. Anthony's, so why wouldn't those reports of their sessions suffice?

Had Matt indicated that he was still a danger to himself during the therapy sessions?

Apparently, this next step was procedural and something that could not be avoided. She told us he would be transported to West Pines, an inpatient psychiatric hospital in Wheat Ridge, about twenty minutes away. This development now added an additional layer of stress to an already packed and stressful Monday. So much for that nice, relaxed state of mind I was in earlier today.

On Monday morning, Enterprise delivered a car to me at 8:00 a.m. as ordered. I set off on the unfortunate mission that I dreaded with every ounce of my being. I tried to distract myself on the two-hour drive with music, prayer, and daydreaming, but couldn't quell the feelings of anxiety no matter what I did. When I got up to Summit County, my first stop off the I-70 was in Silverthorne where there was an Office Max. I methodically selected the boxes and packing tape I would need to do the big job ahead. After making the purchase, I walked down the way to a Hallmark store to select a gift for little Jessica, who I hoped to see while I was at the apartment. I picked out a pretty charm bracelet with a cross and a heart, and selected a card for her. Inside the card I wrote a heartfelt note of apology, telling her how sorry I was that she had witnessed my son's tragic actions. I asked her to please pray for him and told her that I would be praying for her, too. Tears flowed while I jotted this note to her.

Approaching the Vail off-ramp, I could feel my anxiety surge—heart pounding, rapid breathing, hands clutching the steering wheel. I felt sick to my stomach. Returning to this beautiful little town, the source of so much hope and joy just a few short weeks ago, under these current circumstances was nearly unbearable. I made the final turn and was now facing the housing development where my son's life would take a disastrous turn. I had to will myself to keep driving forward while my heart pounded.

I pulled up to the parking lot and slowly allowed my eyes to turn up to the spot on the fourth floor from where he jumped and then down to the steps where he'd landed. I got out of the car and began toting the packing supplies into the apartment. My hand shook as I turned the key.

I entered his place noting that the dinner dishes were still on the dining table, and little Gracie's toys were strewn about the living room. Suddenly, out of the corner of my eye to the left of the doorway, thrown on the chair there, I spotted the pile of bloodstained clothes that the first responders had cut off Matt's body.

As if by some innate, visceral maternal reflex, I gathered up the bloodied clothing and placed it on the floor. I knelt to the floor and lay on top of the clothes, sobbing from the depths of my broken heart. Just seeing and touching the tangible evidence of his suicide attempt was devastating.

After a few minutes, I was all cried out and just lay there motionless, frozen, trying to will myself to get up and start the job of boxing up Blue's belongings. I was up against the clock; needing to get the boxes into storage and then back down the mountain for Matt's transfer to the psych hospital. So, I got myself up off the floor to begin this difficult job.

Before I went out to grab the next batch of supplies from the car, I noticed Matt's cell phone and wallet sitting on the dining table. I decided to search for some glimpse of his state of mind that day, October 11th, thinking I might find clues in the text messages that he had written and received over the days since I'd left Colorado. I reviewed all his conversations and every single one was upbeat and positive. Absolutely zero signs of distress or depression during the days that preceded the Thursday night suicide attempt. In fact, he was communicating with a couple of people he'd met in rehab, and they were sending each other supportive messages. He even encouraged one of

MY 13th STATION

them to apply for a job at the resort so they could "watch each other's backs." I spotted the text conversation with Amanda from that prior Sunday when he had asked if she'd consider reconciling someday, and her reply to Matt was kind, even if it wasn't what he was hoping for.

So, with a heavy heart I placed his personal belongings, kitchen and bath supplies, clothing, stereo and other electronics, and Gracie's clothing and toys into a couple dozen boxes.

While I was in the midst of packing, a man poked his head into the open front doorway and introduced himself as Jim, one of the maintenance workers at the complex. He inquired about Matt and shared his very kind thoughts about what a great guy he is, saying how Matt is always friendly to everyone. He expressed his concerns for Grace, and for me, knowing how devastating this must be for us.

Then Jim told me that he had witnessed the whole thing, stating, "It was literally the most horrible thing I have ever seen in my life."

He had been down on the ground level when he caught sight of Matt climbing up on top of the railing. Before he could even react, it was too late. Carnage. I asked Jim if he happened to know which apartment Juan lived in so I could go and give Jessica the gift. He gave me the apartment number and I went upstairs via the elevator. When I got up to the fourth floor, and I had never been up there before, I was suddenly aware of just how high up it was. I forced myself to walk to the exact spot where my son jumped off and then peered over the rail at the concrete steps below. It was, I have to admit, traumatizing to see it from the actual vantage point. The crazy thing is, Matt has absolutely zero recollection of climbing the three flights of stairs, getting up on the railing, and jumping. None at all. He only remembered slightly coming to for a brief moment in the helicopter, seeing a paramedic bending over him. That was it.

I located Jessica's apartment and knocked on the half-opened front door. Her dad, Juan, was sitting in the living room and Jessica was in the dining room at the table. She saw me and smiled. I asked Juan if I could talk to Jessica for a minute, and he nodded, but I detected in his eyes deep sorrow. He likely felt a mixture of pity for me, the mother of the guy who tried to commit suicide, and sadness that his sweet little girl had been scarred for life having witnessed the awful event. I felt very ashamed, and tears welled up in my eyes. I walked over to Jessica and hugged her, telling her how sorry I was that she had seen such a scary thing. I assured her that Gracie's daddy would be fine and would get the help he needed, and that Gracie will be staying with her mommy now. I handed her the card, with the bracelet tucked inside. When she opened it she put it right on and thanked me. It was such a miniscule gesture, this humble little gift, but I hoped that the bracelet's message of God's love might help her heal, even just a little bit.

Once everything was boxed up I realized I needed help getting it to the storage unit because my rental car was so small that it would take several trips. It was mid-afternoon and I was running out of time. I called Amanda to see if her new boyfriend could come and help me transport the boxes in his truck. Thankfully, he agreed. When he arrived to help load the boxes he was very kind, and told me how badly he felt for Matt and all of us involved. He gave me his business card in case I needed any more help. He was a godsend that day.

As I prepared to leave the now empty apartment, I wept thinking about the month I had spent there, so full of hope. I wept for my son, knowing his life has been deeply scarred now by something he seemed to have no power over. I was sad that he had to leave his apartment and the job he had grown to love so much over the last nearly two years. As I turned to lock the door, I spotted the Halloween pumpkin stickers that he and Gracie had put up on the window that fateful day, when he was feeling so happy.

MY 13th STATION

Once Matt's belongings were safely stored, I headed back to his apartment to meet the babysitter, Denise, who offered to help me move the Jeep over to her property. She had been so helpful and so supportive during this whole ordeal. Even though she felt sad and disappointed that Matt had chosen to drink that Thursday, her support for him had been unfailing. Mostly, though, Denise has been a point of stability for Gracie, who she continued to babysit several days a week. What would we have done without her?

Two hours later I was back in Lakewood sitting next to Matt at St. Anthony's. The discharge administrator and case worker handed us reams of paperwork with rehabs, a list of psychotherapists, a health insurance contact person, and about a dozen other discharge papers, sewing up our time there at the hospital. I was given the address and directions to the mental hospital that Matt would soon be transported to, and told Matt I would meet him there. I left feeling very apprehensive about this next step.

I had decided to keep the rental car for the rest of the week, knowing I would be shuttling Matt to doctor appointments, so I got in the car with my hand-written directions to the mental hospital in Wheat Ridge. I envisioned a sterile hospital-like facility with staff in starched white uniforms. I pulled in to the complex noting a six-story hospital on one side of the property and a collection of low-slung buildings on the other. Maybe it was the gray, gloomy weather, but the facility, situated in a desolate and grim setting, devoid of greenery, gave me the creeps. Possibly due to the upcoming change of seasons, the landscape had taken on a dry, eerie, lifeless vibe that only added to my trepidation about my son coming here.

I parked and entered the hospital structure. Once in the lobby, I approached the desk and told them I was there for Matthew Anthony. She asked me which facility, and I told her he was being transported to the mental health ward. After gaining clearance to enter the mental hospital, she directed me to walk down a hall, make a couple of turns, then pass through a multi-layered system of locked double doors.

When I was finally allowed entry into the mental hospital, I was asked to wait while my son was "processed." Recoiling at the term, I felt my anxiety level ratchet up another notch. While waiting for Matt, I took in the scene in front of me. What I witnessed was unsettling, with about a dozen patients seated around an older model television in various states of seeming catatonia. Possibly drugged into submission, these people exhibited no life energy or presence, as if they had checked their souls at the door when they were admitted. I heard only one lone voice, a guy down the hall yelling profanities. I tried to remain calm.

Finally, Matt was delivered to the nurse's station where I had been waiting. I could tell by his face that he was just as confused as I was as to why he was brought here. He didn't even have to say a word; I know my kid and could easily read his discomfort. The nurse began to relay the various hospital rules and regulations to Matt, and asked him to sign the paper stating that he comprehended them. After all the paperwork was completed, she asked him to remove his belt, so he did. Then she asked him to remove his shoelaces, so he did. As he bent down, in pain, to remove his shoelaces tears stung my eyes. Standing there witnessing this made my heart ache for my son, just one more humiliation, more of the stripping down of his dignity, taking the last vestiges of what was left of him, even though I understood it was done for the patient's own protection.

After they assigned him a room, I sat there with him for a little while. I could tell he was nervous about being in that place. But soon an announcement was made that it was dinner time, so I left, telling him I would try to get him out of there as soon as possible.

I walked quickly to my car, choking back tears. That my son's life had been reduced to this was more than I could absorb or accept.

The place literally made me shudder. I couldn't get out of there fast enough.

I called Francesca on the way back to my hotel to tell her how freaked out I was. She proceeded to warn me to be very aggressive and forceful with the hospital administrators or they could lock him up in there for a very long time. Once someone is in one of these facilities they become like a ward of the state, without rights, and his was an involuntary hospitalization. I felt frantic and helpless. My kid was in a psych hospital and I feared they might try to keep him there.

Once back at the hotel, I rifled through the discharge paperwork from St. Anthony's looking for some information to help me comprehend what was happening. In the pile was one pink form, entitled "Emergency Mental Illness Report and Application," dated today, October 22nd. It was created and signed by the psychiatrist who had been meeting with Matt during his hospital stay. In the notes he had written: 24-year-old male jumped off 4th floor balcony in suicide attempt-He is a danger to himself and in need of inpatient psychiatric care.

Apparently, this doctor believed that Matt continues to pose a danger to himself and had had him committed involuntarily to this mental hospital. I felt confused and betrayed. I didn't know what to do or who to believe at this point. Looking at those listless, soulless patients I wondered if they would turn my son into one of the zombies, too.

I couldn't sleep at all that night. I lie there processing all that had occurred in one day, confronting the scene at the apartment, seeing Jessica, listening to the maintenance guy, Jim, describe the horror he witnessed. I was physically exhausted from hours of packing and four hours of driving. But by far the most upsetting event today was seeing my son admitted to a mental hospital. What has become of my precious child?

At 10:45 a.m. the phone rang and it was the doctor from the facility. I held my breath and prepared to do combat if necessary. No way would my son be kept in that God forsaken place against his will. The doctor proceeded to tell me that he had spent over an hour with Matt this morning, conducting a thorough psychological evaluation and interview. It was his determination that Matthew did not belong in an inpatient facility. He also took him off of the Lexapro, saying that all of his problems stem from the alcoholism. He did not consider him clinically depressed, but that the depression was a result of the many consequences of his alcohol addiction. He said he would benefit from a ninety-day inpatient rehab program. I told him that we simply didn't have the funds for that, even though I wholeheartedly agreed with him. In that event, he said Matt should be participating in an intensive outpatient program and A.A. He told me to come and pick up my son.

I battled the urge to clarify to the doctor that Matt had first exhibited depression a year *before* he had any issues with alcohol, but my instincts told me to just shut up and go get my kid. I just wanted him out of that awful place. I jumped in the car and drove to Wheat Ridge to pick up my son. What a relief!

Matt was in pain and just wanted to lie down, so we drove directly to the hotel room while he shared with me about his experience at the mental hospital. During the night, he had spiked a fever and had actually been transported over to the regular hospital for quick medical intervention, as there was still risk for infection. He had numerous wounds still healing and a serious problem with the hematoma on his upper thigh. After some IV antibiotics, they sent him back to the mental health ward. He shared a couple of humorous stories about some of the patients, which helped lighten the mood a bit.

Because I had spent the past seven days at the Marriott, I was well aware of a liquor store situated right across the street. As we approached the hotel, I felt myself tense up knowing that Matt would quickly spot it. He didn't say anything about it, and neither did I. I just prayed it wouldn't become an issue while we had to stay there at the hotel.

The plan was that Matt would enter a sober living home in the Denver area as soon as he was weaned off the pain medication, OxyContin, which was managing the intense pain caused by the leg injury and hematoma. He had already had the hematoma drained twice, but it continued to fill with fluid and with that came lots of pain. The sober living home would not allow him to move in until he was no longer dependent on the pain medication. This was going to be an issue, because Matt was anxious to move on with his life and start over at sober living. Instead he was stuck in a hotel room with his mom for the time being. Not good.

Soon after we got to the hotel, I received a call from Fr. Matthew. I hastily left Matt in the hotel room, telling him I was just stepping out to chat with Francesca. I walked down the corridor out of earshot so I could talk freely with the priest and also be able to see if Matt tried to escape in my absence. The priest asked for some clarification on a couple of things in my email and then offered to come to my house when I get back into town. I was scheduled to return on Saturday, October 27, so we made an appointment for 3:00 p.m. on Sunday. Just knowing a priest would be coming to bless my home and rid it of bad spirits was huge. I instantly felt relieved.

The next day it snowed! It was so beautiful, like a crystal white blanket that gently covered every surface. When he woke up I told Matt it had snowed, so we both went outside to walk around in it. I took a photo of him standing by the car in the snow—he looked really good. Still, though, his mood was dour and he was extremely restless. His injury was keeping him from entering sober living so he was frustrated and was so over being babysat by his mother. I knew no other answer to the problem than to stay with him. I was no longer ignorant about the grip this disease, and the demons, had on him. That liquor store was beckoning him and if he should begin drinking, another suicide attempt could very well result.

"I'm gonna take a short walk, Mom," Matt stated.

"Okay, sure, let's get out of here and get some fresh air," I replied.

"I meant alone, I want to get some space," he growled at me.

I implored, "Matt, you know I can't risk having you drink. We both see the liquor store on the corner. It is too tempting. Let's just walk together."

"Goddammit, Mom you are as sick as me. It's disgusting."

"What do you mean I'm as sick as you? What do you mean by that?" I felt heartsick to hear him speak to me with such contempt. I did not deserve this.

"Codependent. You are fucking codependent. You need help."

Stunned by the weight of his anger towards me, I stepped back from him and turned so he wouldn't see the pain in my face. I was really hurt that he was attacking me, when all I was attempting to do was prevent another tragedy. I wasn't ready to trust him yet after what had happened just two short weeks ago. Even though his words stung, I tried to remind myself that this was the disease talking.

I texted John and told him he needed to get back here as soon as possible, that he would do a better job managing this situation than me. I was too exhausted and emotionally raw. I felt helpless. Matt needed to get into sober living and to begin looking for work, but his injury was holding him back, keeping him stuck here in the hotel room instead, with John or I having to administer the pain medication to him. He simply was not strong enough to be on his own yet. It was an awful situation.

So, I suggested that we attend an A.A. meeting together. I had looked up the directory for the area the day before, knowing how much he needed to stay engaged in a recovery community. Surprisingly, he agreed to go. It turned out that the A.A. meeting was exactly what we *both* needed.

It was my second A.A. meeting, the first one happening by mistake last September in California. I had decided to try a different Al-anon group and walked in just as a meeting was getting underway. I realized within thirty seconds that this was not an Al-anon meeting, but was an A.A. meeting—I had misread the schedule. But because of where I was sitting, back in a corner, it would have been disruptive for me to get up and try to wind my way out of the room, so I stuck it out. Well, that turned out to be a blessing, giving me a real-world glimpse into the life of alcoholics in recovery. I was really moved by the members' transparency, humility, and eloquence in sharing their personal stories, and learned so much about their daily, if not hourly, struggle.

This A.A. meeting in Colorado was also very moving and informative. Matt didn't actively participate, but he had a good attitude and an open heart as we sat there and listened to the speakers who were very inspiring. This seemed to ease the tension between us, which was a welcome change from earlier in the day.

The next day, Friday the 26th, was my mom's eightieth birthday. I called to wish her a happy birthday and told her I would see her as soon as I returned to California. I still had the pretty necklace I had bought her that last day in Vail when I went shopping before driving home. I felt sad that our plans for her big party had been diverted because of all of the current drama here in Colorado. But she adores her grandson and was more than willing to postpone the festivities so that I could return to help him in his recovery.

I was, frankly, completely fried by this point. I had cabin fever along with Matt. There are only so many TV shows you can watch. But there was much to handle in this last day. I had to file the disability claim, the unemployment claim, and insurance claims. We would have to deal with his D.M.V. registration, pick up his medication, and Matt needed to deposit his final paycheck and buy some groceries. There were paperwork issues with St. Anthony, and I struggled to locate the right person at the hospital to straighten things out. Everything was connected, the medical records, the disability claim, insurance claims . . . and it all needed to be taken care of. Matt couldn't really help with any of these issues, as it was a complicated mess that had been an ongoing fiasco while he was hospitalized. For him to step into the quagmire made no sense. It fell upon me to take care of these loose ends before I left in the morning to return to California.

We had a pizza delivered and watched the World Series together, which was a good way to finish out our time together in Colorado. Even though we were getting along a little better, I could tell he was looking forward to his dad coming—probably assuming he would have an easier time convincing his dad to let him go off by himself. But he would soon learn that his parents had already discussed that possibility and John was well prepared to handle Matt. John would be staying for a week, which he figured was long enough to get Matt off the pain meds and into sober living.

By the time John showed up the next morning, I was all packed and ready to take off. This past eleven days had pushed me way past my ability to manage my frustration and stress. This was not the story I had wanted to tell when I drove away from Vail three weeks prior. I looked back at that day, how I had felt a sense of accomplishment but mostly an abundance of hope for my son. This time as I prepared to leave him I was in knots, stressed out and emotionally drained. I honestly didn't know what the future would hold for my son. So much damage had been done to his life that I truly feared for him, unsure if he would be able to rebound from all of the many setbacks.

Still, I had to hang on to hope. I continued to pray for God's direction and to give all of us the strength we so badly needed.

I gave Matt a hug and passed the baton to John. I couldn't get out of that hotel room fast enough. I needed to get home and rejoin my life, plus I needed to earn a living!

Sipping a plastic cup of cheap red wine on the flight home I allowed myself to rewind the tape since October 11th and process the events of the last couple weeks. Sitting there in my seat, with a tear rolling down my cheek, I wondered how many other people on the plane have loved ones who are battling demons. I closed my eyes and prayed for my beautiful son, so broken in spirit. Please, God, please help him turn his life around. Please pull him out of the darkness and hold him close to You. He is good. Sadly, he just didn't seem to know that at the moment.

CHAPTER 21

Fr. Matthew

AS PLANNED, FR. MATTHEW ARRIVED at my house at 3:00 p.m. on Sunday, October 28th, accompanied by a woman, Michelle, who he brought along to assist him. He said that he brings her to these types of meetings because she has a special sensitivity to the paranormal that he does not have. Okay, I thought, let's do this thing.

I had no idea what to expect when I invited him into the house that day. All I knew for sure was that at this stage I needed to access the spiritual gifts that a Catholic priest would have at his disposal. This problem was far beyond my ability to manage.

Father Matthew, Michelle, and I sat down at my kitchen table where I was asked to recount the various events that had occurred in my house, as well as those I had shared in my email about my neighbors. By summarizing each strange event for them, Fr. Matthew and Michelle would both be up to speed on what had been going on at the house, and on the street, over the past two decades. I shared with them the history of the house next door where the original owner was involved in some type of witchcraft or occult-related practices. After I had shared the unnerving events with them, Fr. Matthew asked me to walk them around the house and show them where these things had occurred. So, we started in the dining room where my oldest, Sarah, at age fourteen, had heard the buzzing words in her ear. The tour took awhile, as there were so many places in the house where scary things had happened.

While we were upstairs, Father Matthew was vehement about my immediate need to discard some pagan décor items I had in the house. At the top of our stairs, in a décor niche, we had a five-foot bronze Kokopelli sculpture, a popular pagan deity used in southwest art and décor. He firmly pointed out that it was no wonder that this was the location where we would smell the stench that resembled a decaying rat. He explained that giving this pagan god a place of prominence in the home had provided a nice little home for a demon. And here we had thought it was just a cool décor accent!

He then pointed at the shelf above my entry door where, among other décor touches, I had placed a ceramic African figure purchased at Pier One Imports. He explained that many of these types of items are shipped here from countries where voodoo or black magic are practiced, possibly cursing the items before they are shipped to America. Again, he told me in no uncertain terms to get rid of it. Immediately, my mind went to the night that Francesca had sensed the evil presence right in that spot in the entry.

While upstairs, I pointed out the place in the hallway where I had experienced a dark column of evil and dropped the laundry on the floor. I pointed out Emma's door that Sarah had heard repeatedly closing one night; my son's former bedroom where my grandson had been terrorized by "the big scary man;" the bathroom mirror where Sarah had seen her eyes morph into cat-like eyes; my room where a demon sat on me during the night and tried to suffocate me, and the area of my bedroom floor that Emma had heard a shuffling sound from directly below on multiple occasions. I showed them the side yard, below both Emma's room and Matthew's old room, where the dog had been relentlessly barking a few weeks ago at something Emma could not see.

Once we completed the walk around the house, Fr. Matthew had us gather at the entry and asked me to open the double-doors. Together, we stood there in the open doorway while he recited old pre-Vatican II binding prayers and exorcism prayers, which are used to bind evil spirits and cast them to hell. We invoked Matt's name in one of the prayers we recited together, inserting it as the beneficiary of graces for that particular prayer. The prayers were very, very intense and thorough, including casting demons out of every crack and crevice of my house, the electrical system, the plumbing, heating system, the attic, the sewage system, the garage, and the yards—anywhere that evil spirits can hide. I was riveted by the power of the words Fr. Matthew read as we stood there, and the ritual itself.

He then explained that he and Michelle would, together, walk the premises while he'd splash the holy water everywhere—which he clarified to me was not just regular holy water, but water blessed for use in exorcisms—including all windows, doorways, corners, closets, and the garage. While he was doing this, Michelle would scatter blessed salt around the house in a similar fashion. Once in the backyard, Fr. Matthew took a bag of blessed Miraculous Medals and set about planting them along my fenced property lines.

Once this step had been completed, we reassembled in the kitchen where they each took turns praying over me, for the spirit of anxiety and fear to leave me, for spiritual protection, and for peace of mind. When the priest was standing over me praying I could literally feel my fears melt away.

After he had returned to his seat at the table, he shared his thoughts regarding the situation in the house.

He asked, "Do you have a special connection with your son?"

I answered, "Actually, I do. Matt was born almost six weeks early and from the first time I held him in the neonatal I.C.U. I had a powerful feeling of fear that something would happen to him. That fear has never left me. Also, my son and I are very compatible. We are wired much the same way, both of us with sensitive and generous natures. We get each other. So yes, there is a special connection. Why do you ask?"

Fr. Matthew replied with a question, "Who in the family still practices the faith?"

Sadly, I had to admit, "Only me."

Fr. Matthew said, "Okay, well I have a theory. I believe that you may be the actual target of the demonic attack; that ultimately it is you that the devil wants to take out. Your ex-husband was easy to pick off. I believe that your son is being tormented or oppressed, because how better to destroy you than by destroying your son."

Wow. I just sat there dumbfounded. It all made perfect sense from a spiritual point of view. I turned to Michelle and asked her to share her observations, if any.

"I picked up a palpable sense of evil in your home," Michelle answered. "However, the effect of the evil was being offset by your obvious love of Christ. In every room there is a symbol of your love for Him or the Blessed Mother."

At this I felt somewhat vindicated, as this woman has a gift for discerning spirits and she felt the evil. Although I always knew that the things we all had experienced here and on the street were one hundred percent authentic, it was good to have a sense of validation.

As they got up to leave, Fr. Matthew ended our meeting with instructions. He warned me that evil spirits often return, and that when they do they will come back sevenfold.

He told me that I should sense a difference in the atmosphere within the house now, but that if I ever feel that the evil spirit or spirits are back I am to pray the Our Father, loudly, the Saint Michael prayer, loudly, and then call him. At that, the priest and his assistant left.

MY 13th STATION

"When an unclean spirit goes out of a person it roams
through arid regions searching for rest but finds none.
Then it says, 'I will return to my home from which I came.'
But upon returning, it finds it empty, swept clean, and
put in order. Then is goes and brings back with itself
seven other spirits more evil than itself, and they
move in and dwell there; and the last condition
of that person is worse than the first."

MATTHEW 12:43-45

CHAPTER 22

Hope

IT WAS TRULY REMARKABLE how different my house felt after the priest had conducted the spiritual cleansing. Like the frog sitting in the pot as the water slowly boils, I hadn't realized just how heavy the atmosphere in the house had become. This was probably because the strange issues we had experienced in the house, the suicides on the street, and the odd activities of our former neighbor had been mounting and compounding over a twenty-year span of time. Living in it day in and day out, with uneventful expanses of time separating the creepy events, the oppressive atmosphere had come to feel normal.

Now, though, the house that I shared with my daughter seemed different. The air felt lighter and more buoyant, hard to describe but very noticeable to me. Was it just my imagination? Absolutely not. The airy feeling in my home after the dark spirits were eradicated was no more a figment of my imagination than any of those paranormal events my family and I had witnessed.

John kept me posted on the happenings in Lakewood, Colorado. Matt had to have his hematoma drained again, another setback that threatened to derail the plan to get him into sober living. But they passed the time watching baseball and taking care of nailing down the housing situation. If all went well, Matt would start weaning himself off the pain medication and rely only on Tylenol by the end of the week. The goal was to move him in on Saturday, November 3rd.

They had located a high quality, well managed sober living home in Aurora, just outside Denver. The house manager told John and Matt that there would be regular, possibly even daily, drug and alcohol testing, and that this was a zero-tolerance house that operated on clearly articulated and strictly enforced rules. The manager lived on the premises, and required that the residents participate in the local A.A. group meetings and weekly house meetings. The cost was $600 per month for a shared bedroom, and there were six men residing in the house.

As planned, Matt was able to move into the house on schedule, but was already struggling with the pain factor. Tylenol wasn't cutting it, unfortunately. But Matt was so anxious to get out of the hotel and find a job that he decided to gut it out without the Oxy. Once John notified me that our son was safely in place in a sober living home, I felt elated, like we had just scored a small victory.

Matt, however, had difficulties and limitations due to his leg injury. First, he was suffering as the hematoma began to swell yet again. He found that he could barely walk, which hindered his goal of getting out and looking for work. He was frustrated about having to sit around and wait until he was able to walk, but at least he was able to apply for some jobs online.

The other issue was his depressed mood. He missed Grace. He had not seen her since that fateful day, nearly one month ago. Going from rehab, where he only saw her for about three hours a week, and then adding another month while in the Denver area, were painful consequences of his disease. He was now aware he'd lost his parental rights, but Amanda was open to supervised visits after he hit ninety days of sobriety, so the two of them were working out a plan for that. Amanda refused to allow him to have Grace alone, which was completely understandable. After all, he had revealed serious emotional instability that had culminated in a horrible trauma that would reverberate for years to come. Between his alcoholism and mental health issues, she had every right to exercise caution moving forward.

Over the next couple of weeks he attempted to go out and apply for jobs at local businesses, but struggled to walk even from the car to the front door of the business. He was relaying this to me and it made me feel really sad. He was doing everything right now; living in a sober environment, attending A.A. meetings several times a week, and trying to get his life back on track by attempting to find work. But his body was not cooperating and his mood was low. I was getting nervous.

Then one day, immediately following an A.A. meeting, he was taken by ambulance to local hospital emergency room because the hematoma had gotten so huge and painful. There was fear at first that it was infected. I was freaked out because initially there had been discussion about possibly having to amputate the leg. Thankfully, it was drained (600 ml. of fluid) and no infection was diagnosed. Thank you, God!

On Thanksgiving, Matthew was extremely depressed. He called both John and me and cried on the phone with each of us, saying how lonely he was out there with no friends or family. It was clear to both his dad and me that there was a serious risk of relapse on the horizon because he was so depressed.

Matt had flatly refused to return to California during the weeks following his suicide attempt. He feared he would never see his child if he moved back to California and could not bear that idea. He believed that if he stayed in Colorado, got a job, and proved himself over time that Amanda would begin to set up the supervised visits. But now, with his current state of mind and his inability to find work, John and I felt strongly that Matt needed to be recovering in

California where he would have a strong support system. It was too risky for him to be alone without loved ones around.

I broached the subject with my son and only got a lukewarm reception. So I called his dad and asked him to take a stab at it. Success! John, again, had the magic touch. He was able to convince Matt to get a ride up to Vail, retrieve the Jeep from Denise's house, and then go to the storage unit and stuff as much of his belongings into the Jeep that would fit. Matt was on the road by November 24th, an amazing answer to prayer. Just knowing that he will be near all of us who love him so much should make a huge difference in his attitude. Even his opportunities to see his little girl might be better here, as Gracie makes several trips back to the East Bay to visit her grandparents. Now her daddy will be here to enjoy those visits as well.

When he arrived in town on November 26th, I was pleasantly surprised by how great he looked. He had shaved off that pathetic goatee, he was slim, and his eyes were once again large and beautiful. John and I managed to locate a sober living home about ten minutes away from each of our houses. We both worked full-time and realized Matt needed to be in a safe, supportive, drug and alcohol-free environment with regular testing as a deterrent not to slip up. Even if for just a few months, this would give us peace of mind.

So, Matt moved in to the house the following day, after attending a local A.A. meeting. He was very anxious to find a job so he could resume taking care of his child financially. That he hadn't been able to for over a month had been bothering him, and Amanda was counting on his contributions for child support. He just needed to get a job as soon as possible to make it happen. Working and being productive is very important in recovery, as it helps restore confidence and self-esteem.

One day, I came home from work to find that Matt had put up the Christmas lights on the house. I hadn't even asked him, but he knew I was beat and wanted to lend me a hand, so I was very grateful for his thoughtfulness. The next week he helped me pick out the Christmas tree, then lugged it into the house to set it up in the usual corner. He also retrieved about a dozen tubs of Christmas decorations out of the attic for me, revisiting an annual chore he used to do when he lived at home. He was such a big help to me that week. I was excited about this Christmas season, and even made plans for a family party that would include Gracie during her upcoming visit.

On December 13th, Matt and I drove to the Water's residence where little Gracie was staying. Liz Waters had been so supportive and kind during the past weeks, not to mention throughout the tumult of Amanda and Matt's marriage. She is a kind hearted, loving woman and I am so grateful for her ongoing graciousness towards my family and me.

Driving to the Waters' house, I felt elated, so excited for Gracie to finally be reunited with her daddy after a two-month separation. Grace's babysitter, Denise, had been sending regular emails, keeping me updated on how she was doing. Apparently, Gracie talked about her daddy a lot and really missed him. The reunion was bound to be emotional.

Matt brought along a little stuffed elephant to give Grace when he got to the Waters' house. When we arrived at their home I stood back behind Matt so he would be the first person she'd see when the door opened. In an instant, her arms where wrapped tightly around his neck as she clutched the little elephant. Matt was moved to tears being able to hold his dear child again. It had seemed to each of them like an eternity since they'd last been together. I glanced at Liz and she, too, had tears in her eyes right along with Matt and me. It was a tender, joyful moment in time.

For the next couple of days, Matt and Gracie spent tons of time together, going to the park, playing Legos, reading books, and just hanging out. We had the family party the next night, so Grace got to see her cousin, Jake, her aunts and uncle, and her grandparents all in one place. We had a lovely dinner and exchanged gifts with Christmas music playing and a fire roaring in the fireplace. It was a wonderful evening. In all, Gracie spent three days hanging out with her daddy, and what a difference that made in his spirits.

After we returned Grace to her other grandparents, Matt went back to his sober living home. He was still looking for work, and thankfully his leg wound was finally healing. He was excited about getting back to the gym to start working out again. A couple of the guys at the sober house would eventually join him at the gym, and they also attended the almost-daily A.A. meetings together.

He got along with the guys in the house, and had a heart for one of the residents in particular, a fellow in his later fifties who was disabled and had become addicted to alcohol and painkillers. He was cleared to remain on some type of painkiller, but the house manager would be the one to administer it. Don loved to rail about politics and Matt just thought he was hilarious. I stopped by the house a couple of times just to say hello, and the guys seemed to get along well. The house manager, Jeff, was a former Marine and managed a tight ship, so I didn't worry about Matt's safety. I was just so grateful that Matt had a supportive place to stay while he became stronger both mentally and physically.

A family wedding in early January was the first event where I had to consider Matt's alcoholism. It's so strange how being exposed to alcohol addiction completely changes your perspective about our cultural celebrations. Now I knew that for someone in early recovery for alcoholism, just being around alcohol could pose a potential trigger for relapse. For this reason, I had purged my home of any alcohol, including, not only booze but Nyquil, vanilla extract, mouthwash, and even hand sanitizer.

I picked Matt up at the house and off we went to join the festivities in Tiburon, a lovely seaside enclave that provided a perfect venue for a wedding. On the long drive, Matt and I discussed openly how to manage the alcohol situation. We devised a strategy; that he would sip sparkling water and focus on socializing with the family but if at any time during the reception he felt being around booze was threatening his sobriety, he would discreetly motion to me and off we would go.

I shared this plan with John so he would know what happened to us if we suddenly vanished. We got through the wedding and about an hour of the reception when I got the signal, it was too much for him and we needed to leave. I was just grateful that we stayed long enough to be included in the large family group photograph taken on that special day.

The above example is a healthy mother-son dynamic that demonstrates mutual love, trust, and my desire to support his sobriety in every way possible. Unfortunately, over the ensuing months, I allowed my fear of a reenactment of the horrors of October in Colorado to affect my ability to practice restraint, and I became increasingly co-dependent in my behaviors. If I wasn't helping him rewrite his resume I was online searching for job postings for him, coaching him before interviews, or brainstorming career goals for him—not with him, for him. My need to control the outcome was intense, but as a mother who had seen firsthand the life torching consequences of his alcoholism, I was terrified of any future missteps at this juncture. This fear is what drove my need to navigate many of his decisions. He was probably right. Maybe I *was* as sick as him.

Matt was on a health kick. He had lost all of the excess weight by mid-January and was eating chicken and rice and salads every single night for dinner. He was also working out at the local gym several days a week and had also discovered a network of hiking trails that he could access from his sober living home. Seeing him taking care of himself and dedicated to the daily A.A. meetings filled me full of hope . . . until the day I got the call from his house manager, Jeff.

Apparently Matt was missing, having not come home for two days. He had given Jeff some bogus story that his sister, who he said was moving, needed his help and that he'd be back the next day. Jeff had my phone number as a contact, so was checking on Matt's whereabouts. As all sober living homes, they have a zero tolerance policy and would have to kick him out if he had relapsed.

My heart sank. No matter how many Al-anon meetings I have attended, nothing can really prepare you for the roller coaster ride of loving an addict. In an instant, the feelings of hope I had been enjoying for weeks were now dashed. I knew Matt had basically run away, as the story about his sister moving was a bald-faced lie. This, of course, meant he was off somewhere drinking. If he was drinking then he was likely feeling suicidal. As I processed what was happening I felt sheer panic rise up in me.

I tried calling and texting him multiple times over the next two hours, and then decided to call the police. After about fifteen minutes, a male officer arrived at my door and I let him in. We sat in the dining room as he interviewed me, but he had such an antagonistic attitude towards my son and me that, after one final insult, I told him to leave my home. I kicked out the cop! I was not going to have some jerk sit there and make me feel even worse about my life.

After he left, I got a call from the dispatcher that another officer would be arriving momentarily. The lady on the phone asked what my complaint was with the first officer, so I summarized it for her. The guy must be totally burned out at his job and has no compassion left in him, to the point where he is literally rude and disrespectful to citizens in need of help.

Soon the doorbell rang again and this time there was a female officer on my doorstep. Her name was Mary, so I instantly liked her. She asked to come in and we sat at the kitchen nook table where she asked me questions about my boy. Mary was kind and gentle, the polar opposite of the rude cop. She patiently listened while, I told her, sobbing, about his recent suicide attempt and how afraid I was. My son had been missing for two days and was not responding to my calls, so obviously I feared the worst.

Mary had a technique that she used in these situations. She asked for his number and then called and left him a message. She told Matt who she was and that she is sitting next to his mom who is about to file a missing person's report. She said that if we do not hear back from within ten minutes she would be forced to take that next step, and then described to him what all it would involve—all points bulletin, helicopter search, check hospitals, jails, interview people and more. She politely asked Matt to please call us back when he gets this message.

Five minutes later, the phone rang. It was Matthew! He was completely obliterated, but he was alive. I asked if he would tell me where he was so I could come get him. At first he refused, saying he was drinking himself to death and didn't want anyone to stop him. I pleaded with him to give me his whereabouts. I had been told to keep him on the phone for a certain period of time so he could be tracked down through his iPhone. It didn't work; he hung up on me.

I just collapsed there at the table, sobbing and feeling helpless. Mary was so kind. She said she would begin the process of filing the missing persons report, but just then the phone rang and it was Matt again. He told me where he was, some dirt-bag motel on the south end of town. I told him I would be there in ten minutes. I thanked

Mary profusely for all her help and off I went to pick up my very drunk son. On the way, I contacted Jeff at the house and told him I had located Matt, and he said he would have to give some thought about how to proceed.

I got to the motel and spotted Matt outside leaning against the door of his room. He could barely walk from there to my car. I knew it would be pointless to ask him any questions or to chastise him for screwing up his sober living arrangement by relapsing. He was so intoxicated there was no way he would be coherent or rational. I felt so disappointed and sad driving us to my house. I told him he could sleep it off in the guest room and then go speak with his house manager in the morning.

The following morning, Matt humbly apologized to Jeff and asked if there was any way he could still stay at the house. Apparently, Matt was so well liked by the manager and the other housemates that Jeff was willing to give him a second chance. What a blessing this was!

Matt doubled down on his A.A. efforts, devoting more time at meetings and on working the steps. He realized what a gift he had been given and worked diligently to earn back Jeff's trust. For the next thirty days he was on fire. He also intensified his efforts to find more consistent work than the driver gig he'd been working the past few weeks.

On his twenty-fifth birthday he hiked all the way from the sober house to my house, which took him over two hours. I had already attended an 8:00 a.m. Al-anon meeting, so was in a good frame of mind and happy to spend time with him on his birthday. We had such a great visit, and I made him his favorite meal for dinner, tuna casserole. I drove him home after dinner and felt so much better. He seemed really strong now.

Matt told me the next week he had scheduled an appointment with our family physician, Dr. Davidson. He said he is going to ask the doctor to put him on Antabuse. I had no idea what that was so he explained that it is a medication that acts as a deterrent to drinking and can help prevent a relapse. While on the medication, if you drink you become violently ill. I liked that he was being proactive in trying whatever it takes to stay sober.

After that appointment he was really down. He said that Dr. Davidson refused to give him a prescription for Antabuse, stating that it is too dangerous. Instead he put him on Xanax to help manage his anxiety and gave him a referral to a psychiatrist. Although I was irked that the doctor would not get him the Antabuse, I hoped that meeting with the psychiatrist would allow Matt to examine his emotional pain, to process it and heal.

It was mid-February, time for a much-needed break. After all the stress of the past few months I looked forward to a nice relaxing weekend in Monterey for a music and arts festival. I had arranged for my daughter to take care of the dogs, but waited to tell Matt about my plans until the last minute. I felt confident that he would be fine, based on the positive frame of mind he was in, but wanted to give him minimal time to be tempted. I left feeling very excited about the carefree weekend ahead.

How I needed the diversion! Being with friends in such a fun atmosphere was the perfect release for pent up stress and worry. For two whole days I just had fun—and it felt wonderful. I didn't have the constant cloud of fear and uncertainty looming over me while there in Monterey. I pushed all thoughts of Matthew and his problems into a box in my mind and locked it up tight. The weekend was all about rediscovering me through my passion for music and art.

I arrived home on Sunday evening, pretty exhausted from the two-hour drive and a weekend of frolicking. I looked forward to playing with the dogs for a bit and then going straight to bed. As I pulled into the driveway I spotted Matt's Jeep on the curb and immediately froze. Why would he be here at this time, knowing he should be at the sober house? My mind went first to a rational explanation; he loves the dogs and possibly wanted to keep them company for a couple of hours until I got home. That is actually something he would do.

Sadly, hope vanished instantly when I entered the house to find him passed out drunk on the couch. I couldn't even handle it. I knew I would lose it, come completely undone. So, I said hello to the dogs and headed to my room, just leaving Matt there passed out in the family room. I would deal with my son tomorrow. I crawled into bed in tears, the joy of the weekend evaporating in an instant. I was devastated that he had fallen down again, barely thirty days since his last relapse.

I felt trapped. How can I ever leave town or have a life if I always have to worry about my son relapsing? And each time he relapses he moves farther away from his ultimate goal of reclaiming his parental rights. No matter how deeply his loves his daughter, it seems he cannot muster the strength to wrest himself free from the vise grip of the devil. I felt so full of despair that February night as I drifted off to sleep. So utterly beaten.

The next day I wrote his dad an email. It is clear in my words that my outrage had not dissipated after that fitful night's sleep:

February 11, 2013
Bad news. I was away this weekend and I had Sarah taking care of the dogs. When I came home last night Matt was here passed out drunk at the house. This morning he told me he had started planning his drinking binge the minute I told him I was leaving town. It made me sick.

The said he drank a half-gallon of vodka in those two days. I sat there stunned as he told me this, not knowing what else to do and feeling my stress level shoot up. He was crying and saying how would get kicked out of the house, since they had already given him a second chance. He said he hates to wake up every day—wants to be dead, that he's felt that way since he was nineteen. He said something happened that year (at SLO). He realized back then that something was wrong with him. He said his anxiety and insomnia were so bad that he drank just to function.

That shrink that he saw last week spent all of five minutes with him. He told me the guy didn't engage him at all. He told Matt not to continue with the Xanax that Dr. Davidson had prescribed ten days ago because it's addicting. Then just sent him on his way. No talk therapy, nothing. Bet he billed for the full hour, though.

I am this close to an absolute breakdown myself. I am tied in knots and hyperventilating and feel like something is choking me. He is mentally ill, this I believe no matter what that other shrink in Colorado told me. Until his mental problems are dealt it is ridiculous to think he can stay sober. He needs the alcohol to just survive the torment in his head.

I had suggested he not tell Jeff he relapsed, because if Jeff knows he relapsed again he would surely kick him out this time. But Matt said he didn't want to go back to the house and be full of lies. So, thankfully, later today after confessing, Jeff took him back. But he is on borrowed time.

He can't make it without serious help. I don't know what to do. No one seems to really want to help him! I do know that I am about to come undone. I go to Al-anon but that isn't enough. I got a massage hoping that would help,

and the gal said my neck was basically frozen. I do not know what to do anymore. I am ashamed. I feel hopeless. He seems bent on self-destruction. Last night I went to sleep preparing myself for his death.
T.

Matt dreaded going back to A.A. and having to admit, yet again, that he is a newcomer. That he had stepped out . . . again. He was deeply ashamed and felt very weak to the addiction's power over him. This was his third newcomer chip. I joined him at his next A.A. meeting, just to be an extra layer of support. He seemed to enjoy when I attended the meetings with him.

One day, I decided to make him a wall calendar through Walmart's photo services. Each month in the calendar featured a large photo of him with Grace, and I added an A.A. saying at the bottom. I felt that the visual of him with his daughter would provide additional inspiration for staying strong in sobriety. He loved the calendar and put it right up on his bedroom wall at the sober house.

Over the next months he was doing really well. We started going on hikes together, just the two of us. These hikes will remain some of my fondest memories, walking the trails in the beautiful hills with my son in the spring of 2013. We talked about everything; no topic was off limits. That had always been the centerpiece of our relationship, open and honest communication.

On one of the hikes I told him I was having trouble understanding why he couldn't muscle back the urge to drink when it would hit. He explained it like this, "It's like walking all day in the desert, and you have no water left. It is scorching hot and you are dying of thirst. Finally, you spot a little pond and you run over to it and start lapping up the water, feeling like you can't get enough. You just keep drinking and drinking the water, trying to fill yourself up from the terrible thirst." Wow, this gave me a visual of what alcohol cravings must feel like, and how alcohol is used to "fill yourself up" where a deep void exists.

On another hike, he admitted to me how much he missed baseball. He was now twenty-five, but he was in fantastic shape. I encouraged him to join a club team just for recreation, while secretly I still harbored that image in my mind of my son playing professional baseball. He just looked like a ball player, his build and his overall appearance screamed baseball player. When he was a senior in high school, fully grown, he would go out onto the field and, seriously, looked and moved just like a professional.

As we walked, I told him about a pro baseball player I had read about who battled alcoholism and made a comeback, and told him he should seriously consider joining a rec team. He pretty much balked at my rosy picture of how he would be the guy who overcame all these obstacles to return to the game. He said he was just too old at this point. This made me very sad. But for a few minutes, just a few, I saw the spark return to his eyes. That spark of Matthew's spirit was missing in his recovery. He looked like his old self, he was now fit and healthy and active again, but the essence of his spirit was, sadly, absent. But while walking along in the hills that day, chatting about baseball, I got a glimpse of the old Matthew.

Thankfully, his beautiful Grace had visited twice in the past month, so we just milked those opportunities for them to be together. He was still unable to have her unless another family member was with them, but he did understand. That I got to hang out with the two of them was a special blessing that I will always treasure.

When he and Gracie were together it was so very sweet and beautiful. She adores him. He is a wonderful daddy, very gentle and kind, but teaches her and guides her, also. He was very engaged when he is with his daughter, and had abundant patience. It always melted my heart to watch them interact. She was seriously all he lived for, all that really mattered in his life.

He was continually working on himself that spring. He got a full-time job in March and was able to finally start sending Amanda some money, a little here and a little there. It was a start, and it made him feel better. He knew it was the least he could do, and said he hoped to increase the support soon.

In April, Matt had become discouraged with the sober living house. He had seen heroin paraphernalia in the outdoor trash can one day, and later that week his roommate came home completely intoxicated before passing out in bed. He began to feel that sober living was a waste of money and asked his dad if he could live with him. He told John he would be able to pay Amanda more support if he wasn't paying for the sober living. It sounded like a reasonable request, so John agreed to let him live at his house.

At the end of April, I was able to gather all three of my kids together, a very rare opportunity since Emma now lived in San Francisco, and spend a wonderful weekend together in South Lake Tahoe. It was so special for us, this family trip. We had spent many family vacations in Tahoe over the years before the divorce, so being back there together again, although minus their dad, was a really wonderful treat.

Matt had just picked up his 90-day chip when the wheels fell off again. Matt relapsed at John's house, badly. Apparently, he had fallen off and had been drinking for about three days. I don't think John really knew what to do. He didn't tell me at first that Matt had relapsed, but later described the horror in witnessing his son pass out on the front step, falling hard to the ground. But on the third day, things became dire. John described how Matt completely lost it, and was out in the middle of his street, head thrown back, and a deep guttural yell, almost a growl, came out of him. John described it as if he was trying to expel something from inside him.

Matt told his dad he wanted to go run across the freeway, and actually fled the neighborhood on foot. John called Sarah and together they located him at a nearby park and then called for police assistance. The officers placed him on a mandatory three-day psychiatric hold, called a Code 5150 in California. John and Sarah were kind to handle this without my knowledge because I was dealing with a very difficult personal matter on that very same day, May 13th. Mike, my amazing boyfriend of two years, had been diagnosed with a rare form of leukemia.

Mike was the answer to many prayers during the years following my divorce. I had tried the online dating scene on and off for a couple of years and had become entirely disillusioned about the whole dating thing. It was awful. Disappointing first dates, meeting weirdoes who were nothing like their profiles, and being ghosted a couple of times left me cold. I had given up ever meeting a new guy that I could actually develop a real relationship with.

And then walks Mike into my life. I met him through a work function and found him so charming. He was funny, handsome, smart, and kind. A rare find. Our first date was on May 13th, 2011. Wow, those Fatima dates! Over the ensuing two years we became so very close, developing a loving bond that was based on mutual love and respect.

Mike was very fit and athletic, so when he struggled to finish a mountain bike race the last week in April he initially chalked it up to the flu. But as the week wore on, he became so ill that he was unable to go to work. He developed a strange rash on his face and a fever, which prompted him to visit an after-hours urgent care facility. They sent him directly to the emergency room at the local hospital.

After ten days of extensive testing we received the awful news on May 13th that he had the CMML form of leukemia. This was a horrible blow to him, his family, and to me. I knew nothing about leukemia, other than it is a form of blood cancer. Well, anything associated with cancer is enough to scare me, especially after losing my little sister to it and other family members and friends. I was devastated by this diagnosis.

So John and Sarah were kind to delay the news of Matt's latest setback, knowing I had enough to deal with. When I talked to Matt a few days later, I told him I just couldn't understand why he kept relapsing. Why would he continue to undermine his chances of being with Grace? I am a logical person so I asked him why he didn't reach out to someone for help when he knew a relapse was coming on.

He calmly looked at me and said, "Because the cravings overpower you . . . and you *don't want* anyone to stop you." I just sat there with a stupefied look on my face.

John and I realized that Matt's only hope was to re-enter a rehab program. We knew Matt needed extended treatment, several months, so we decided to check out the Salvation Army adult rehabilitation program. It was a six-month program that costs nothing, as the client basically works full-time in exchange for room, board, and therapy. Convincing Matthew was going to be difficult, though. Even though he needed it, and obviously knew he needed it, six months is a long time.

One day that June, before Matt went back to rehab, John came over to pick up something from the house, although I cannot remember now what it was. I do, however, vividly remember the scene as he was leaving. I walked out the front door with my ex-husband, and we walked the path to the driveway. He mentioned he'd been asking Matt to throw the baseball with him, like the old days. At that, John broke down. He said part of what motivates him to continue to ask

MY 13th STATION

Matt to play catch is the fear that he may never get to do that again, that we may lose him. It killed me to see him acknowledge his own fears and sorrow, but it also endeared me to him. We had become partners to save our son.

CHAPTER 23

Rehab Revisited

MATT RESISTED AT FIRST, but John and I convinced him of his need for long-term treatment and eventually prevailed. After the benzodiazepines were out of his system, which the hospital had treated him with during the detox, he could be admitted to the Salvation Army program. The representative had told us that he needed a Bible, the Big Book, a dress shirt for chapel days, and stationary and stamps if he wanted to communicate with anyone, as phones were not allowed during the first month of treatment.

During that rehab stint, John and I would meet there every Wednesday for the family meeting in the chapel. The program was very impressive, with excellent guest speakers and lots of useful advice. One of the things they taught us was that if our loved one shows up at our door saying they got kicked out of the program, they would be lying. They instructed us that if this should occur, to kindly inform our loved one that they cannot live with us and to try to convince them to go back to treatment where they have a nice warm bed and three meals a day. They told us that giving them a soft landing back at home would be the worst thing we could do. Instead, the emphasis should be placed on guiding them back the program to continue in treatment.

We hadn't seen Matt at all for the first two weeks when we went to the rehab to attend the family meetings. The meetings are held in an adjacent chapel, so our paths didn't cross. Then on the third week, we caught a glimpse of him. He looked so good, so healthy; how it warmed my heart to see my son. They were not allowed to speak with us, so we just snuck a little wave and smiled at him. Seeing him smile back made my day.

I had given Matthew a list of our addresses, and also the address for Gracie. Matt ended up writing to all of us. He wrote his dad three letters and me just one. Oh well. He also wrote three letters to his three-year-old daughter, to be read to her by her mommy. In those letters he poured his heart out to Grace, telling her over and over how much he loved her. He called her his Little Princess.

What I found very sweet, in addition to his words to Gracie, were the short, friendly notes at the bottom of each letter written to Amanda. Amanda was expecting a baby with her boyfriend, and even though that had to be very painful for Matt to accept, he still displayed such kindness toward her. That was who he was. No matter what he was struggling with, he was a good person with a kind and thoughtful nature.

While he was back in rehab I decided to re-read *Beautiful Boy*. The first time I had read this book Matt was very sick and I was grasping for some basic information to help me understand addiction. Now, eighteen months later, I was firmly in the thick of the nightmare, an eyewitness to the horrible consequences of addiction. Re-reading Sheff's engrossing story of the roller coaster ride he lived through during his son's addiction somehow, oddly, gave me a sense of grounding. After all, the author lived through the horrendous saga of his son's battle, and even though the book ends once again in relapse and disappointment, his boy, Nic Sheff, did eventually make it. Nic overcame a horrible meth addiction and later became a successful author himself. This gave me hope that, no matter how dire the situation seemed at the end of that book, David's beautiful boy ultimately survived.

MY 13th STATION

I also continued to explore Al-anon groups, hitting different meetings across three nearby towns. It is important to locate the right fit; for me it had to feel safe and inviting with the right mix of personalities or I just wouldn't connect with the group and open up. During the summer of 2013 I finally found the right group for me, which allowed me to really share. Al-anon is a valuable asset for the loved ones of an addict who live in fear and emotional pain every single day. The organization publishes excellent resource material for members, and the meetings help us to conduct our lives in a healthy manner while in the orbit of our addicted loved one. Members bond over shared pain and offer each other helpful suggestions, or just a shoulder to cry on. I felt grateful that I had finally found just the right Al-anon fit in California, although the group in Colorado was my very favorite.

On Friday, July 12th, just one month after entering the Salvation Army program, Matt appeared on his sister Sarah's doorstep. He lied, exactly as the guest speaker had forewarned us only a couple of weeks prior, telling his sister that he was kicked out for not complying with the strict housekeeping rules. She let him in, and then went to her room, closed the door, and called me while her brother played with their now three-year-old son, Jake. Sarah was beside herself knowing she would have to turn him away; it killed her. But because we had all agreed in advance to practice tough love, and not give Matt a soft landing should he arrive at our front door, she realized she had to hold the line. She was so sad, having to send him on his way knowing that he would get the same response from each of us. She followed through, as painful as it was, telling her brother that they couldn't have Jake exposed to his ongoing issues. That afternoon I wrote their dad an email:

July 12, 2013
Sarah used the strategy I told her to use, so he confessed that he had left voluntarily. She offered to take him back to rehab but he refused, says he will "do it on my own." Yeah, right. So she let him know that we all love him but won't give him a place to stay. He chose to leave on his own and now he has to deal with the consequences or go back with the right attitude. She said he seemed surprised that no one would help him. Remember the lady telling us that they would not like that we were being taught these things. Since he hasn't relapsed, maybe he could go back in today. Can you talk to him and see if he would go back?

Sure enough, our son called his dad next hoping for a better outcome than he had gotten at Sarah's house. John gently but firmly told him no, that he cannot stay with him but that he would be happy to drive him back to the rehab. Matt politely declined the offer.

I guess he knew he would get the same response from me, but he called me anyway. As a mother, I can say that telling my son that I would not give him a place to stay broke my heart. I was afraid of what he would do next. He was stable at the moment, being now about fifty days sober, but I was now painfully aware how that could change on a dime. I hung up the phone, laid my head on my desk, and cried my eyes out. It was one of the most difficult things I have ever had to do, turning my son away.

For the next several days, no one heard from Matt. It was excruciating, not knowing where he was, how he would eat, where he was staying, or if he was even alive. Every day, I prayed that he remained sober, but in the back of my mind I visualized him homeless, drunk, living under the freeway overpass. All I could do was pray. I prayed my heart out several times a day that his guardian angel would keep him safe, and that Jesus would not let anything happen to him. As a mother, my prayers to the Blessed Virgin were the most fervent. "Please wrap your mantle around my boy and keep him close to you," I would pray.

After five days of constant worrying, he called. He sounded good, his voice clear and strong. He told me he was living out of his Jeep for now until he can get a job and find housing. He had called to let me know that he was safe and to ask me to bring his blue blanket, the blanket that was actually a comforter he had on his little twin bed as a young boy. I still had that comforter in the linen cabinet, so I agreed to bring it to him. He also needed a toothbrush.

Apparently he had found a really great A.A. group that meets at a community center a couple of towns away, and some of the older guys, around my age, had taken him under their wing. I was so relieved to know that he has met some nice people who can keep an eye on him. He told me he joined them every morning for the 7:00 meeting, and also attended an afternoon meeting. Thankfully, the guys he had befriended knew his situation and would bring him sandwiches and water.

Later that day, I drove the twenty-five minutes and met him at his car in the community center parking lot. Matt looked really good. He was really tan from skateboarding during the daytime hours. He looked healthy and trim. It was evident that he was still sober, thanks be to God. It broke my heart, though, to see the newspaper taped up in the windows of the Jeep, evidence of just how far his life had fallen from the golden boy he once was. I asked him why he left rehab, and he said it was because he knew that Grace would be in town next week and could not bear not to see her.

Before I left, I asked him if I could put one gallon of gas in his car so if he got a job interview he would be able to get to it. He graciously refused my offer of even one gallon of gas, thanked me, and said he is determined to do this on his own. He had a job lead and would keep me posted. I hugged my beautiful son, and then drove away feeling very proud of him. I prayed that he could indeed do this on his own.

The next week he called to let me know he had gotten the job. It was a graveyard shift, unfortunately, but he was just grateful to be earning an income again. I was really happy for him and asked him to keep me updated with his progress.

One of the problems of being both homeless and working a graveyard shift is trying to sleep in the car during the day in the middle of the summer. Not only was the heat a problem, but about a week into his new job, he was cited for a vagrancy violation. The next week, a friend of his said he could park in front of his home on a private street, which was fine for a few days. But the heat and sunlight basically prevented him from getting any real sleep and it was taking a toll on him. I became worried that he would lose his job if he couldn't get a decent amount of sleep, so I invited him to use his old room to sleep for five or six hours a day if he wanted to. He was very grateful that I would offer him this opportunity.

I had moved Mike into our house because I had become his primary caregiver while he was undergoing treatment and receiving transfusions. When I mentioned to Mike that Matthew would be grabbing some sleep in his old room before his shifts, he graciously suggested that Matt just come home and stay until he gets his legs under him with the new job. This made me very happy, to have this supportive man at my side. So, in early August of 2013, Matt moved back to his old room. I established some house rules and a three-month time limit, and also told him that if he relapses he would be asked to move out.

One August afternoon, soon after he'd moved back home, I was standing in his doorway while we were chatting. He was sitting on the side of his bed with his laptop and we were just catching up with each other, chatting about his job and Gracie's upcoming visit. While we were talking, something out of the corner of my eye caught my attention. I turned and noticed a thin strip of dirt inside the wooden door jam. The dirt started at about shoulder height and went across the top of the jam and back down the other side. My first thought was that I had never seen dirt in the door jam before, and peeked at the other two bedrooms' door jams that once were occupied by his sisters to see if they were dirty, too. But the dirt was only on Matt's, which was no big deal at the time, just odd. I wondered, after twenty-two years of living in the house, why suddenly dirt was collecting there. While we were still chatting, I reached behind me where the linen cabinets are and grabbed a rag, wiped the dirt off, and threw the rag in the hamper. I didn't give it another thought.

He crossed the threshold of ninety days sober, yet again, and picked up his chip. Progress. During this period while he was living with me, I would come home on occasion to find him in the backyard with his Big Book and a spiral notebook, working on the steps. He always seemed to get hung up on the fourth step (taking a brutally honest personal inventory), but was really making an effort. He now had a sponsor, one of the guys from his A.A. group, which I hoped would help him continue to progress in the program. He never missed that 7:00 a.m. meeting, now showing up immediately after getting off the graveyard shift. He was in great spirits, having just spent about three days with Grace during her recent visit. Amanda's family had a party that I also attended, and there was Gracie, sitting on her daddy's lap eating a Popsicle and giving him every other bite. Precious.

On Sunday, August 25th, we attended my mom's annual summer barbeque, always a super fun party. We took a family photo in the backyard with the self-timer on my camera, me standing proudly between my tall, smiling, handsome son and my beautiful man, Mike. Matt was one hundred days sober, and Mike seemed to be in remission, so everyone in the family was cheering for them.

What an amazing weekend was had in Napa for the Labor Day holiday that year! I was feeling so happy and encouraged by Matt's progress, and I never get tired of the earthy, sensuous beauty of the wine country. Before leaving town, I arranged for Matt to stay with his dad for the weekend, just as a precaution against temptation. I learned from my last attempt to leave town how to be much more vigilant and strategic where my son is concerned. The mind of an addict is a wily one. The disease seeks the tiniest opening, an opportunity to barge back through the door and wreak havoc in the victim's life once again. As I have become more educated, mostly through the addiction school of hard knocks, I now anticipate potential problems and try, anyway, to be proactive and take the offense.

Sunday afternoon, Mike began to spike a fever, which was cause for concern. We cut our trip short and headed back to Walnut Creek. When we arrived back home Sunday evening, I saw that Matt was already home from his dad's house. I then remembered that he was scheduled to work that night, so I figured he probably just came home to grab fresh work clothes before heading off to his 10:00-6:00 shift.

I began unpacking my car from the road trip feeling happy to be home. I was increasingly worried about Mike, and just wanted to get him situated before calling the triage nurse at the hospital. With leukemia being so unpredictable, it is necessary to stay in contact with the emergency department when issues pop up outside of doctor office hours. Once upstairs, after getting Mike in bed with a cool washcloth over his forehead, I received a text—from Matt. It was 8:30 p.m. and he was in the house. It read, "Can you come in here?" I thought, geez what a lazy bones, why can't he just come to my room if he wants to talk. So, with an eye roll, I headed down the hallway toward his room.

MY 13th STATION

I opened his bedroom door to find him highly intoxicated in his bed, vodka bottle on the nightstand. He was lying in the fetal position. It was obvious to me that he was seriously inebriated, maybe poisoned. I didn't know what to do! I just knew he needed immediate medical attention. I told him I had to get him up and couldn't do it myself, and Mike was in bed sick. Matt weighed two hundred pounds.

He lay there sobbing, just sobbing. I managed to pull him up into a sitting position and pulled his arm up over my shoulder to keep him upright. I told him on the count of three we would stand up. This took three attempts, but eventually we succeeded to get him off the bed. From that point the real challenge lay ahead, where I would try to negotiate getting this large man down my staircase.

Making it down the stairs without both of us falling down was going to be really tricky. Taking one stair at a time, then pausing to regain my balance, and leaning into the wall for support, I managed to get Matthew down the stairs. The next challenge was to get out of the house through the laundry room. This was the most expedient way to get to my car, so I was determined to succeed. I managed to maneuver my son past the washing machine and had him lean against the dryer while I propped the door to the garage open. He nearly tumbled on his way through the door by missing the small step inside the garage. I feared he would fall and sustain a head injury on the concrete. During the entire episode he had been talking gibberish. He was agitated, then gentle, then agitated. I had never seen him so drunk.

I was able to shuffle him towards the passenger side of my car. I opened the door in hopes he would just sit down inside the car, but instead he began flailing his arms and knocked his sunglasses off, which he had still been wearing even though it was about 9:00 p.m., sending the glasses flying to the ground and causing a lens to pop out. Somehow, I managed to get over to the other side of him and just began to push him into my car until he would sit down. Once I was successful in getting him seated, all I had left to do was pick up his feet, one at a time, and place them on the floorboard while slowly turning his body so it would face forward.

I ran over to the driver's side, jumped in, and began to pull out of the garage with a strong sense of urgency. As I was backing out of the driveway, Matt suddenly opened his door and jumped out of the car, stumbling down the driveway and rolling to the curb. I was just furious at this point. I was tired, spent, scared, and angry all at once. He looked like a pathetic drunken bum lying there on the sidewalk.

I pulled the car back into the garage and yelled loudly at my son, "I am SO OVER THIS!"

I then went back inside the house and closed the garage door and locked all the doors to the house. At that moment I was so angry and disappointed that I just didn't care anymore. He could live on the streets.

I went upstairs to check on Mike and called the hospital. They said he seemed to be having a reaction to the Cipro (antibiotic) and told me at which point I should bring him to the hospital. I then walked to the front of the house and looked out a bedroom window to spot Matt sitting on the curb, head down, appearing to be crying. Oh my goodness, my heart just sank. I stood there looking at my pitiful son, tears streaming down my face. But, I didn't act. I just walked away and began unpacking from the road trip.

I was blown out at that point, worried sick about both Mike and Matt. I did text John to fill him in on the latest development. He said that Matt had given him some story that he would be working both nights while I was gone and would be staying at a friend's house to get some sleep during the days. John tried to convince him to adhere to the plan that was made before I left town, but Matt assured his dad that all was good. Not to worry; he would be working all through the nights and sleeping all day. When your kid is twenty-five years old there really isn't a whole lot you can do. So, John had trusted his son.

After about ten minutes had passed, my anger dissipated and morphed into fear. I called Matt and, thankfully, he answered. I asked him if he still wanted me to take him to the hospital. He told me that he had already called the police to come and get him and was over at the local elementary school parking lot waiting for them. I asked if he would prefer for me to take him, and he said yes. So I drove the few blocks to the school.

When I arrived the squad car was already there, and the officers were chatting with Matt. I approached and introduced myself as his mother. I told the officer, Deputy Jaime, a summary of what had happened and that when I attempted to take him to the hospital he'd jumped out of the car. The officer was very kind.

"Ma'am, your son is as gentle as a lamb. He is obviously sick but is very cooperative. I suggest you allow us to transport Matthew, if only to avoid another incident like what happened earlier."

I knew he was right, and quietly acquiesced. Deputy Jaime then warned me that when they do put him into the vehicle they would have to cuff him, and that it might be difficult for me to witness that. I told him I totally understood, and to do what they needed to do. So, from my car, I watched the police officers put my son in handcuffs, a disturbing sight I thought I'd never see. Tears stung my eyes seeing this young man, someone who had everything going for him in his youth, ushered, exceedingly drunk, into the rear seat of a police car. He would, yet again, be placed on a mandatory seventy-two-hour psychiatric hold. This was his sixth relapse and his third 5150 involuntary hold since leaving his first rehab stint just eleven months ago.

On the second day of the hold he called to let me know which hospital he was at, as the first hospital had no beds available in the psychiatric wing. He shared with me what happened over the weekend. Even though we had all agreed that he would stay with his father for the weekend, he nimbly wiggled out of that with a lie, saying he would be working. In fact, he never went in to work at all, but began an alcohol binge that would last for two solid days. Of course, he was fired from his job immediately. This was a very significant setback on every level. He was lucky to have found that job, and now, through his own stupid actions, he had lost it. On the phone he expressed remorse and embarrassment and apologized to me for ruining my life. I knew that I had one day to think about the next step.

When I had invited Matthew to stay for three months at my house, it was with a caveat that he remain sober. I had learned so much in Al-anon about co-dependency and enabling behaviors, and surely didn't want to make matters worse by enabling him. But this was a very difficult decision to make, and I knew that I would have to consult Jesus and the Blessed Virgin before making it.

That next day, I sat in Adoration for an hour. Instead of reading or writing, I just sat there, staring at the Blessed Sacrament, fixated on it as a life source. I was all out of ideas. I was out of energy. I was losing hope. Something far stronger than me had its grip on my son. No matter how hard he tried, how committed he was to reining in the addiction so he could be a reliable father to his child, he just couldn't overcome the demon that sat there on his shoulder chirping at him all day. I prayed my heart out in the little chapel that day, weeping for my boy and begging for a sign from Jesus. What should I do next?

The following day, Matt got a ride home from the hospital and, after greeting the dogs and giving me a hug, apologizing profusely for letting me down again, he went upstairs to his room. After a few minutes I saw him carrying bags of his clothes down the stairs and then placing them into his car. At first I ignored him, trying to decide if I should just allow him to leave. He knew he had violated my rule and that he needed to move on. He didn't even ask for another chance, he just set to packing up to prepare to live out of his car again.

When he came back into the house and walked upstairs again, I let the Holy Spirit lead me. I felt a powerful signal from God not to allow him to leave. I walked outside and pulled the bags out of his car, and brought each one back inside. He came downstairs and looked at me questioning what was going on. Then he sat down on the bottom stair and put his face in his hand and just cried. He told me he didn't deserve to be allowed to stay. He told me I was the best mom in the world to even consider giving him another chance.

I looked at my son, sitting there broken in spirit, and told him, "Matt, I will never give up on you, ever! As long as I live, I will love you and be your biggest fan. I will *never* give up on you."

Later we sat down at the kitchen table to talk about his new plan. I had learned enough to know that this had to be *his* plan, not mine. He needed to own his plan for sobriety; he needed to own his recovery. He knew he had to do whatever it would take to achieve a sustained recovery.

My confused demeanor must have been evident to him, as he suddenly said, "I know it is hard to understand why I keep relapsing. Just read the Big Book pages 21-24[5] because that is the best description of what it is like to be an alcoholic."

Later that night I read those pages, nodding in bewildered recognition.

I had asked him a few months back to go with me to church, or even just meet with a priest to talk, and he politely declined my invitation. So, on this day, September 5, 2013, I figured I would ask again while we sat together at the table. I knew in my heart that by abandoning church and the sacraments six years ago he had put himself in a spiritually compromised position; he was clearly under attack by the devil. I had come to believe that no matter how much time someone spends in rehab or going to meetings, if they don't reclaim or develop their faith in God all efforts are likely to fail. But, he wasn't there yet. Wasn't ready to turn his life over to Jesus. I knew I couldn't force the issue, no one can. So I just amplified my efforts in prayer that he would soon reach out to God for strength and healing.

He realized that he must immediately find a new job, so together we set up expectations. By now I was all too aware of how important boundaries are when living with an addict. He was very receptive to my request that he physically go out to look for work three days a week and spend the alternate days applying for work online. I set down rules to have him show me his completed job applications by taking a photo of it at the business where he was physically applying and, when applying for jobs online, to have me witness the submission of the applications. Sadly, this reminded me of parenting a young teenager, but it was, unfortunately, a necessity under the circumstances.

Matt also made the admirable decision to meet with his former boss and apologize in person for not showing up for work on Labor Day weekend. Now sober, he realized what a burden he had placed on the boss and his coworkers by abandoning his job, and on a holiday weekend no less. He knew that his boss would not reverse his decision about the termination, but he just felt he owed him a sincere apology. He followed through and apologized to his employer that day. He told Matt how upset he was being left high and dry over the busy weekend, but he wished him all the best in his sobriety and future endeavors.

As the weeks progressed, Matt adapted a healthy daily routine. He started his days at the 7:00 a.m. A.A. meeting, went to the gym, and then came home to shower and change clothes before going out to look for work. It would be difficult for him to find a job, as each job he had held over the last three years was lost due to his alcoholism and mental health issues. He had only completed one year of college and two semesters of the fire science program. Not impressive. My heart hurt for my son. I knew he had an uphill battle and was becoming discouraged as each setback put him deeper into the hole. So, I just kept praying for someone to take a chance on hiring him.

Matt ended up being a wonderful gift to me during a very, very difficult time in my personal life. Mike was back in the hospital. His leukemia had morphed into the deadly AML, amazingly the same exact leukemia that his first cousin, Kathy, had also been recently diagnosed with. I had created a CaringBridge online blog for his many friends and family members to follow the course of his illness, but just trying to find the energy to write the updates became nearly impossible. I was so exhausted and frazzled trying to manage the sad and trying situation with Mike's cancer treatment, and Matt really stepped up to take care of the house for me.

One day, I came home to see he had taken it upon himself to steam clean the carpets, this in response to an offhanded comment I'd recently made that the carpeting was in dire need of a good cleaning. He took care of the laundry and cooked meals for us. He kept up with the yard work and the dogs' needs. The long drive to the hospital and the eight to ten hour visits demanded so much of my time and energy I don't know how I would have managed without Matt's help.

Matt crossed the days off the calendar I'd made him, which now hung on his bedroom wall at our house. Soon it was time to turn the page to October. The photo on the calendar for October was one I had snapped of him and Grace grinning on a silly arcade ride at Chuck E. Cheese's earlier in the year. The A.A. slogan I placed on that page was "Let go and let God." He had written a large "G" on October 29th surrounded by exclamation marks. Gracie would be arriving that day for a five-day visit and he was really looking forward to taking her to the pumpkin patch.

Over the next weeks Matt was in good spirits. He and Kevin, a close friend from their baseball years, were hanging out a lot and enjoyed watching the baseball playoffs together. He met up with another close baseball friend, Justin, to hit balls and play catch at the local middle school ball field, which gave Matt much joy. He came home smiling, complaining that Justin, who played professional baseball at that point, was merciless in throwing heat while Matt struggled to make contact. Ironically, it was Justin that Matt had inadvertently hurled that wild pitch at when they were eleven-year old Little Leaguers, injuring him badly enough to send him to the hospital. Even so, Justin had forgiven Matt and the two shared an enduring friendship.

I was very grateful that I did not kick him out that day after his Labor Day relapse, as his company ended up being such a blessing. While Mike was in the hospital in preparation for a stem cell transplant, I spent most of my days at his side. I was very sad watching the suffering that Mike endured, and so fearful of losing this special man. Driving home late at night, I would struggle to stay awake at the wheel, totally drained. I would come home and there Matt would be, a caring person to talk to about Mike's ordeal, as well as my own worries and fears.

One particularly difficult day I came home depressed and exhausted. I saw my son there watching TV and, suddenly feeling sentimental, asked him if we could just sit together and watch skate videos like we used to when he was fourteen. His eyes lit right up. He got out his laptop and set it up on the coffee table in front of the couch where we sat, side-by-side, just like the old days when we watched skate videos via VHS tapes on a clunky, old TV monitor in his room. This night, in early October 2013, mother and son sat together watching his current favorite skater, Chris Cole, and found quiet solace in each other's company.

MY 13th STATION

It was a gorgeous autumn day. The neighbor on the corner had a deciduous tree that, every year like clockwork, dumped its annual pile of glorious golden leaves all over their front lawn. For twenty-two years I have walked past that corner house and smiled, knowing the holidays are on their way when seeing the leaves scattered about.

So that day, October 16th, was just a typical fall day in the East Bay—crisp and lovely. I took my two dogs for their usual jaunt, which I am sure they were sick and tired of since I rarely changed up our routine. But it was such a nice trek that I looked forward to it each day, giving me a nice twenty-five minutes of quiet time to say my daily rosary and offer up my prayer petitions for Matt and Mike.

On the way home that Wednesday, as I walked the dogs down the street that faces our house, which sits at the top of a "T," I was ambling along when I happened to glance forward at my house. Terror suddenly gripped me. I sensed an ominous darkness over my house, as if a huge, heavy black tarp had been laid over it. As I approached the house, I felt a deep sense of dread. Immediately, I knew in my gut that the demon, or demons were back.

I had almost forgotten about that whole experience over this past year, as I had felt absolutely zero signs of evil in my house since Fr. Matthew had cleansed it last October. Absolutely none. My home felt light and sunny and friendly and comfortable for nearly a solid year, which is why the stark change that day was so riveting.

As I entered the property, I immediately recited the two prayers that Fr. Matthew had instructed me to pray, loudly: the Our Father and the Saint Michael Archangel prayer. I did this inside the garage. I then entered the house and saw Matt there in the family room watching TV, as he often did at this time of day. I unleashed the dogs and went upstairs to my room to grab the little holy water bottle only to find it nearly empty. I jumped in the car and drove to our church, where a cistern of holy water is provided right outside the Adoration chapel, and refilled the bottle. I felt a distinct sense of urgency setting in.

When I re-entered the house, I didn't say anything to Matt, I just climbed the stairs as if on a mission. I went directly to his bedroom where I proceeded to douse the room—corners, windows, closet, doorway, and his bed—with the blessed water, stating in a firm, commanding tone, "Be gone, Satan, you have no power over my son. Be gone in the name of Jesus Christ! You cannot have my son!" For good measure, I also threw the water in the hallway in the same spot where I had dropped the laundry that day, years ago, and also sprayed some in both adjacent bedrooms.

I stood there shaking, adrenaline flowing like I was literally in a battle with the devil for my son's life. I had been so preoccupied of late helping my dear man with his health crisis, spending so many hours at the hospital, that I simply didn't have the energy to handle anything more. Between my son's disease and Mike's cancer, I was completely worn out. Anyway, I felt sure that I had adequately handled the situation that evening.

While I was in Matt's room casting out evil spirits, I noticed his Crucifix missing and then remembered that I had hung it, the one he'd received when he made his First Communion at age 9, in Mike's hospital room when he was first admitted in mid-September. I remember thinking that he would find comfort in its presence while facing such frightening health issues. That Crucifix had been hanging on my son's bedroom wall for the last sixteen years, and at that particular moment I wished it was still there.

Mike was released from the hospital two days later, on Friday, October 18th, for a three-week respite to gain weight and strength before his scheduled return on November 5th for the transplant. He had wasted away, losing all muscle tone and about forty pounds. His daughter brought him home that day and I remember we just stood there hugging each other and crying, so happy to be together outside of the sterile hospital environment. We caught up on the details surrounding his health and ongoing treatment, and then I asked if he had remembered to pack Matt's Crucifix when he left the hospital that day. He checked his bags and replied that, unfortunately, he and his brother, who'd help him pack up, must have missed it. Dang.

So, I called the hospital to ask if the staff had found the cross when cleaning room #505. I was very distressed when, after carefully checking the room, they reported that it was nowhere to be found. The nurse suggested I check with the lost and found at Security, so she connected me. Unfortunately, there was no sign of Matt's Crucifix in the lost and found. I waited until the following Monday and called the fifth floor again, hoping that by then someone might have found the simple wooden Crucifix. Again, I was told that it had not been found or turned in. In fact, the nurse said that many times items of small monetary value are simply tossed out by the cleaning crew. That made me really sad.

CHAPTER 24

Loss

ON WEDNESDAY, OCTOBER 23RD, Mike and I were up early because we had to get to an 8:00 a.m. appointment at the hospital. He had numerous appointments and tests scheduled throughout the day and I wanted to be there for him. I was also going to participate in a training session designed for caregivers who will be tending to the needs of a stem cell transplant patient.

Matt was up early too, as usual, getting ready to dash off to his early meeting. I asked him what his plan was for the day and he gave me the rundown: Meeting, gym, look for work, tennis with Kevin, and babysitting his nephew, my grandson, Jake, from 4:00-8:00 p.m. Wonderful, a full and productive day. I told him I would see him later, and Mike told him what a great job he is doing and to keep it up, and then off we went.

At about 10:15 a.m., between the first two appointments at the hospital that morning, as Mike and I headed toward the lobby to wait to be called again, I suddenly, inexplicably, began having what I could only guess was a panic attack. Out of thin air, a splitting headache came over me. My chest tightened and my heart pounded. I struggled to breathe and my hands began to shake. I knew I had to immediately sit down.

I began to weep, scared at what I was experiencing. Mike went over to the coffee cart and got me a cup of tea, but when I attempted to reach for it I managed to spill it all over the floor. It took me several minutes of deep breathing and Mike's quiet consoling voice to just settle myself down. Never had I ever experienced anything like that before. It was so strange. I wondered, wow, maybe I am just freaked out about the caregiving thing?

After the next doctor appointment was completed, as we headed back to the central lobby, I realized I hadn't checked my phone since we had arrived at around 8:30 a.m. So I fished my phone out of my purse to find just one text message there, from Amanda. She wrote, "I think something is up with Matt," and it was time-stamped at 10:11 a.m. It was now about 11:15 a.m., an hour after she had reached out to me. My initial thought was, please God, please tell me he didn't relapse again.

I immediately called Matthew, but he didn't pick up, so I sent a text, but got no response. I walked outside for better reception and called Amanda, asking her why she thought something was up with Matt. She said was worried because Matt had sent her a cryptic-sounding text message, and that she was concerned about him. I asked her to forward the text to me, which she did.

When I received that text message seconds later I felt icy panic run through me. It sounded virtually like a goodbye message, directed to Grace through her mother. I then acted swiftly, calling Amanda right back to convey my fear. She offered to call in a citizen check with the police, from Colorado where she lived, which she proceeded to do. I immediately called John to ask if he could leave work as soon as possible and go to the house to check on Matt, as I was over an hour away, versus his thirty minutes. Thankfully, he said he would leave right away.

After arranging for Mike's daughter to take over with him at the hospital, I went to get my car from the valet, trembling, telling the attendant there was a family emergency and to please, *please* hurry.

He quickly got my car and I was on the road home within ten minutes of my call to John. As I drove, I recited over and over, "God please save my son. Please don't let him die." After about twenty minutes on the road I got ahold of John, who had just arrived.

John's voice was calm and controlled as he informed me that the police had arrived first on the scene, and kicked in the garage side door to get our son out. Matt was found unconscious inside his car in my garage, the garage full of carbon monoxide fumes. By the time John arrived Matt was out on the front lawn receiving CPR and other life-saving measures performed by the paramedics, and that he had a light pulse. John did tell me, however, that it didn't look good. His voice broke. He told me they would be transporting our son to the emergency room at John Muir Hospital, so I was to meet them there.

Driving at 75 mph I clung to the tiniest shred of hope, knowing there was still a heartbeat. But as the gravity of this event began to sink in, I began to feel faint with the telltale sparkles that presage a fainting spell. I was in the fast lane on the freeway, so slowly I made my way to the right hand shoulder where I stopped for a minute to practice deep breathing, and then convinced myself to get back on the road. I got back on the freeway, shouting my pleas to God, "Please save him, please save him, don't let him die!"

After a few minutes, I got my wits together and called our oldest, Sarah. I told her in the calmest voice I could muster that her brother has attempted suicide and is being taken right now to John Muir, and to please call the church and have a priest sent immediately. Sarah began to freak out, wanting to know what happened. I told her I would tell her details later, but to hang up and call the church now, and to pray hard for Matt. He still had a heartbeat, so he could still receive the sacrament, the anointing of the sick through which a multitude of graces can be conferred. I got off the phone so my daughter could make that important phone call.

It seemed like days that I was on the road trying to get to my son. I could not get there fast enough no matter how fast I drove. Finally, about seventy minutes after I left the other hospital, I arrived at John Muir. I pulled into the emergency lot and ran into the emergency department. Breathlessly, I told the gal at the front window that I was there for my son, Matthew Anthony.

She said in that calm, practiced, professional tone, "Okay, just one moment," and with that she disappeared through a back door into the emergency ward. After a couple of minutes she reappeared saying, with a completely neutral face, "Ms. Anthony, they will be right out. Please have a seat."

Hooray! I thought, "Oh, my gosh, John and Matt would be right out. Thank you, Jesus! Thank you!" As I began to seek a chair, the door opened and out walked two people I didn't recognize, a man and a woman. I initially ignored them, sure that my son and his dad would be following behind them soon. Instead, these two strangers walked over to me and asked if I was Matthew's mother. My heart seemed to drop to the floor, anticipating the gravity of their next words.

The man said, "My name is Joel and I am a volunteer grief counselor. I am so deeply sorry, but your son didn't make it."

At this, they ushered me to a nearby chair where I sank like rock, defeated and sorrowful. I had been so sure that God would save him. I had been so confident.

Joel and Ruth were grief volunteers who provide solace for parents who lose a child to suicide, as they each had. They attempted to console me as I sat there racked with sobs. They asked me if I would like to see my son, and I said, "Yes, please." At this, we entered into the emergency ward toward a closed black curtain, the death curtain, behind which lay my only son.

There, before me, my eyes rested upon the beautiful creation that God had placed into my life on that stormy night in February

1988. His heart no longer beat. This young, beautiful man started his journey in my womb, where I was thrilled to listen to the rhythmic woosh-woosh, woosh-woosh of his tiny beating heart transmitted through the ultrasounds that preceded his birth. As a little boy, I held him tight enough to feel his heart beat when he ran up to give me hugs. That heart of his would dance when he hit a home run or nailed a skate trick, and melted when snuggled up with his favorite dog, Bailey. Finally, that big, generous, amazing heart simply soared when he gazed upon his precious daughter. His heart, his lovely heart, was stilled.

After the agonizing deathbed scene, I returned home and entered Matthew's bedroom with my daughter, Sarah. As we entered the room, my eyes immediately caught sight of the dirt that had reappeared inside the door jam in the exact same configuration, starting from a height of about four feet and following the inside of the doorway up and around to the same height on the opposite side. A surge of intense anger welled up inside me at the sight of this. I knew, without a shred of doubt, that this was some kind of residue from the demon that was attached to my poor son. This time, I grabbed a rag, and, after wiping the dirt, folded the rag and placed it into a baggie with a sticky note on which I scribbled, "Residue found inside Matt's bedroom door jam on 10/23/13. First appeared Aug 2013 and wiped off. Reappeared two months later. Get tested" I sealed the baggie and vowed to someday get the dirt analyzed at a lab.

The next thing I noticed was my mini ironing board and iron on his bedroom floor, which he'd apparently borrowed from my bedroom closet that day. Across the ironing board lay his black pinstripe dress shirt. Obviously, he was preparing to go out and look for work, as he had stated earlier that morning when telling me his plan for the day. The fact that he had gone to my bedroom closet to fetch the ironing board and selected a shirt to wear on his job hunt struck me as hugely significant. Before I left the house that morning he'd asked where I kept the old tennis rackets. He also told me how pleased he was that his sister was going to pay him to babysit Jake later. These were not the actions of a person planning to kill himself.

I then looked up at the calendar. All month long he had placed firm x's in each day's box, as the day approached that his Grace would be here. On this day, Matthew only completed half of the X, placing just a weak diagonal slash in the box of the 23rd, just six days away from her arrival. On his desk was a passionate letter written to his daughter, which will remain private, that absolutely ripped my guts out to read. In it he parroted the lies that the devil had bored into his mind, like a devious serpent, convincing him he was a worthless failure.

As promised, John handled the awful task of informing our youngest, Emma, of her brother's passing. Emma was completely crushed by the news. She and her big brother shared a close bond, and she adored him. Emma was enrolled in a demanding art program at a top design school in the city, which left no room in the schedule for mourning. She soldiered on, but her performance in school suffered terribly.

That evening, as I lay balled up in the fetal position in bed, processing this somber, dark day, it dawned on me that my panic attack at 10:15 a.m. happened just as my son's life was slipping away. I had actually *felt* Matthew dying; I physically experienced him leaving us. I am so attuned to my children that the horrible tragic energy somehow transcended space and communicated with me. I had never prior, or ever after that frightening event, experienced a panic attack.

Lying there in my bed that night, I just needed to feel my grief and acknowledge and honor the beautiful life that had been lost that day, in the thirteenth year of the century. Of course. I struggled to comprehend the events of the day. I couldn't wrap my head around it at all. Matt had been doing so well, and was so looking forward to Grace's upcoming visit. I lay there in bed, catatonic and numb.

Thankfully, Mike was home that evening, after an eight-hour slog of tests, transfusions, and meeting with doctors. He, too, was devastated by Matthew's suicide. We were all in a state of shock. While chatting with Mike about the events at the hospital that day, my thoughts suddenly returned to the missing Crucifix. Although I was very sad last week when realizing it was gone, this development now filled me with sorrow. That little cross now had even more sentimental meaning in the wake of losing my son.

Matthew's was the third completed suicide on our street, all occurring on the same side of Meadow Lane and within an expanse of two blocks, or sixteen homes. One of the many awful things about losing a loved one to suicide is never nowing what might have triggered it. I had my theories regarding demonic influences, but, obviously, had to remain open to natural motivations or causes as well. So, two days after his death, I set about going through Matt's phone, just as I had done a year ago after his first attempted suicide. It was sad to see all of our texts to him on that fateful day, October 23rd, when we were frantically reaching out to him. Dozens of texts from both sides of the family, imploring him to not give up, sent in vain, as it was already too late. All of his recent text conversations with friends were, just like the last time, upbeat and positive. There were several conversations with his local friend, Kevin, and also with his friends from A.A. and the sober living house. Some texts, including Matt's, chatted about how many days of sobriety they had under their belts. All were just normal conversations between buddies, planning beach time, tennis, baseball, football—just regular guy talk.

One conversation that jumped off the phone was the one he'd had with his dad the week before his death. It was absolutely beautiful, and I knew when I read it what a treasure it would remain for John.

In his text to his dad, Matt said, "Hey Dad, I wanted to tell you something last night, but I didn't have the guts to do it in person because it's still very emotional for me. I am very, very sorry for what I put you through a year ago [first suicide attempt]. And also what I did in May [relapsing at John's house]. I am so sorry that I put you through that."

His dad replied, "I know you are, Matt. I just want the best for you and for you to be healthy and safe is all. I love you."

"I love you, too."

Was this text to his dad a sign that he was giving up? Or was it simply part of the process of making amends in the program? We will never know.

Early the following week, I realized that the guys at the 7:00 a.m. A.A. meeting were probably worried about Matt. He rarely missed these meetings, and surely, after not showing up for several days at that point, they must be concerned. I decided I would go there and tell them in person what had happened.

I entered the A.A. room just before they were going to begin the meeting. About a dozen men sat around a rectangular table sipping coffee, idle chitchat filling the room. I walked over to one of the guys and told them that I was Matt's mom, and had some sad news to deliver. All eyes were suddenly on me. I mustered up the strength to tell them about Matt taking his life the prior Wednesday, somehow remaining calm when speaking these awful words.

One by one the men got up out of their chairs and walked over to me, encircling me, hugging me. Some had tears running down their faces, others stared at me in total disbelief. It was obvious how much they cared about my son by the kind words they spoke to me that day, telling me how special Matt was to them. I thanked them for taking him under their wings in August, and welcoming him into their group.

They asked me about the memorial plans, so I told them I would keep them apprised. Several men stated they would attend, to pay their final respects to this young man who had become a friend and fellow warrior against the hideous disease called alcoholism.

The next few days I walked around in shocked disbelief. As word got around and phone calls and emails came rolling in, the reality of my son's passing hit me very hard. I was not the only person in shock. Everyone was devastated by this unbelievable turn of events. But amidst the outpouring of grief and disbelief that Matt would suddenly, shockingly, have taken his own life came beautiful little nuggets in the sentiments expressed. I had the presence of mind to make a copy of every text and email, and kept every card sent by the people who loved Matthew, knowing that I would someday want to share them with his little girl. I wanted Grace to know how beloved her daddy was.

Among all the kind, loving messages two stand out as significant. I will include excerpts from these:

From his close friend, Kevin:
When you say that you are mystified and confused because there were not any warning signs, I cannot tell you how much I agree with you. I was blindsided by the news of Matt's passing. It doesn't add up. The things that you mentioned, like the ironing board in his room and the

commitment of babysitting Jake, and Grace coming to town within days, are just a few of the things that really stump me as to why Matt chose now of all times to leave us. Another thing I find confusing is that we actually planned to play tennis that day.

Matt has been talking non-stop about the baseball play-offs this year. He seemed to really be into it this year, so it confuses me why he didn't stick around to watch the rest of the playoffs, to see who would be crowned World Series champs this year. Two nights ago, when the Red Sox/Cardinals game was on, I was home alone. I moved the pillows off the spot on the couch where Matt usually sits when he comes over. I sat there alone, making comments throughout the game to Matt as if he was there watching the game with me.

I keep thinking back to that Monday when we last hung out to try and remember if there were any signs that would indicate that he was depressed, but I cannot think of anything. He seemed fine! But Matt always wore a happy face in front of me. I just wish I had asked how he was feeling, if everything was okay. I would have done anything to help him out of the dark place he was in.

I miss everything about him. I miss skating with him at the skate park. I miss texting him. I miss sitting on the couch watching TV with him. I miss his laugh. I miss his smile. I miss the skate videos. I miss the metal music. We would just enjoy laughing together. Those were some of the best times. The list of memories we had together is endless. Matt was such a good person. He was loving and kind. I just wish that he saw what everyone else saw in him. There is always going to be a part of my heart

missing. I will never stop thinking about him and I will never forget him.
Kevin

From Evan, one of the group of men at the 7:00 a.m. A.A. meeting:
Hi Mrs. Anthony,

Over the past five months I had the privilege of getting to know Matt well and it is an honor to call him a true friend. When I first moved here from Miami I was in a great deal of physical and emotional pain. Matt's friendship helped to heal some of that pain. Not only did we attend meetings together, we played football until our arms hurt. We went to the gym together, the pool, played tennis and basketball.

The last time I saw Matt we had just returned from a day at the beach. Something seemed to be bothering him but he wouldn't talk about it. He had difficulty opening up and asking others for help. Most of us who struggle with alcohol have great difficulty with this. I watched him come out of thirty-six days at the Salvation Army and live in his car in front of our house for three weeks until he got the job. He did not complain once. I have been through a number of detoxes, rehabs, and sober living homes over the past fifteen years. His was the most inspiring and courageous effort to get sober I have ever witnessed.

The disease of alcoholism, however, is a formidable yet subtle foe. It's cunning, baffling, powerful, and speaks to us in our own voice. I hope you can take solace in knowing that by no means did Matt meet with a cowardly fate. He died of a fatal disease. He lost the battle to alcoholism.

Your son was very strong. On that morning he was in his disease and it overcame him. Matt was loved by all of us. I have never heard anyone say an unkind word about him. He was a true friend and I will always remember him for his huge heart.
Evan

One morning, a few days after Matt's death, there was a knock on my door. My dear friend from two doors down, Suzanne Peterson, was on my doorstep. I invited her inside and she gave me a big hug while we both cried about Matt. She said she wouldn't stay, knowing I was probably not up to visiting, but wanted to let me know she was there for me if I needed to chat or cry. She then handed me a card, gave me another hug, and headed home. Once back inside, I opened the card and in it was a check for $3,000 to help with the burial expenses. Standing there stunned, I immediately burst into tears. This was nothing less than a gift from heaven.

When I went to meet with the representative at the Catholic cemetery I was still in a fog. What the heck was I doing sitting in a cemetery waiting room? I sat down with the saleslady and together we made the selections for the plot and the marker. I asked her if there was a plot available next to the one I chose, and she asked why. I told her I would like to be buried next to my son when the time comes. She suggested that we both use the same plot and share the marker, that this would save the extra expense of purchasing a second plot. I immediately loved the idea, so the marker has his information on the left side, Saint Anthony in the center, and the right side will remain blank until my day arrives to be buried there with him. I drove away feeling a little more at peace.

MY 13th STATION

The following days were consumed with making plans for Matthew's memorial service. This just shouldn't be happening to our family. How could it be that we lost the heart and soul of us? I was informed that in California an autopsy is mandated when there is a suicide death. The thought of my perfect son lying on some sterile, steel table while someone sliced him open and analyzed every part of him made me literally sick. But apparently, the family has no say in this, so they gave us the timeline as to when he would be available for his rosary, memorial service, and burial.

I contacted four people to speak at his service, but could have had double that number. It was very difficult to narrow down the speakers but time constraints were in place. For music I scheduled a lovely cellist, a young lady who was part of our homeschool community, who would play gorgeous, melancholic selections, many of them of Irish tradition. I also arranged for a soloist to sing the Ave Maria. When writing the obituary for the newspaper, even though a solemn assignment, I managed to smile a little while recalling and writing about the sweet details of my son's life.

My sister, her husband, and I worked feverishly to assemble a photo slideshow with over two hundred carefully selected photos. I chose the *Memorare* as the prayer for his memorial cards, my favorite prayer. John took care of the casket selection and program, and my dear friend, Anna, offered to have the reception at their beautiful home. John also created large mounted photos for the memorial service that would also be available at the reception for friends and family to sign.

I walked through these days in a cloud of confusion and disbelief, going through the motions because I had no other option. I would spontaneously burst into tears when the reality hit that the project I was working on was for my deceased son's memorial. I willed myself each hour to just put one foot in front of the other. I so wanted to create a beautiful memorial service to honor Matthew.

During the fury of making arrangements, I found some time to contact that hospital in hopes that Matthew's Crucifix had somehow been located. I was transferred from the nurse's station to the housekeeping department to the security department, spending about a half hour of time only to be told it was not there. I was crestfallen. I tried to remind myself that the weeks it had hung in Mike's hospital room gave him solace, so it's purpose had not been wasted. For all the years that the Crucifix hung in my son's room, it provided a constant reminder of God's love for him. With those thoughts, I managed to accept the loss of this blessed and sentimental little object.

No one can prepare a person for the day that they are to view their child lying inside a casket. The viewing and rosary were to take place on Friday evening, at the little chapel within the mortuary building. When I arrived a little before 5:00 p.m. I was alone in the chapel with Matthew. I had requested that he be holding the awesome WWI army-issued rosary I had bought on eBay for his 18th birthday. He was wearing the black pinstriped dress shirt that had been lying on the ironing board in his room the day he died.

I took with me the Divine Mercy prayer book, the same little book I had carried into the emergency room that fateful day. I knelt before my beautiful son, lying there so peacefully with the antique rosary placed in his folded hands. As I took in the scene I felt myself begin to convulse. I struggled to regain control, knowing that soon the little chapel would be populated with family and friends. I proceeded to quietly read aloud the prayers from the book, looking up at his face after every so many words in hopes that he would have opened his big beautiful brown eyes.

At some point, thinking I was alone in the room, I spotted someone sitting in a pew behind me to the right. It was my dear friend and coworker, Desiree. She adored Matthew. She and Matthew shared a mutual love for Iron Maiden and were Facebook friends. She was always so caring and supportive throughout his ongoing struggles. She sat there in total reverence. Seeing her there in the chapel, the two of us alone with my boy, meant more than words can express. I will always be grateful for her quiet, loving presence, supporting me in my darkest hour.

I had informed friends and family in advance that the casket would be open between 5:00-6:00 p.m., so if that was a source of discomfort or pain, they could arrive at 6:00 for the rosary, at which point the casket would be closed. Some braved the discomfort of viewing their beloved friend and family member, while others waited until the casket was closed.

Soon, the room was full. Francesca sat with Mike, providing comfort to each other, which made me smile. Little Gracie sat with Amanda, her grandmother Liz, and Amanda's aunts. I asked my friend, Jo, to lead the rosary—the Joyful Mysteries, selecting those because his birthday is the same as the Feast of the Presentation of the Lord, which is the fourth mystery. So, Jo graciously led the rosary as we sent up the collective prayers to heaven for God's Mercy on my son's soul. There is great peace and merit in these Catholic traditions.

The following morning was the day of the memorial service. Because Matthew had not been a practicing Catholic for six years, and because of the manner in which he died, the priest suggested we do a hybrid-type memorial service. There would be the readings and the Gospel, but no Communion service. Also, with this truncated format we would be permitted to present the slideshow in the church.

I was thrilled that the local newspaper had published a story about Matthew that morning, so a friend drove to the newspaper's office to grab a stack of the papers to offer to mourners at the church. I stood out in front of the church hoping to thank people for coming. Instead, I was mentally out of it, unable to even process what was happening. I still cannot remember seeing many of the 400 people who had attended Matt's memorial; my mind just draws one big blank. A do, however, vividly remember my friend and neighbor, Laurie from two doors up, embracing me and fervently telling me, as she hugged me close, to draw some strength from her strength. How beautiful.

I also have a clear memory of his close friends, those that I asked to be the pallbearers, lined up along the wall of the church. The faces, all, were cloaked in shock, sorrow, and grief. These were young men, each just twenty-five years old, given the grim task of accompanying their deceased friend into the church.

The first person to eulogize Matthew was his baseball coach, Brett Johnson. Two of Matt's closet friends followed the coach, and then his uncle spoke. Matt's cousins bravely recited the Scripture readings, fighting back tears. But it was when the slideshow was rolling that an unforgettable moment ripped through the silence of the church that day. The slideshow progressed through the images of Matthew's childhood and teen years accompanied by John Lennon's "Beautiful Boy." When they reached the recent photos that included his beautiful daughter, suddenly there was a guttural cry from the pew about four rows behind me on the opposite side of the aisle. It was little Gracie. She was wailing, crying out for her daddy, and then asking for her Nana, me. Amanda picked Grace up and delivered her to me, where she would sit for the remainder of the service. She had connected me with her daddy, since the past year every time she got to spend time with him, Nana was there, too. So, sitting next to me during the emotional slideshow gave her a sense of peace and connection with her daddy. But I remember thinking, oh, this child's pain is just beginning.

MY 13th STATION

The reception that followed was just beautiful. The mood was somber, but not depressed. We all loved Matthew, and wanted to come together as a unit, as his fan club. People lined up to sign the large posters that John had made, and we smiled and laughed recollecting good times together with Matthew. This gathering was helpful in gently restoring the broken spirit, reminding us that Matt had touched so many lives and will live on through each one of us... especially Gracie.

The burial two days later was very difficult. It was brutal. Seeing the gravesite prepared for him was when the finality of his life on earth really hit home. I thought how someday that site will house both of us, mother and son, and that gave me a little solace. My daughters and John, our friends and family members, all of us wept in stunned silence while the priest recited the prayers for the dead over Matthew's casket. Francesca happened to snap a photo of me in my deep grief, just as I was leaning over the casket, kissing it, and placing a red rose on top. Matthew's earthly journey ended there, in that hole in the ground.

Later that week, the first week of November, I was back with Mike at the hospital, this time on the 4th floor. He was there in preparation for the stem cell transplant that involved intense chemotherapy 24/7 for a solid week prior to the procedure. Although I had already exhausted all possibilities of ever finding my son's childhood Crucifix, left here a month ago, I couldn't help but visit the nurse's station on the fifth floor just one more time. Again, I tried to describe the missing item to a nurse—this time an Asian nurse, who evidently had no idea what I was even talking about. She rifled around the drawers and stepped out to look inside an office adjacent to the station, but came back empty handed. By this point I didn't expect success, I just had to give it one last shot. With tears in my eyes I told her that it had belonged to my son, who had just passed away, and that it was very special to me. I told her that I would be visiting my friend on the fourth floor in the coming days so if they should happen to find the wooden cross to please contact us. With that I left and headed back to his room on the fourth floor.

No sooner had I arrived back in Mike's room, just sitting down to watch TV with him, that the hospital phone on his nightstand rang.

Surprised, Mike said to me, "It's for you!"

I picked up the phone, confused, while the person on the other end asked me to return to the fifth floor to look at an item that they had found. I sprinted to the elevator, praying Hail Mary's as I ascended to the next floor. The elevator door opened and there, standing behind the nurse's station, was the Asian nurse holding up Matthew's Crucifix! I just burst into tears! I could not believe that, a month after it had gone missing and given up as gone forever, someone had found it. The nurse sensed my joy and emotion, getting tears in her own eyes as I reached across the desk to hug her. Apparently, the cross was stashed away in a drawer and this crew of nurses had found it. Of course, I thanked St. Anthony, who I had been pleading with all along to find it. Now that God has returned my boy's Crucifix to me it will hang next to my bed for the rest of my life.

CHAPTER 25

Grief

THE WEEKS THAT FOLLOWED Matthew's death and burial are just a thick, gray blur in my memory. I struggled to keep up with thank you notes to all the friends and family members who graciously cooked dinners for us, gifted me with massages, housecleaning services, and dropped off my favorite wines, who pretty much propped me up emotionally during those dark days.

I am an independent person by nature, not one to ask for help. I am accustomed to using my own resourcefulness and inner strength to handle difficult life events as they pop up. During this period of my life, however, I willingly and humbly accepted the kindness that was being bestowed on me by loved ones. I knew how withered my spirit had become, deflated by not only Matthew's death, but by the cumulative weight of his battle over the last few years. Add to that my efforts to be a source of loving support for my man since his diagnosis in May and it was all just too much. I felt emotionally wiped out. So, during those days I learned how to say yes to offers of help.

During the early weeks of experiencing the intense grief that only another grieving mother would recognize, I truly resembled the walking dead. It was as if my soul had been surgically removed, and all that was left was a sad shell of me. I hesitated to leave the house because I dreaded running into someone who knew Matt or me. When I did bravely venture out to run errands, I'd cringe when I spotted someone I knew. Their outpouring of affection and sympathy, though kind and generous, triggered a flood of tears that would explode right there at the bank, the cleaners, the grocery store, the gym, shattering my carefully crafted veneer of fake normalcy. The pain was just sitting there, right below the surface, waiting for any little thing to set off a fresh cascade of tears to blow my cover.

I have a clear memory of going to the grocery store one day. It was all I could do to muster the fortitude to drive to the store and handle this mundane chore, but my cupboards were bare. Sitting there in the store parking lot, I had to give myself a pep talk just to get out of the car. I had a list of only a dozen items. I sat there staring at the list in my hand, calculating how fast I could grab the items and get back to the safety of my car. In my mind I plotted the most expedient trek through the store. It took every ounce of energy I had to open the car door and make my way into the grocers. In record time, I grabbed the necessities, got through the line, and, once back in the safe cocoon of my car, exhaled.

One of the first constructive things I did following Matthew's death was to create a My Daddy book for Gracie. I spent about two weeks gathering dozens of photos from all stages of his life, culminating with the many precious photos I had taken of the two of them over the three-year period while he was her daddy. I wanted to create a tangible testimony to his life, something that she could refer to throughout her life when curious about who her daddy was.

Interspersed through the pages of the book was a narrative, written for a child. I wanted Gracie to know about her daddy's life, with all the details that made him who he was. His best friends in childhood, his prom dates, his amazing baseball years, his favorite color, favorite animals, favorite baseball team, favorite foods, and any little detail I could think of. Most importantly, I included copies of the heartfelt letters he had written her from rehab in July 2013.

For the cover of the book, after much consideration, I selected a picture of the two of them at a stream in snowy Colorado, she in her bright pink puffy jacket and her daddy holding her hand. Near the end of the book I wrote, "Daddy suffered from a disease that made him very sad, and that no matter how badly he wanted to get better, he just couldn't, and he died." I ended that page writing, "Somehow we will manage to live our lives without Daddy, but every single hour of every day we will miss him."

There are other memories of the early grieving period that stand out. I remember one day I decided to use the generous gift card a friend had given me to treat myself to a well-deserved ninety-minute massage. How I looked forward to that massage! But while laying face down on the table, without warning, a torrent of tears began to fall to the floor as the tension was released from my body. I apologized to the therapist, telling her that I had recently lost a loved one. She was so kind, telling me to just let those tears flow. It was the body's way of releasing the sorrow stored up inside. I was grateful for her compassion.

I also remember my valiant attempts to go to Mass. Knowing that I would benefit from receiving the Eucharist. I would jot the word "Mass" on each Sunday on my calendar, fully intending to go. During the early weeks that followed Matthew's death I never even made it out of the house those Sundays. After about a month, I decided to will myself to go to church. I made it inside, only to burst into tears as soon as the music began. I made two more failed attempts before accepting the reality that I was simply not up to sitting in church yet. Eventually, about two months later, I went back to church and got all the way through the Scripture readings before falling apart when the choir started singing during the Offertory. It was no use. Finally, thankfully, I was able to return to Mass, but it was probably another three months before I was strong enough.

That first Christmas without my son was excruciating. I made no attempt to decorate the house and could barely muster up the effort to shop for gifts for my daughters, grandkids, and immediate family members. I remember one day in December, when exiting the local Walmart, spotting a Salvation Army volunteer in that spiffy white suit they always wear while ringing the little bell. In years past, I might have stopped and placed a dollar in the bucket, making no real connection with the volunteer. This year was different. I strode over to the man ringing the bell and placed a twenty-dollar bill in the bucket, and thanked him so much for helping people. I got tears in my eyes as I told him that my boy had been in their wonderful program for a little while, but, sadly, didn't make it. I told him my hope is that many people would overcome their disease through their program and live a long, fulfilling life, and wished him a Merry Christmas.

When it came time to visit my son's grave on Christmas Eve, I stopped at the store and selected a few cute little Christmas decorations and a single red rose to place on the grave where Matthew's remains had lain for two months. I remember thinking, as the smiling cashier checked out my order, how shocked she would be if she knew that these items are destined for my son's grave.

When I turned into the cemetery I was moved to tears of joy seeing the beautiful decorations that sparkled across the expansive grounds.

My heart swelled with happiness thinking that so many people remembered their loved ones at Christmas and made the effort to go there and decorate the graves. When I arrived at Matthew's grave, I saw that his dad had already beaten me to it. I added my own décor touches to his handiwork and smiled. To this day, we still join efforts, sometimes, although unplanned, showing up at the same time, to dress up our son's resting place.

One day in early 2014, a few months after Matt's passing, I had a yearning to go back to the little chapel that features the traditional Latin rite from the 1962 missal. I had attended the traditional Mass for years after discovering it in 2002, but hadn't been there in about two years. This little chapel, St. Margaret Mary's, fills up fast so I knew from experience that I needed to be there at least twenty minutes early to get a seat. Well, I must have dawdled that morning because I got there just five minutes before the Mass was to begin. My bad. I wandered up and down the aisle hoping for a spot, realizing that I would be standing or kneeling for an hour on the hard tile in the rear. My next thought was, no worries, it's my own fault; I will offer up my sore knees for my Boy Blue's soul.

    As I was standing back there waiting for Mass to begin, I noticed an usher looking at me. He held up one finger and motioned to me that he had located a spot. Yay! Thank you, Jesus! So, I walked back up toward the sanctuary and gleefully slid into the pew, taking the seat against the wall of the little church. I put down my purse and glanced up to my right only to see that I had landed, you guessed it, right under the painting depicting the 13th Station. Instantly, tears sprang into my eyes and I smiled. It was just so perfect, that I would, after a two-year absence from this church, end up sitting there, right where God wanted me.

I very much doubt that most mothers who lose a child to suicide would bother to request the police report or the autopsy results. For whatever insane reason, I needed to know every little detail regarding my son's death. As difficult as it would be to read these findings, I felt compelled to know everything. I guess I felt it would somehow help me with processing his death and arriving at some modicum of closure.

I received the autopsy report first. It was incredibly painful to read this, actually making me feel physically ill. I found myself holding my breath as I read through the pages that described each organ and part of my beloved son, including his tattoos. The toxicology report confirmed that his blood alcohol level was .25, about three times the legal limit. All other drugs listed on the panel were negative. Matthew had simply given in to the demon that fateful day, given up on life, believing the lies that Satan's minion had whispered in his ear. Sadly, he had seen no other way out.

When I received the sheriff's report, I braced myself. My primary concern was that Matt might have been listening to that satanic music as he passed away. The thought of him absorbing such vile filth at the time of his death was abhorrent to me and filled me with fear. Thankfully, there was no mention in the police report of any music playing when the sheriffs discovered him in the car. Just to be certain, though, I actually contacted the sheriff who had arrived first on the scene and asked him if he recalled any music playing in my son's car, and he said no, there was no music playing. That was a relief for me. Sadly, the police report did mention that his laptop was open on the passenger side of the car, with a photo of his daughter on the screen. Grace was the last person he was with, if only in this way, at the time of his death.

MY 13th STATION

After a couple of months had passed I began the sad task of packing up Matthew's clothes, shoes, hats, sunglasses, and miscellaneous personal effects. I opened his wallet. In addition to his driver's license, ATM card, various other cards, and $31.00 in cash was the Miraculous Medal, still tucked inside, that I had given him two years prior. This made me smile, that he had actually kept that medal on his person throughout his horrific struggles until the end.

When I carried the bag of Matthew's shoes into the house Bailey, the dog that adored him so, began to sniff the bag and wag her tail. I carefully folded each item of clothing, placing them with the shoes into two tubs, deeply breathing in the scent of my son. Two months later, Bailey was diagnosed with cancer and we had to say goodbye to this sweet companion and family member. The only thing that assuaged my sorrow was my firm belief that our dogs go to heaven, too, and that she would be reunited with Matt.

I decided to rummage through the boxes of his belongings that he'd brought with him when he came to live with me in August, still stacked in my garage. I came upon a file folder that contained the worksheets from his therapy sessions during his first rehab stint in Colorado. These worksheets provided an intimate look into his state of mind in late 2012 when he was at his worst, and were heartwrenching to read. People look at addicts or those with mental health disorders with such disdain. If only they knew what was going on in their hearts and minds!

One of the therapy exercises had the clients list traits to describe themselves prior to addiction and then after. Matt described himself before the alcoholism as "polite, happy, friendly, approachable, and fun." In his alcoholism he described himself as "lonely, sad, tired, and resentful."

In another exercise, called The Baggage Cart, he was given ten descriptions of a piece of luggage from which to select the one he self-identified with. The options included a paper bag, hardcover shell, a knapsack, luggage with wheels, softcover shell, colorful, tattered, an overnight bag, and faded color. Matt circled "faded color." The feelings that he listed as contents inside the luggage included embarrassment about his alcoholism, fear of losing his daughter, love for his daughter, family, and friends, and being proud of his daughter.

Some of his most poignant answers were on a worksheet regarding spirituality. When asked to list the things that give meaning and purpose to life, he wrote "My daughter Grace, and the rest of my family." Asked about the most special events in his life, he answered, "When Grace was born was the happiest day of my life. Also, marrying my wife, because I felt like there was a great future for us." When asked who were "the most significant people in your life," Matt replied, "My mother. She taught me how people should be treated, especially women. Also, my friends who showed me that they care about me a lot."

On the worksheet entitled "Powerlessness" Matt described how after going away to college his drinking became "much more frequent and I started smoking pot." Later, after his wife left him he "felt more lonely and isolated and the amount of alcohol consumption increased." Asked what he felt guilt and remorse for, Matt replied, "Many times I would drink while my daughter was sleeping." Also, "Being verbally abusive to my wife because I was angry when she left." He also wrote that he felt ashamed and scared "because my health is bad and I don't want to miss any more time with my daughter." He felt ashamed because "I used to be very fit and now I am fat, unattractive and unhealthy."

Regarding work (his job in Vail) he cited examples of how his disease was causing problems at work, including "Coming to work with very red eyes and not being social," "Calling in sick when I was so hung over that I got sick," "It was obvious I was hung over at work and it was embarrassing," and "Having tremors at work that I know were noticeable."

He also described how he became increasingly obsessed with drinking, the financial problems it caused, and how he hadn't been able to make many friends in Colorado because his priority was getting drunk. He wrote that he felt sad because "I am a fun, friendly person but my disease has taken that from me. I have very low self-esteem because of my physical appearance. I isolate myself so I don't have anyone to share my feelings with. I am ashamed because now I look like an alcoholic and I know my family is worried."

These are just some of the entries in his therapy worksheets, but these examples should cause us all to take a minute before condemning someone who has succumbed to addiction, and consider the person they are beneath the disease, as well as the immense emotional pain they are in. No one starts out with the goal of becoming an addict or alcoholic. Many times, the genetic predisposition toward addiction, something invisible and unknown until it is too late, directs this tragic outcome. Sometimes it is a co-occurring mental health disorder, like depression and/or an anxiety disorder, causing them to self-medicate the emotional pain away. And sometimes the lies of the devil, through the spirit of addiction or the spirit of despair, bore their way into the person's mind and seduce them into self-destructive behaviors.

A bright spot came in February, when the high school baseball coach, Brett Johnson, announced the team would be hosting an alumni tribute game to honor Matthew's memory. Usually, the high school alumni games were held in April, but Coach Johnson purposely selected February 22 for the event because Matt wore #22. Matt's friend Kevin had spearheaded a project to have an eight-foot memorial banner made that would be installed on the outfield fence where Matt played countless ball games. Kevin solicited donations from two key faculty alumni who graciously covered the cost, and Kevin himself designed the banner. On the day of the memorial alumni game, two news reporters were there to report on and take photos of the thirty-eight alumni players who showed up to honor Matt. There was a moment of silence before the game commenced. I was then asked to throw in the first pitch, which I lobbed underhanded and skyward, which we all got a chuckle out of. He sure didn't get his baseball talent from me!

Just before the game, when all the players from the alumni team were assembled on the field for a photo, I stood behind the batter's box looking through the wire fencing, just taking in the beautiful sight, and almost trying to will Matt to suddenly appear amid the group. I was wearing one of Matt's old jerseys with #22 on the back. My daughter, Sarah, snapped a photo from behind, showing me peering out onto the field wearing Matt's number, while also capturing the whole group of players. What a precious image that is.

Two of Matt's closest friends and teammates, Kevin and Mitchell, ceremoniously attached the banner to the fence, and photos were taken of the players, the coach, Grace, and me. It was an amazing event, heartwarming, bittersweet, and beautiful. All our family members, Mike and his brother, and many close friends came out for the game, as well as my fellow baseball moms from all those years we sat in the bleachers together. I felt Matt smiling down on us that day. A few days later, I got to read all about it in the paper, which included a photo of me, wearing #22 and carrying Grace out on the baseball field.

MY 13th STATION

Because I had lived in the same city for nearly three decades, raising our family here, everywhere I looked triggered memories of my boy. I was inundated daily with these emotional grenades, going off as I passed a baseball field filled with eight-year-old Little Leaguers, or Matt's favorite Mexican restaurant, or his high school campus. Everything around me, no matter which route I took through town, reminded me of my son. This was so painful that at one point I was tempted to pack up and run away, to start a new life in a new town. But in the end, I knew deep down that I needed my friends and family now more than ever before, and that it would be a mistake to leave.

Emotions were all over the map during those first few months. My days were often colored with heavy sorrow as I still struggled to process what had happened. None of it made sense to me. Interestingly, although consumed with grief, I never felt angry that Matt had taken his own life. On some level, I was certain his actions were not really his own. I even came to believe that God had allowed Matt to peacefully leave us that day. God was merciful, knowing full well that had Matt run across the freeway or laid on the train tracks to die, both of which he threatened to do when he'd relapsed, I would have never made it out of the hospital on that tragic day. I have no doubt that my poor heart could never have survived a violent, bloody end to my son's life.

My daughter, Sarah, did grapple a bit with feelings of anger, which is a very common response among suicide loss survivors. While standing in my kitchen one evening, she opened up about how angry she was that he took that selfish route instead of bravely battling his issues. I didn't attempt to discount her valid feelings. Instead, I talked to her about how much anguish he was in, how much suffering he endured every single hour, suffering that she just couldn't imagine. I shared with her the words from his suicide note, which sum up the despondency he felt about being a failure and a burden to us.

Sarah and Matthew had formed a beautiful bond once they had both become parents. They hadn't gotten along well in their teen years, but in adulthood as parents they shared a common interest that allowed them to overcome past animosities and become quite close. She cared deeply for her brother and felt robbed when he took his life, both for herself and for her little boy, Jake, who adored his Uncle Matt. I hoped that eventually her anger would be replaced with pure empathy and compassion, and although it took some time, I know now that it has.

My daughter, Emma, struggled with depression following the loss of her brother. She barely limped through the fall term at school. When it came time to show her work and be juried by classmates, they mentioned that it wasn't up to her usual standard. She had never told her teachers or classmates of her brother's suicide, instead choosing to gut it out and do the best she could without looking for excuses or sympathy. I will always be very proud of Emma for sitting there while her sub-standard work was being critiqued, and taking it like a trooper. Indeed, her grades took a beating that term. But, although emotionally raw at the loss of her big brother, Emma managed to push through the pain and eventually graduate that demanding program. He would be very proud of her.

Tragically, while I was still in a very tender emotional state, Mike, who had courageously battled leukemia for fourteen months, passed away. This was a tremendous blow, losing this beautiful human being, the love of my life, just nine months after my son's death. As God would arrange it, Mike died on July 13th, not only my birthday, but also, yet again, an important Fatima date. It was my 58th birthday, 5+8=13.

Grief became unbearable. I remember one night walking the dog along a fairly busy street while fervently praying that God would send a truck careening off the road to take me out. Losing the most significant men in my life so suddenly just crushed me. I felt like a wounded animal, barely limping though the days only partially alive.

In hopes of finding some inner peace, I set off in August for a four-day trip to Ojai, California, a beautiful valley located inland of Santa Barbara. I selected a hilltop retreat, which consisted of a small collection of quaint bungalows with sweeping views of the valley. There were no amenities to speak of; the place was simply a serene location for emotional healing.

Although I allowed myself the luxury of just lying around and getting some much needed rest, my journal entries from those four days expose the depths of my pain. Among the sad entries, I wrote about the experience of sitting in a local restaurant alone, sans Mike, feeling like a lost, lonely soul and realizing that no matter where I go I cannot escape my broken heart.

For months I had been subconsciously in denial about Matt's death. Whenever I spotted an older dark green Grand Cherokee I would stare intensely at it, attempting to will Matt to miraculously materialize in the driver's seat. I would actually check to see if it was his Jeep, looking for the "Ski Vail" sticker on the rear window. In fact, once when I went to Colorado to visit Gracie in 2014, while driving up the mountain on I-70 there was an exact copy of Matthew's Jeep following me. When I glanced in my rear view mirror I was absolutely convinced that it was Matt in the driver's seat.

I returned to my job as a staff writer for a behavioral healthcare provider. I made the purposeful decision to direct my career toward writing in the addiction recovery space soon after losing Blue. Now, following a short bereavement period after Mike's death, I forced myself to return to work. I made a valiant effort to carry on as if I was fine.

Although I tried to continue working in that corporate environment, I soon realized that the profound grief I was experiencing forced me to expend huge amounts of energy just to function there. It takes a lot of effort to pretend to be okay for the sake of your coworkers when you are actually dying inside. Some days I was unable to even think straight. Other days I simply couldn't converse with anyone. I kept pictures of Matt and Mike at my desk, so intent on not allowing the distractions of work to allow me to forget them. Counterintuitive, yes, but that is how I was able to find peace at that particular place in time.

I had enlisted the help of a grief therapist, someone who specialized in working with parents who have lost a child due to addiction. Nancy was a kind, compassionate psychotherapist who patiently endured my weekly sob-fests in her office. I was grateful to have found her, as the first therapist literally told me my issues were too much for her scope of training. Oh my. Thankfully, Nancy happily took me on, issues and all, and for a whole year she was like a guiding light as I wound through the grief journey under her watch.

Although two different physicians had encouraged me to go on antidepressants, I adamantly refused. I realize these medications can be very helpful, lifesaving even, to many people who go through depression following the loss of a loved one. But for me, I felt that experiencing the emotional pain was a necessary part of healing and didn't like the idea of changing my brain chemistry or personality with the drugs. So, I leaned on psychotherapy instead.

During one of my therapy sessions I mentioned to Nancy how difficult it was to work a nine-to-five corporate job in my emotional state. I told her I was exploring the idea of going solo, of starting my own contract writing business. She was very supportive, and told me how impressed she was that I was not dwelling in my grief, but was proactively managing it. Nancy possessed the perfect blend of compassion and guidance, and while a consummate professional, I would sometimes notice tears in her eyes when I'd talk about my son or Mike. Eventually, after a year of therapy she and I agreed that I was ready to go it alone.

After about eight months at the job, of carrying on that charade of pretending I was fine, I decided to pursue the idea of working from home. I reasoned that if I was working at home when grief overcame me I could just go with it; impulsively plop myself on the kitchen floor and sob when the waves of sorrow would inevitably wash over me. It wasn't good for me to force myself to function in a structured workplace like everything was hunky dory. I needed the freedom to grieve.

While visiting Francesca one day, I ran the idea of starting a contract writing business by her. Franny had been my co-pilot throughout the entire Matthew saga, as well as through my man's difficult cancer journey, so she had witnessed first hand the horrendous suffering it had entailed. Seriously, you had to be a very strong person to be my close friend during that stretch of time.

Franny couldn't believe I'd lasted that long in a corporate workplace while experiencing such intense grief. She encouraged me to go for it, to trust my skills and start my own freelance business. She reminded me that God would provide. I valued her opinion very much, so, in February 2015, I said a little prayer and gave my notice at work.

During that same period, to fill the empty, lonely nights, I took up making crafts and jewelry using antique and vintage Catholic holy cards and medals. Creating these little confections kept my heart squarely focused on Jesus, Mary, and the saints, which I found very therapeutic and comforting. So, in March 2015 I officially launched both small businesses, which, by God's grace and blessings, continue to thrive. This reprieve from the nine-to-five work world did not result in a reduction in work hours, but allowed me the flexibility I craved to mourn and wail at will when the grief bombs hit.

Grief is potent. It felt like I'd lost two full years, losing all awareness of month or season, mostly feeling off-balance and disoriented as one sorrowful day blended into the next. Grief is unpredictable. One day you might wake up and feel the clouds beginning to lift, only to find it a head-fake, a brief respite before slowly sinking back down into the quicksand of heartbreak. Grief takes you to unfamiliar places within yourself, to the deep caverns of darkness and despair you never knew existed.

I yearned for my son and pined for my man. Anyone who has lost someone they love understands this profound ache that pierces not just the heart, but the soul itself. While gripped in the clutches of grief, we would give *anything* to spend just one more day, one moment, with our cherished deceased.

So, about eighteen months after losing my son I was contacted by a family member who told me about a medium that she and her sister had gone to see a couple of times in the past. She began the conversation apologetically, stating that she was aware of my strong faith beliefs and would drop the subject immediately if I was uncomfortable discussing it. Interestingly, I conveniently acquired momentary amnesia, ignoring all the scriptural and magisterial admonishments regarding the occult. After all, it is clearly stated, in no uncertain terms, that as believers we are strictly forbidden to participate in any aspect of these types of psychic practices, including seeing a medium. All my life I had avoided palm readers, card readers, the Ouija board, and psychics of all kinds. But right then, in that moment, my heart leapt at the possibility of communicating with my loved ones, so I simply chose to ignore all biblical warnings and called the medium to make an appointment.

I had to wait about three weeks to get in to see him, during which time I had plenty of opportunity to back out. I began to ask friends for advice about whether to go through with the session. Some adamantly answered, "No!" while others cheered me on. I didn't know what to do, to go or not go.

I had some idea how mediums operated, mostly through episodes of *The Long Island Medium* on TV. It seemed harmless enough, so I not only decided to keep my appointment, but also, God help me, invited my daughters to join me. In the days preceding our session, I continuously prayed about it. I asked God that if going to the medium was really against His will, to somehow impede this session from happening, to make the guy sick on our scheduled date, or to cause a huge traffic jam that would cause me to miss the appointment. I told God to block me from going if it was in any way demonic. Well, no sick call from the medium or traffic jam happened, so the three of us met at his upscale office. No cheesy strip center for this medium, he was a first rate practitioner, and pricey.

On a subconscious level, aka, the Holy Spirit, we must have realized it was forbidden because all three of us admitted to feeling very nervous. Regardless, we wanted to hear from our loved ones, so in we went to join the medium for our one-hour session. The medium was a fellow in his forties with a kind and gentle demeanor. We sat across from him and, for the next hour, were completely blown away by the accuracy and detail of things he shared about our loved ones that he in no way could have known. Even Google couldn't have provided these kinds of facts and identifying details, had he been a deceiving charlatan. He was definitely not a charlatan; he was the real thing.

When the spirit of Matthew was present, the medium relayed that my son was tapping on his head, indicating that Matt suffered from mental torment. He described it as like a bad piston in a car, that his mind was mixed up and misfiring. He specified, "Depression, depressed thoughts, mental chaos." He conveyed that Matt said his, "mind wouldn't follow his intents, but rather did its own thing." He said that Matt suffered from not only depressed spirit but also anxiety. Regarding treatment, the medium said, "He is showing me that it was extremely frustrating, that nothing worked, nothing he tried made any difference, saying, "It felt like my brain was crumbling." Matt relayed that the smallest things were stressing him out, the smallest little things. He said he "had to get out of that body." He told the medium, "Now my mind isn't playing tricks on me anymore," He said he just couldn't live that way any longer.

The medium also stated that Matt got into a car and did not get out. He said he used to have a small car (Audi A4) and that he loved that car. He wants us to remember him in that car. He liked his life when he had that car. The medium suddenly asked if Matt was ever homeless. I replied, "Yes." Apparently, Matt had shown the medium an underpass or a bridge and told him "That was my home for awhile," indicating homelessness.

When my daughter Sarah asked why Matthew had picked that particular day to leave us, the medium told us that Matthew had wanted to die since age nineteen, which immediately caused me to recall the day when, at age nineteen, he told me on the phone from Colorado that he didn't want to live anymore. During the session, Matt alluded to his difficult relationship with his dad, and offered some uncanny details when speaking of his dad, including his first name. He asked us to tell his close friend, Justin, who Matt had played baseball and golf with the week prior to his death, to thank him for always caring for him and for having his back. He mentioned the three-day cruise that Justin and two other close friends had gone on after graduating high school. The medium asked if there was something significant

MY 13th STATION

about that cruise. I immediately remembered him telling me about one night on the cruise when, at about 1:00 a.m., Matt was on the upper deck. He spotted a young woman who was apparently preparing to jump overboard. He rushed to her and convinced her to not jump, to get back down on the deck. It was pretty incredible, especially in hindsight, that he would be the one to commit suicide.

At the end of the session, Matthew's "spirit" stepped behind me and hugged me, thanking me for being "the best mother, the very best mother." He said, "Tell her this had nothing to do with her mothering, this was because of my mind."

In addition to Matthew, both Mike and my sister also came through during the session, revealing stunningly accurate details that were nothing less than mind boggling.

The session was incredibly emotional, with lots of tears cried by the three of us throughout the hour, as was evident by the audio recording of the session that I later received. I left there feeling emotionally exhausted, but strangely comforted. I felt even more confident that eternal life after death is real, believing that the soul is an energy source fueled by love; and that love, our soul, never dies. The experience satisfied my desire for contact with my son and deepened my faith in the concept of life everlasting.

Soon it was Lent and time to go to confession prior to Easter. I headed to the Christ the King Institute for confession, since I always got really great spiritual direction from the priests there. These priests were not as easy on the penitent as the diocesan priests, which I actually appreciated.

While confessing my sins that day I included the fact that I had visited a medium with the desire to communicate with my deceased son. Well, the priest had a heyday with that one. He minced no words, telling me that the spirits that claim to be our loved ones are none other than demonic spirits straight from the pit of hell. He explained that there are people who do indeed have special sensitivities to the spirit realm, such as this medium, who can be used as tools of the devil to dupe us into thinking that our loved ones are either lingering here with us, or flitting back and forth between heaven and earth. He explained that upon the moment of death, our souls are immediately directed to heaven, hell, or purgatory. He assured me there are no exceptions to this biblical truth, and explained that our loved ones do not bounce back and forth between heaven and earth.

The priest told me that by being there in that room, we had exposed ourselves to dark spirits masquerading as our loved ones. Because the demons were indeed present in Matthew's life, they witnessed all of the things relayed to us through the medium in the session. Here we were so blown away thinking the medium could legitimately relay detailed minutia about our loved ones with amazing accuracy, when all he was doing was communicating what a demon spirit was conveying to him through words and imagery.

Needless to say, I vowed never to use the services of a medium again, or any other form of psychic, and dutifully said my penance. I will admit, though, to wondering at times if it really was Matthew's spirit, and Mike's and my sister's, there in the room with us that day. Still, I will humbly acquiesce to God's truths as stated in the Scriptures and choose obedience.

I was blessed with a strong survival instinct that has served me well, helping me to lurch furtively forward, even under the heaviest grief burden imaginable. There are days, however, when I am keenly aware of my vulnerability, knowing how precariously I walk that tightrope. On those days I realize I am just *this close*, as if about to cave in to it, to fall into a deep dark hole that could swallow me right up. So far, with the help of God's amazing grace, I have managed to fight my way through the worst of those despairing moments.

That first year of the grieving process wasn't all horrible; indeed it was punctuated with many beautiful moments. There were unexpected little gifts and blessings from the people who loved me and cared about my family. Sometimes a friend would suddenly appear at the door with a warm meal. A group of my close homeschool friends blew me away, delivering a little decorative tree covered in gift cards and cash gifts. My friend Jo's eldest daughter and husband sent an exceptionally generous financial gift to help me through this dark period. Friends of Mike's who had gifted us with $5000 so he could enjoy his bucket list during his remaining months, refused to take the money back when Mike passed away before he could enjoy the gift, telling me they wanted me to have it. My next-door neighbor had a beautiful custom necklace made with blue beads in honor of Blue, and two angel's wings; one wing for each of my lost fellas. Friends would treat me to lunch and then present me with sweet gifts, such as inspirational books, cards, or a meaningful trinket. My sister showed up with a gift bag full of self-pampering products, and my mom sent me a big box of the delicious Omaha steaks. My wonderful hair stylist even gave me two complimentary haircuts. I was just bursting with gratitude for the loving people in my life that each contributed so much to my healing.

One Sunday in early 2016, I walked into the church and could not believe my eyes. The church that I had been a parishioner at for fifteen years had, in the last week, added new statuary to the niche adjacent to the sanctuary. Amazingly, it was a replica of the Pietà. I took one look at it and felt the tears well up in my eyes. Of all the pieces of sculpture the church could have selected to feature in that niche, here was the image that had initially drawn me so close to the suffering of the Blessed Virgin back in 1979 when I was a fallen away Catholic visiting the Vatican in Rome. That famous sculpture that had so intimately spoken to my soul for all those years would now accompany me at Mass every Sunday. I secretly felt like it had been placed there just for me, a renewed bond between Our Lady and me. There she was speaking lovingly to me that she knows my pain, she understands my sorrow. She lost her Son, too.

A little breakthrough of sorts in my grief journey happened in mid-2016 while I was doing housework, of all things. I had recently rekindled my old habit of playing my favorite music while engaged in the drudgery of cleaning, so one day I had put on some old school R&B from the 1970s to power through my housework. While scrubbing the kitchen, and without giving myself permission, I noticed I was dancing and singing along to the tunes! When I realized that I was actually *dancing* I knew, in that moment, that I was going to survive. What power there was in that revelation! If I could survive such unspeakable pain and loss, I could survive anything.

Soon after reaching this important turning point, I added Zumba classes twice a week to my gym schedule. At first I resisted smiling along with all those other Zumba devotees during class. I mean, should I really be smiling and dancing at all, I wondered? I didn't know the moves and felt as stiff as the Tin Man before he got those squirts of oil to help his hip joints move.

But one day the Zumba instructor, a beauty who hails from Peru, exuberantly told those of us who were new and fumbling with the steps to just "fake it until you make it." This oft-used saying resonated deeply with me. I knew she meant to fake the steps, but to me it meant I should just fake my smiles until my true joy eventually returned. Today, now two years later, I dance with gusto, wearing a big, *authentic* smile on my face. I attribute Zumba classes to playing an essential role in my grief recovery.

Navigating the grief journey is a learn-as-you-go process, kind of like stumbling blindfolded among the hidden landmines that populate the fields of mourning and loss. In the summer of 2016, my friend Francesca came for a visit. We went downtown to have dinner, and did a little shopping while we were there. We ambled into a boutique where Francesca decided to try on some clothes. While she was in the dressing room, I stood just around the corner and waited.

As I was standing there, a woman, waiting for her daughter to come out of the dressing room, engaged me in conversation. I had learned to resist small talk with strangers because one of the first questions they ask as the conversation unfolds is, "So, how many kids do you have?" Each time over the past couple of years, I would swallow hard and tell the person the truth, that I have two daughters and had recently lost my son. At that point, I would have to witness their sad expression as they processed this response to their innocent question. It is a very hard call to make on the fly. You want to be honest, but it is painful and awkward to share about the death of a child, especially a stigmatized death like suicide.

Well, Francesca was taking her time in the dressing room, giving this lady ample time to get to that dreaded question. For whatever reason, I decided to lie to her. Smiling away, I told her I have two daughters, one then aged twenty-four and one who was thirty. With this omission I got to bypass the process of watching the woman, who just wanted to chitchat, awkwardly grope for the right words. At that moment, I thought that was pretty darn smart move.

Franny then emerged from the dressing room and we eventually left the store. I was sullen through dinner. I felt rotten. While she drove me home I broke down and sobbed. I felt such incredible guilt for having not acknowledged Blue, as if he had never existed. Indeed, I had "a beautiful son who would be twenty-eight," I wished I had told that lady. So, I vowed to never, ever again exclude my boy when answering that question. From that point on, I would simply state that I have three children, two beautiful daughters and a beloved son in heaven.

Sadly, in April 2017, my sweet friend and neighbor, Suzanne Peterson, lost a four-year battle with breast cancer. She was just sixty-three years old. As a matter of fact, several neighbors had untimely deaths, one as young as forty-six. Can the devil cause physical disease, too? Who knows? Suzanne was a godly woman with twinkly eyes and a huge, loving heart. I am grateful for our decades-long friendship, and our valiant teamwork in the trenches of spiritual warfare when our families were clearly under attack. I look forward to meeting her again someday in heaven.

I will always have a deep connection with the Peterson family, now scattered across the East Bay area. We shared an unusual and unfortunate space in time during which evil forces caused us to feel afraid within the walls of our homes. We, and fellow neighbors, experienced torment, pain, and loss attributed to something intangible and unseen. Now, sadly, Suzanne was gone, but these memories are permanently etched in the memories of those of us who survived.

One day in the summer of 2017, I was with seven-year-old Gracie during one of her visits to her grandparents in Rockridge. We took a day trip to the beach and found ourselves on the swings near the snack bar. Side by side we swung, soaring higher and higher. There in that moment, I was that little girl again, pumping my legs and feeling the warm ocean breeze blowing on my face and tossing my hair. Together, Gracie and I were smiling broadly as we swung back and forth in tandem, in each other's "bathtubs." I thought to myself how amazing and powerful that moment was, almost as if a second chance at life had been gifted to me, a renewal of hope—a *new* launch pad to the future.

CHAPTER 26

Return to Fatima

BACK IN JULY OF 2001, as our tour bus was pulling out of the Fatima, Portugal complex, I had promised Our Lady that I would return in 2017 for the centennial celebration of the famous apparitions at Fatima. I didn't just make a promise; it was more like a vow, an oath. I knew back then that I would definitely return to commemorate that special milestone.

Who knew, when I made that vow to return, that my life would take such twists and turns over the ensuing sixteen years? When I was in Fatima in 2001, my marriage was difficult and troubled, but I was in warrior mode, determined to make it work. I had three beautiful children then aged nine, thirteen, and fifteen, a beautiful home, a healthy family, a dog, and many wonderful friends. For all intents and purposes, my life was incredibly blessed. I had been drawn to the story of Our Lady of Fatima quite out of the blue one day in the year 1999, leading me to study the subject and become a sincere devotee of the daily rosary as a result. My pilgrimage to Fatima in 2001 was like a calling, or a mission, and even though I didn't know the exact purpose, I answered the call and made the trek with Sarah.

Oh, how Jesus and His Mother work in our lives! God knew what the fate of my son would be, and that I would need to be fortified for the pain that would someday deeply afflict me. That first pilgrimage to Fatima sparked an intense faith journey that has yet to falter.

As promised, I arrived back in Fatima, Portugal on July 11, 2017. This time Emma joined me, and we would be soon meeting up with Sarah, her husband, Cameron, and their two adorable sons. Sarah, who joined me there at age fifteen back in 2001, was now a beautiful thirty-one year old wife, mother, and middle school teacher at the local Catholic school. Introducing such a special place to Cameron, the boys, and Emma made the trip even more meaningful.

Returning there, and stepping down into that enormous quad, I immediately felt the familiar soul-level stirring, and got choked up. I was full of emotion, being back in Fatima again after all those years, saying aloud, "I made it! I made it back." I had kept my promise. Silently I prayed, "Blessed Mother, thank you for guiding me back here."

In 2017, now sixteen years older, I was a somewhat beaten down version of my former self. The casualties of my life—divorce, financial strife, and devastating loss—had taken their toll on me. But standing there that day, surrounded by strangers, each on their own personal journey, I felt totally alive and energized. I had come to give thanks with a pure heart filled with gratitude. Although I had lost my precious son and my man, I was alive with my faith intact, and still had purpose in my life.

That evening, my daughters and I purchased tall memorial candles that were to be placed in a huge pyre adjacent to the Chapel of the Apparitions. We lit the candles in honor of Matthew and Mike, sending up prayers for their souls. Cameron took our picture as we lit the candles, a poignant image of mother and daughters honoring their lost loved ones.

The next night was the amazing candlelight vigil, as beautiful as I remembered. The crowds were enormous, there to usher in the centennial anniversary of the July 13, 1917 apparition. To be there in Fatima that night was such a precious gift. Under a glorious summer sky, tens of thousands of pilgrims recited the rosary, each in his or her native language, moved by the stirring music that reached deep into our souls. The rosary and the candlelight procession were nothing short of mesmerizing.

The next morning, July 13th, was my birthday. I had to pinch myself that I was really there again, this time on my sixty-first birthday. It was a dream come true for me. We attended the outdoor Mass, replete with its pageantry and splendor. It was the topping on the cake, to be celebrating the Eucharist with thousands of pilgrims in that sacred space on this once-in-a-lifetime occasion, the centennial anniversary.

After Mass, we had lunch and strolled the little streets, poking our heads in the shops. I was on a mission to try to locate the store where, back in 2001, I had befriended the shopkeeper whose name was also Teresa. My eye was drawn toward a storefront that looked vaguely familiar to me; we entered it, and lo and behold, there she was. Amazingly, Teresa remembered me, too! She knows not a lick of English to this day, but just as sixteen years prior, we managed to communicate through Fatima love energy.

While I was "chatting" with Teresa, and she was showing me various items to consider as souvenirs, my daughter, Emma, had whipped out her sketchbook. Standing in front of a statue of Our Lady, she whipped off a beautiful drawing in a matter of minutes. I took a photo of it before she handed it to Teresa.

As we left Fatima the next morning, Emma and I off to the Algarve on the southern coast, and Sarah's gang off to Italy, I once again felt that sorrowful pang of regret, not wanting to leave. I do believe there is a mysterious spiritual connection between my soul and Fatima, Portugal, and I know in my heart I will return again someday.

CHAPTER 27

Lindsey's Story

AFTER MATT'S MEMORIAL SERVICE back in 2013, I had received a private message on Facebook from Lindsey, the girl whose family had once lived across the street from us. She is the girl who had those very dramatic raging tantrums as a young child. The family had moved away when Lindsey was twelve, after the parents divorced. After they moved, I only saw Lindsey a handful of times, and eventually we lost touch altogether.

In her private Facebook message to me she expressed deep sympathy for Matthew's death, and as I read on I was simply stunned. She wrote that she, too, had become fully alcoholic by the age of twenty, and at age twenty-two had also attempted suicide. By the grace of God, she wrote, she was saved from ruin through a powerful conversion that led her to Jesus. She attributes the fact that she is still alive today to her strong faith. I was very grateful that she was so open with me, generously sharing her own horrible experience so similar to Matt's.

Nearly five years later, when preparing to write this memoir, I reached out to Lindsey as I had the other "kids" who had lived on the street, asking if she had any memories of interesting or odd events while living on Meadow Lane for those seven years. I mentioned that I was preparing to write about Matt's struggles, which also included spiritual warfare. I reminded her that we had a practicing witch living next door to us and had experienced some strange events over the years. I didn't want to say too much or to lead her in any way, so I kept the message pretty general.

Lindsey replied the next day, saying that she never knew that the lady was really a witch. She thought the kids called her the "witch lady" because she was just really mean. She said she definitely had something to share with me but preferred we meet in person. So, we set up a date to get together the following week.

When she arrived at my house in September 2018, I wasn't really sure what to expect. After all, she and her family had moved away in 1999 and I hadn't seen her in years, except for a brief glimpse at Matt's memorial nearly five years ago. When I answered my door I was pleased to see the lovely young woman Lindsey had become. She came inside and we began to share our stories.

I began by giving her an overview of occurrences in our house, the Peterson's house, Mr. Peterson's sudden drug addiction in the late nineties, the suicides on the street, and Matt's story. She sat across from me listening very carefully, with incredible focus and a serious expression on her face. While I was describing the events, Lindsey would at times nod knowingly after something I said. Then it was her turn.

Lindsey started off by saying that, after hearing my tale it all made sense to her now. She believed that demonic spirits had undoubtedly attached to her family, too, following them to their next place of residence. She described her early teens, during which she became fascinated by goth-inspired imagery, like dragons, witches, warlocks, and darkness, even taking to drawing these dramatic images. She described how she felt compelled to sit up on the roof-deck of their home at night and burn candles, then purposely burn herself with the hot candle wax.

There was an awful sense of discord in the home due to a dysfunctional relationship between her mom and a new beau, and she felt increasingly uncomfortable and depressed. She described her sudden descent into alcoholism, how it came on very fast. With the alcoholism came all the usual consequences, such as successive job losses, promiscuous behavior, emotional instability, homelessness, and ending up married with a child at a very young age.

The marriage was doomed. The alcoholism escalated and eventually her child was removed from her. Distraught, one day Lindsey had a sudden impulse to kill herself. She felt that everyone would be better off without her and saw no reason to go on living, so she grabbed a big butcher knife and thrust it into her abdomen. Her guardian angel saved her though, as the injury she inflicted managed to only slightly penetrate the small intestine (she admits she was overweight at the time, which helped).

The following year, her behaviors became much more erratic and self-destructive, but she felt powerless over the addiction. She truly felt she was a loser and a burden to her family. She had an extremely low sense of self-esteem and was consumed by feelings of despair. One day, just six months after her first suicide attempt, she decided to end it. She hatched a plan to hang herself this time. She planned to drive to the mountains and find a remote spot, deep in a forest where no one would find her body.

As she began to drive toward the freeway, she passed a large, wooded local regional park. Suddenly, she decided that the long drive to the mountains would give her too much time to think and possibly allow her to change her mind, so, she impulsively pulled into the park. She drove through the park seeking a distant corner within the property, and located a tree with a tall enough branch to complete the suicide.

Lindsay climbed up the tree and prepared the rope. She didn't know how to make a noose so she wound the rope several times around her neck and tied it off, certain that it would do the job. She had typed two text messages on her phone, one to her mother and one to her now ex-husband. She hit "send," threw the phone down on the ground, and jumped.

Lindsey said that after what seemed like about a minute, "it got dark." The next thing Lindsey remembers was glancing down at her body from above, seeing the lower part of her body faded out and the upper part in clear focus. She turned her glance upward and felt herself traveling straight up, entering an energy field of immense static and turmoil before spotting a bright, pure white light. Immediately Lindsey was enveloped in a blissful sense of peace and joy, feeling completely at rest. She said she could not begin to describe it, as there is nothing here on earth to compare it with, this sublime joy.

She delighted in this amazing essence of light and love for what she thinks was just a minute or two before feeling herself being physically pushed downward. She described it to me as a huge spiritual hand that forced her back down, pushing her back down through the static and noise. Lindsey started fighting this, angrily yelling, "Let me go, let me go!" over and over.

She then heard a powerful but loving voice say, "Lindsey, it is not your time."

Meanwhile, a woman running after her off-leash dog in that section of the park happened upon Lindsey hanging there from the tree. As consciousness began to return, Lindsey became aware of her screams for help. As God would have it, an off-duty female police officer jogging through the park heard the woman's screams for help and rushed over. She quickly cut the rope and took Lindsey down, and began to administer CPR while they waited for the ambulance.

Lindsey began experiencing pain and just wanted to go back to sleep, trying to will herself back to that celestial state, but couldn't.

MY 13th STATION

She slowly regained consciousness, hearing the police officer state, "I got a pulse," and "Okay, she's breathing." Lindsey remembers the lady officer asking her questions, after opening Lindsey's wallet, to test her cognitive functions, such as "What is your name," and "Tell me your address." Soon, after, the paramedics arrived and Lindsey was placed on a 5150 72-hour psychiatric hold at a local hospital.

For another year, Lindsey would continue to struggle on and off with her addiction and mental health issues before finally getting sober. Her life had been reduced to living out of her car. In December 2011 Lindsey decided to attend an A.A. meeting and told her story to the group. After relaying the years-long struggle with addiction, depression, and suicide attempts she humbly asked for help. A female attendee stepped up, telling Lindsey that she had a neighbor who might be willing to take her in.

The woman's neighbor, Kristine, agreed to have Lindsey come and stay with her while she looked for a job and got back on her feet. A Christian woman, Kristine also invited Lindsay to join her at Sunday service. Lindsey wasn't quite ready for religion though, so she politely declined the invitation. But Kristine just kept inviting her until three months later on Easter Sunday Lindsey finally acquiesced and accompanied her to the Easter sunrise service. On that day, Lindsey felt driven by the Spirit to submit her entire life to the care of Jesus Christ, and has remained sober now for seven years.

Lindsey emphatically believes that she had been under diabolical attack and that it was likely launched while living there those years on Meadow Lane. The evil that was pervading our section of the neighborhood, stoked by a wicked woman who'd intentionally wished us harm, had been incredibly successful. Both Matthew and Lindsey's trajectories ran an uncannily parallel pattern, although Matt had no symptoms until his freshman year in college where Lindsey displayed erratic behaviors at a young age.

Lindsey visited a deliverance ministry, in response to the guidance of a pastor. Her deliverance experience was very intense, attributable to the high degree of psychic attack that she had been under since childhood. She described herself during the deliverance process as "flopping around on the floor like a fish."

With her permission, I am sharing her story as a final punctuation point in the long list of strange occurrences and serious afflictions that have taken place on Meadow Lane. Although Lindsey has struggled through so much torment and countless trials in her short thirty-one years, thankfully, God's pure love for His child has prevailed and she has returned to Him.

CHAPTER 28

Spiritual Warfare

"I AM NOT STRONG ENOUGH." "I am a failure." "I am weak." These were the words my son used on the last day of his life, conveyed to his three-year old daughter in a letter, a text message (through her mother), and in a thirty second video message he recorded on his iPhone while waiting for the carbon monoxide to put him to sleep. The devil had convinced him that his life was not worth living, that his daughter would be better off without him. The lies of the devil tormented Matthew incessantly, causing mental turmoil, confusion, and finally, his decision to give up the fight.

Addiction is a spiritual disease, a symptom of a wounded soul. Oh, the medical community assures us it is a disease of the brain, and there is no doubt that the structure of the brain's chemistry and neural pathways are altered due to alcoholism. But what sets up the compulsion to drink in the first place?

Of course anyone reading Matthew's tragic story could point to a number of natural causes that led to his demise. Yes, there is some alcoholism in our family—I think most families would have to admit to this. Yes, there is some depression on my side of the family. And yes, there was a family member also took their own life at age fifty-four. Yes, our family endured divorce and the subsequent discord and sadness that so often follow divorce. Yes, Matthew was brokenhearted when his marriage ended. Taken as a whole, the case could indeed be made that Matthew's short life was the result of bad genes and heartbreak.

He truly wanted sobriety, he knew he *needed* sobriety to survive, but he could not get the demon off his back. It taunted him relentlessly, goading him, tempting him. The demon stops at nothing to take a soul down, to destroy someone baptized in the Holy Spirit. Since his teens, Matt had absorbed so much evil messaging tucked into the dark music he was exposing his soul to that he had become desensitized to it. Between the menacing music and the demonic imagery he tattooed onto his skin, he had put out a welcome mat for dark spirits to become the ugliest of houseguests. He just didn't know he had.

The spirit world is real. All around us exist invisible beings, both angels and demons, abiding in a space between the earth and heaven called the preternatural realm. While difficult to grasp and accept, our efforts to deny the existence of these celestial beings are truly made in vain. Admittedly, it is hard to imagine that wherever we are there is an invisible world layered right over that which our eyes can see. But, believe it or not, this realm exists.

In the case of our family's story, we had someone living next door literally summoning dark spirits and placing curses on various neighbors, including us, and possibly the whole street. It is safe to say that our section of the street was infested with demonic activity that resulted in emotional affliction, mental chaos, addiction, and despair.

Lest anyone attempt to deny the reality of the devil, Blessed Archbishop Fulton Sheen's comments can offer a cogent reminder:

> Do not mock the Gospels and say there is no Satan. Evil is too real in the world to say that. Do not say the idea of Satan is dead and gone. Satan never gains so many cohorts as when, in his shrewdness, he spreads the

rumor that he is long since dead. Do not reject the Gospel because it says the Savior was tempted. Satan always tempts the pure—the others are already his. Satan stations more devils on monastery walls than in dens of iniquity, for the latter offer no resistance. Do not say it is absurd that Satan should appear to our Lord, for Satan must always come close to the godly and the strong—the others succumb from a distance.[6]

One of the most important lessons I have learned from my son's tragic sufferings is that evil spirits, such as the spirit of fear, the spirit of anxiety, the spirit of self-hatred, and the spirit of suicide can latch on and overwhelm the unaware, unsuspecting victim. The suicidal thoughts are not their own, they are the result of the demon methodically whispering these thoughts in the victim's ear. It is a misconception to believe that a demon would, for example, push someone off a building. On the contrary, the demon, through its lies and deceptions, convinces the person to jump off on their own volition.

For a basic understanding of the demonic realm, a mini-primer on the topic is helpful. This is important information, as most people are simply unaware of the dangers our souls may be in.

I. How Satan's evil spirits can gain a foothold or stronghold in your life:
- Habitual sin. The world tempts us with all sorts of goodies that are nothing more that sinful activities or behaviors wrapped up in a veneer of worldly delight. We are fed a daily diet of tantalizing opportunities to sin, and using our free will, we may succumb. These temptations can be provided and perpetuated

by evil spirits, encouraging us to acquire sinful habits that take us further from God.
- Trauma. Traumatic events that cause intense feelings of fear, anxiety, anger, or guilt have the potential to leave deep scars on the soul. An evil spirit seizes the opportunity to attach itself in a moment of weakness. Because the pain of the traumatic event is stored in the soul, an evil spirit can entice a person to eventually turn to drugs, alcohol, or other addictive behaviors to ease the pain.
- Occult practices. Participation in or exposure to occult practices can result in direct contact with evil spirits. These activities might include practicing Wicca, witchcraft, new age practices, Transcendental Meditation, visiting fortune tellers, psychics, mediums, tea leaf readers, palm readers, card readers, or using Ouija Boards. Practicing any form of the occult, or being present when occult practices are taking place, can open up a direct portal to dark spirits.
- Exposure. Being consistently exposed to the sinful behaviors of another can create vulnerability. Living in families where there is substance abuse or addiction, physical, sexual, or psychological abuse, manipulative behaviors, or exposure to pornography or adult entertainment as a child, can give evil spirits a stronghold by setting up a sense of confused values, making one vulnerable to sin.

II. Types of diabolical involvement:
- Oppression. Diabolical oppression can range from mild to severe, and is usually recognized by afflictions caused by an evil presence in the victim's life. These oppression-related sufferings can impact health, relationships, the family, or one's career. The appetite might be stoked to participate in evil activities

related to pride, lust, carnal appetites, drug or alcohol abuse, pornography, or the occult, while the demon whispers lies that these activities are acceptable. With oppression, demons may manifest as a dark cloud or shadowy black figure, or give the sense that someone is watching them. The incubus attack, when a demon assaults the victim in their sleep, is a sexual type of demonic attack. With oppression there is no involuntary action or possession of the person.

- Obsession. Diabolical obsession involves sudden or ongoing attacks of the mind. To some degree the victim has lost function of their will, and giving themselves over to whatever the obsession is, such as addiction or suicidal thoughts. The obsessive thoughts may be irrational or absurd, but the victim seems powerless to shake them off because an evil spirit has attached itself to the victim's will. The demon's temptations and the victim's weakened will allow for power to be yielded to the evil spirit and self-destructive behaviors and desperation can result. The demon's lies such as, "You will never overcome addiction," can prompt suicidal thoughts and attempts. The victim cannot distinguish between their own thoughts and the thoughts that are introduced by the demon. Diabolical obsession can be the result of a curse, or contact with cursed objects.
- Possession. Diabolical possession occurs when the devil has taken up residence within the victim's body. The evil spirit can exert control over the actions of the victim. Those who are demonically possessed may appear normal at first glance, but they reveal the evil within through certain behaviors. They may acquire a deep, or growling voice, speak in languages the person doesn't know, have supernatural strength, has knowledge of things they couldn't otherwise know, and recoil at any sign

of holiness. The victim is under the control and influence of the evil spirit, and is unable to throw off the demon. An exorcist is the only hope for someone who is demonically possessed. The Rite of Exorcism is the ritual sanctioned by the Catholic Church to assist the possessed individual. Exorcists are specially trained to perform the Rite, and many archdioceses and also the Vatican have trained exorcists on staff.

III. Signs of demonic presence
- Foul odors. Sudden wafts of strong putrid odors, such as rotten flesh, decomposing animals, sulfur, human feces
- Shadowy figures. Sightings of black or dark shadowy forms that vary in size and shape, and may move by lurching at supernatural speed
- Nausea. An overwhelming sense of nausea when being in an oppressed home or room
- Voices or whispers. Hearing voices in one's ear, speaking in a language unknown or in one's native tongue
- Knocking or banging sounds. Knocking sounds that come from inside the walls without an explanation
- Unusual pet behavior. Dogs may be barking at something not visible, or exhibit aggressive behavior like growling at something unseen by its human
- Sudden drops in temperature. A sudden chill in a room for no reason; no window or door open to allow for a cold wind
- Noises. Strange sounds such as rattling, shuffling, growling, creaks
- Sense of dread. An overwhelming feeling of dread or doom when entering an oppressive house or room
- Difficulty praying. Experiencing mental disturbance while attempting to pray

- Moving objects. Items that have been moved to another location without explanation

In late 2014, I decided to contact a deliverance ministry. Why? Because, even though I had not sensed any presence of darkness or evil or experienced any strange events since October 2013, I wanted to be totally sure that there was nothing attached to me! I realize this may sound paranoid, but after all that had happened, it just felt like an insurance policy to me. So, Nancy, my grief counselor, referred me to a local deliverance ministry. Deliverance is not intended for people who are possessed by a demon, it is for casting out generational sin and for liberating someone who has a demonic attachment—a hanger on, so to speak. So, I contacted the ministry and made an appointment, not really knowing what to expect.

This was a husband and wife team with a lengthy history of deliverance ministering that performed their services out of a non-denominational Christian church. We met in a small conference room where we had privacy for the deliverance process. I admit I felt a little apprehensive going into their office, not knowing what exactly deliverance ministers do. They asked me to fill out a very detailed accounting of all my past sinful inclinations and sins, asked if there was any family history of mental illness, suicide, abuse, addiction, and more. It was disturbing, and embarrassing, to have to write down an accounting of past sins and bad behaviors, but I figured this must be the roadmap they use when homing in on each particular demon that might be attached to a person through generational sin or mortal sins committed during one's lifetime. It was not a comfortable experience filling out that long questionnaire.

The ministers did prep me by explaining what was to transpire and how I was to clearly and honestly answer each question as the process unfolded. They warned me that the process is very intense, but necessary, as they are confronting evil spirits and casting these entities off of me, should any be lurking. They prepared me, saying that sometimes the process makes clients nauseas and that I may actually vomit. They told me that some people cry, some shake and shiver, some collapse to the floor, and various other strange responses that can happen as the evil spirits are cast out.

Well at that point, feeling freaked out, I almost got up and left. But then I decided, no, after what I have been exposed to the last twenty-three years I would be stupid not to make absolutely sure that there was nothing attached to me in any way. So, I hung in there.

The male proceeded to forcefully, loudly, name each and every evil spirit related to all my particular sins and generational sins and demanded that they exit in the name of Jesus Christ. The woman chanted prayers over me all the while. It was very surreal. I never threw up but at one point my right leg twitched and right arm began to tingle and shake. That was very bizarre. So I guess that indicated that there was *something* hanging on to me.

I left there feeling light and safe. I marveled at my bravery in doing this thing, so far outside of my comfort zone. But even though it was a bizarre experience, I felt it was a necessary ending to a period in my life when evil had invaded my home and harmed my family so grievously.

Remember the dirt that appeared inside Matt's bedroom doorway on two occasions during the last two months of his life? To remind the reader, I had lived in that house for twenty-two years by 2013. I had never seen any dirt accumulate inside any of our door jams, the wood framing of an interior door, ever, until that August in 2013 after Matt returned home to live with me. I had wiped it off, thinking it was odd at the time. But the day he died the dirt was back, just two months after the first appearance, and one week after I had detected the heavy evil presence over my house. Instinctively I was certain it was some sort of residue from the demon that was attached to my son. To further drive home the point, since Matt's death, the dirt has never reappeared.

This summer, nearly five years later, I located the baggie that contained the rag with the dirt on it and contacted a lab to have the specimen analyzed. I asked the chemist if it had been too long to get an accurate reading of the elements. He seemed to think not, and suggested I mail the cloth to him. He said once he sees the smudges he can determine if the sample is viable to analyze.

When the chemist received the sample he called me and said that there is, indeed, sufficient material to analyze. I could tell he wondered why I would spend $300 to analyze what appears to be simple dirt smudges, so I told him that I am mostly interested to know if there is any sulfur in the sample. He asked in what geographic location the sample was collected. After telling him where the house is located he stated that it was unlikely that the household dirt sample would include sulfur. This Ph.D. chemist explained that sulfur might be present inside homes that are in proximity to natural sources of sulfur, such as near a volcano or hot springs, where ours is not. Still, I proceeded to move forward with the analysis.

You may wonder what the significance of sulfur is, and why would that have any bearing on this narrative. While researching demonology for this book I read in several sources that traces of sulfur were sometimes found in locations where there has been recorded demonic activity. This is also referenced in the phrase, fire and brimstone, a reference to hell, with brimstone as an archaic term to denote sulfur.

When I received the chemical analysis I couldn't decipher it, as it was written with those long-forgotten elemental table abbreviations we all had to memorize in high school. So I emailed him and asked that he provide me with a key describing the chemicals for each symbol listed. When he did, I admit I was a little freaked out. Sulfur *was* on the list. Not sulfur dioxide or sulfites, but sulfur. Of course, I cannot use this analysis to prove a thing, but I add it to an already long list of other unnerving supernatural phenomena that occurred in the house.

> "Now in my vision this is how I saw the horses and their riders.
> They wore red, blue, and yellow breastplates,
> and the horses' heads were like heads of lions,
> and out of their mouths came fire, smoke, and sulfur.
> By these three plagues of fire, smoke,
> and sulfur that came out of their mouths a
> third of the human race was killed."
> REVELATION 9:17-18

In June 2018, just as I was gathering material to write this book, I attended an event at my parish. Outside the hall stood Fr. Matthew, the priest who six years prior had exorcized my house! I had not seen him since that day, as he had moved on to become pastor at a church in the next county.

I approached him, wondering if he would even remember me. I shook his hand and asked if he recalled visiting my house in 2012 to expel evil spirits, and he said he did. He asked how everything turned out, so I told him the sad news that Matthew died a year later there at the house. I told him I regretted not contacting him as he had instructed me in the event I felt the return of the dark spirits, and shared with him how, one week before Matt took his life, I had indeed sensed the presence of evil once again. I explained to him

MY 13th STATION

how I attempted to manage the situation on my own because I was overwhelmed with my loved one's cancer treatments and exhausted from the ten hours a day spent at the hospital. He consoled me. Just then, someone approached him and our conversation ended. But right before we parted he looked at me and said, "Yes, spiritual warfare is very real."

When Fr. Matthew had posed his theory back in 2012, that I was the ultimate target of the demon, I didn't really grasp it fully. I do now. Satan hates the souls who cling to God. He despises those who seek holiness through devotions and prayer, especially the daily rosary. And for those who sit in Eucharistic Adoration there is a huge bulls-eye on our backs. The devil will stop at nothing to take a person like me down, even destroying my child.

Even with all we went through, I do not fear the devil. I am clothed with grace and suited up with the full Armor of God. My guardian angel protects me 24/7. Nothing will ever succeed in taking my faith from me. It is my treasure, a gift from God.

> "Finally, draw your strength from the Lord and from his mighty power. Put on the armor of God so that you may be able to stand firm against the tactics of the devil. For our struggle is not with flesh and blood but with the principalities, with the powers, with the world rulers of this present darkness, with the evil spirits in the heavens. Therefore, put on the armor of God, that you may be able to resist on the evil day and, having done everything, to hold your ground."
>
> EPHESIANS 6: 10-13

CHAPTER 29

God's Plan

GOD IS THE ETERNAL MASTER POTTER. He shapes the clay vessel held lovingly between His hands, the ultimate look and shape it eventually takes unknown until it is finally revealed in His perfect timing. Meanwhile, we are to trust as He kneads us over time into the desired shape. Only God knows what His plans are for us, where He is leading us. He knows our life path before we take a single step, and has assigned us each our own unique gifts and talents to help us successfully navigate that path and make it to heaven.

As for me, looking back on my life story, I can see how God has been masterfully equipping me for a much more challenging existence than what my lowly little mind would have ever guessed. Back in my twenties, all I had wished for was to be a small business owner, to have kids, and to have a nice, normal, intact family. How little I knew of what was actually in store for me.

Since reclaiming my Catholic roots twenty years ago, and then methodically acquiring the knowledge that would teach me the nuts and bolts of my faith, I have been on a personal journey toward holiness, in fits and starts, warts and all. I am a flawed, struggling sinner like anyone else, but I refuse to abandon hopes of doing better, stubbornly striving to achieve a higher, more refined state of holiness. We are created to be givers, to be loving servants of God and neighbor, a role that I have embraced in the aftermath of losing my son.

I find it fascinating how the paths we take in life seem to eventually coalesce into something seemingly preordained. God gave me a gift for expressing thoughts, facts, opinions, and just random musings using the written word, which I have been dutifully utilizing in the role of a freelance writer since the mid-nineties. My education happened to be in the humanities, so I have a general knowledge—very general—of psychology and the various treatment modalities employed for treating mental health disorders. For six years, I got a firsthand and very intimate look at what addiction and mental health disorders look like up close. These life experiences now come together, by God's design and perfect timing, to allow me to help others using my acquired skill set.

So, with God's careful preparation, I can now devote the majority of my writing career, about eighty-five percent of my work, to the fields of addiction, mental health, and dual diagnosis. I produce content for a myriad of clients in this realm to honor my son's memory by informing and inspiring others to get the help they need before it is too late. After several years of firsthand experience and study I have become a fairly knowledgeable resource for others who may need some guidance. I hope to educate parents who may not yet recognize the signs and symptoms of substance abuse in their child. I want to discuss these sensitive issues openly to help reduce the stigma associated with them, allowing for honest dialogue and encouragement for those afflicted. I hope to increase suicide prevention awareness. I want to help save lives.

For those parents in the throes of the hellish nightmare of having a child with a substance use disorder, I hope to be a sounding board and source of support. I know all too well the roiling undercurrent of fear that these parents live with each and every day. I know about the thin veneer of "normal" pinned on their faces like a cheap mask, hiding the constant dread of the next shoe to drop. I know that for these parents, any momentary peace they are gifted with is clutched with a vise grip, because in an instant that peace can be obliterated. I know these parents' suffering, and I want to share what I have learned through my own experience, including how crucial it is to attend to self-care, to protect one's own mental wellness, and to learn to "detach with love."

Living through Matthew's illness has left me very sensitive to others who suffer. One day, I was stopped at a signal in front of the local Costco. A pedestrian began to cross the street and while I watched him slowly walking I felt tears come to my eyes. This young man, in his late twenties, was clearly an alcoholic. I recognized the ruddy skin tone, the bloated belly, the glassy eyes. My heart went out to him. I thought to myself, he is someone's son, someone's best friend, or brother. He might be someone's daddy. I wanted to jump out of my car and plead with him to go get help. Instead, I just said a little prayer for him, that he finds his way to treatment, and to God.

In our local communities, it is hard to ignore the escalating drug overdose deaths and suicides among young adults. It is as if Satan has engaged an all-out demonic assault on our young people, trying to drag down an entire generation with his lies and deceptions. Too many parents are burying their children, each with their own sorrowful tale to tell. What we parents have in common is that we adored our kids, no matter what mess they had may have made of their lives. No matter how afflicted, addicted, and sinful, we parents never stop loving these cherished, if troubled, souls that God had gifted us with.

As someone who is, unfortunately, familiar with the grieving process, I have occasionally been called upon to write about my personal grief journey. These requests were very difficult for me to accept at first. My knee-jerk response to such a request, to write about, say, approaching the holidays without my son, or enduring Mother's Day minus a child, was usually a quick "no way." But each and every time, I would eventually deliver the goods. Though I would sit at the keyboard bawling my eyes out while writing these tender articles, I learned that doing so offered me an opportunity to not only process my own pain, but to also be of help to others who are dealing with loss.

Through my artwork, I also find opportunities to serve others. It gives me so much pleasure to know that my humble creations now hang on people's walls. In repurposing antique prayer cards and other vintage religious items, I love that these precious objects are finding their way out of dusty attics and back out where they can be enjoyed as visible sources of grace again.

God has abundantly blessed me with my two wonderful daughters, Sarah and Emma. In addition to Grace I also have three other grandchildren, all four of whom are the light of my life. In these precious children I can see God's imprint. With each birth, I could almost hear Him say, "Here you go, my faithful servant, here is another gift from Heaven."

> "God is faithful and will not let you be tried beyond your strength;
> but with the trial he will also provide a way out,
> so that you may be able to bear it."
> 1 CORINTHIANS 10:13

CHAPTER 30

Matthew's Legacy

WHEN WE HEAR THE WORD LEGACY it might conjure up thoughts of a long life well lived, someone who has made a major contribution to society. Someone's legacy may refer to a significant career accomplishment, the creation of great works of art, or of authoring some important public policy. Some people may connect the word legacy with financial bequests, as in money or property left to heirs or institutions. So what kind of legacy could a twenty-five-year-old young man who died by suicide, penniless, unemployed, and drunk, possibly leave behind?

I understand why some might question the title to this chapter, with the indisputable facts of Matthew's state, his life in shambles at the end. But limiting one's focus to those sad facts ignores the much bigger picture of who my son was and how he impacted the people within his sphere during those twenty-five short years. It also ignores the most obvious legacy, his daughter, Grace.

It is not due to my total lack of objectivity that I make the claim that his little girl is incredibly special, because special she is. Gracie is now nine years old and physically resembles both parents in equal parts. This means that Grace is a beautiful child, tall and graceful and poised beyond her years. Grace is smart as a whip, affectionate, talented, and keenly perceptive. But it isn't her physical beauty or innate intelligence that make the child unique. It is her spirit.

Here is a young girl who has experienced not only family instability and strife throughout her childhood, but whose daddy died by suicide when she was just three and a half. We all—her family members, her mom, and her teachers—just marvel at her coping skills, resilience, and level headedness, putting most adults to shame. She sees only goodness in anyone and everything, and openly articulates her observations about the goodness she witnesses in the people she encounters. In church, she sings passionately and prays fervently at my side. When I take her to church, we always stop to say a Hail Mary at the beautiful statue of Our Lady of Grace near the entrance, sometimes bringing flowers to leave there. On our walk over to the statue, there is Gracie turning cartwheels as she approaches the shrine. She is joy-filled, and absolutely emanates what her daddy wrote to her on his last day, that, "You are the very best of me."

When Grace and I are together we celebrate her daddy's life in many little ways. We mention him in conversation often, keeping him alive in our consciousness. She knows that his favorite Ninja Turtle was Leonardo, that his favorite color was green, and that he loved Nana's tuna casserole and BLT sandwiches. We have decided that the yellow butterflies we see floating by when we are together represent her daddy saying hello. She sleeps with his "polka dot doggy," Matt's favorite stuffed animal from his childhood. When she plays on softball teams she always requests the #22 jersey in his honor. Grace will continue to radiate her daddy's spirit throughout her life. I look forward to seeing how she will use her many gifts. This amazing Grace is Matthew's primary legacy.

Matt's legacy also includes the permanent mark he left on the hearts of those he cared about. His kind, loving disposition resonated with so many people who now carry his memory around with them. To this day, I still receive occasional emails and Facebook messages from Matt's closest friends. They write to share a dream they had of him, or to tell me they have been feeling him around of late. I was invited to Kevin's wedding this summer and, after the ceremony, when I approached him and his bride, he put his arms around me and sobbed. To him, my being present was as if one of his best friends, someone he misses deeply, was attending the most important day of his life. Another of his closest friends, Mitchell, got married last year. He reserved a front row seat by placing on it the carefully folded #22 jersey that I had given Mitchell after Matt died, with a small sign that read, "Reserved for Matt Anthony."

The impact Matt made on the lives of his friends was profound. In the days and weeks following his death many reached out to me. Here are just a few of the sentiments conveyed:

"My heart is broken in losing one of my best friends in Matt." [close friend]

"Your son helped my son who was also in recovery, offering to him help, and gave him rides to meetings and back home." [mom of a fellow A.A. member]

"He was all heart." [neighbor in Vail]

"Your son was an angel on earth." [high school friend]

"Matt was always one of the stand up guys and I cannot imagine what was happening in his life that lead to this" [one of the baseball dads]

"I will never forget the special times I got to share with Matt and the memories we made through baseball." [former teammate]

"I am brokenhearted over the loss of a beautiful person." [coworker]

"I didn't know Matt as a father, but if he was a dad to Grace the same was he was a son to you or a brother to Sarah and Emma, or a ball player, then he must have been the best dad ever." [childhood friend]

"Melanie [his senior year prom date], my husband, and I have always thought very highly of Matt. He was such a good person" [from Melanie's mom]

"Matt was a wonderful human being that I loved dearly" [his first girlfriend]

"I will always remember Grace's pure joy at seeing her daddy. She loved him so dearly. He will be forever in our hearts" [Amanda's mom, Liz, Matt's mother-in-law]

"Matt was just a doll—you raised an amazing man." [coworker]

"I ache knowing your daughter will never get to know the sweetest man, and that your mother lost the biggest part of herself" [friend to Matt on his Facebook wall]

"Matt was one of the coolest guys and nicest friends I have ever had." [friend]

"He will always be the brother I always wanted. I loved him dearly." [Amanda's sister]

"Even though Matt and Amanda did not stay together he became a part of our family forever. We all loved and cared about him and prayed for his happiness after they split. But know he will live on through his beautiful daughter and we will never let her forget how much he loved her." [Amanda's aunt]

"I, and the A.A. community are deeply saddened with the loss of Matt. I shared his story at a meeting last Saturday and it touched many, and made an impression on a number of newcomers. Matt has made a difference in our lives." [Matt's sponsor]

"He was my best friend. He was so beautiful and perfect" [Amanda]

Matt has gifted all of us with a treasure trove of beautiful memories. We will carry them with us, throughout our lives, those profoundly edifying moments we were blessed to spend with this beautiful soul. When sharing our memories of Matt, sometimes we laugh and sometimes we cry, but either way we *feel* him. We feel his love with us at every gathering, and we smile at the mention of his name.

And finally, Matt's legacy includes the lesson, even the warning, which he has left for us all to ponder. No matter what was the reason that he ultimately lost the will to live, whether due to the consequences of addiction and depression or due to demonic attack, it is clear that the role of faith is intrinsic in overcoming trials and adversities. Only by attaching our wagon to God's love, and subordinating our will to His will, do we have the fortitude to survive the slings and arrows that could otherwise take us down. Sadly, Matt was not practicing his faith those last six years of his life—and oh how much he truly needed God.

Matt's legacy serves as an urgent reminder for us to recognize that there is evil in the world, and that it often comes in the guise of pleasures and past-times that are not aligned with goodness. Whether it is the music we listen to, how we speak, how we comport ourselves in the world, what movies or Internet content we expose our souls to, or the tattooed images we brand on our bodies, these are the ways we push ourselves further and further away from God. Spiritual warfare *is* real. Let Matthew's story be a lesson for us all to have a healthy fear of evil, to be able to recognize it for what it is and cling to Christ and His Blessed Mother every step of the way.

On New Year's Eve back in 1999 the whole world was on pins and needles in anticipation of Y2K (aka, the year 2000). A crazed fear had seeped into the collective consciousness that pandemonium would break loose on the first day of the new millennium. This was predicted because of a glitch discovered in computer programming that would, the prognosticators warned, result in pure chaos when the clock struck midnight on 1/1/2000. Most people took this theory with a grain of salt, but still, there was some lingering, and legitimate, concern that something bad might actually happen.

As did many people that New Year's Eve, we attended a party with friends and family members to celebrate the quirky incoming of the New Millennium. The hostess of the party handed out questionnaires to the children present to fill in answers to questions about their favorite things and tidbits about themselves, accompanied with firm instructions not to open the envelopes until the year 2025. Matt was eleven.

After his death I found his Y2K time capsule when packing up his belongings, still in his top dresser drawer all those years later.

I opened the still-sealed envelope. Among the various questions about his favorite this or that, were these:

#7. Who do you admire most? *My mom and my dad*

#9. What do you want to be when you grow up? *A baseball player*

#12. Describe yourself. ***I am a person***

THE END

Afterword

SOMEDAY I WILL LOOK BACK on these past months and be amazed that I was able to persevere through the indescribable emotional pain that writing this book entailed. During the final few weeks of writing, having to revisit such painful memories, I could see in my haggard, drawn face the toll it was taking on me. It had felt for weeks like I was tugging around a wagon loaded with a huge, heavy, bloody, broken heart—the weight of it was nearly unbearable.

Interestingly, although so very difficult, I found that going through the arduous process of parsing each twist and turn of Matthew's story was extremely therapeutic. This endeavor turned out to be more helpful to me than the entire year of grief therapy, as it forced me to really process the trauma that has been sitting just beneath the surface since his first suicide attempt when jumping off that building six years ago.

While sifting through my old journals and recounting the disturbing events in the manuscript, I realized in hindsight that I had been engaged in a vicious spiritual battle during the entire time my family lived in the house until Matthew's death. As my faith grew deeper over the years, the intensity of this spiritual warfare ratcheted upward, the stakes getting higher and higher. I do believe that the evil one sought to take me down through any means, culminating in his final diabolical attack, convincing my son to end his life.

In reading the journals I also revisited the unusual events I experienced and wrote about as my faith deepened, so carefully documented within. For example, the amazing glimpses of the face of Jesus in the Exposition of the Eucharist in my little Adoration chapel on various occasions. Certainly, those were likely figments of my imagination, or of my eyes playing tricks on me. But at the time I experienced each occurrence, it seemed absolutely real. In fact, since 2004, I have not seen His face, even though I attend Adoration at the same chapel, with the same tabernacle, lighting, and monstrance all these years since—and trust me, I look for His face every week, yearning to see it again. Regardless, whether these perceived "visions" were real or not doesn't matter. The fact is that I was completely enraptured while in His presence, and that was undeniably real. Still is.

Matt's suicide remains a dagger in my heart, a special kind of suffering reserved just for the mother of the deceased child. During all the years that Matthew battled the depression and alcoholism, after falling away from the Church, I prayed so hard for him. I know that God heard this mother's prayers and will honor them. I have to believe that in His Infinite Mercy, God will eventually permit Matthew's soul to enter heaven's gate. My prayers were not, and are not to this day, wasted. Knowing that, I continue to pray for God's mercy on my son, who'd committed the grave sin of suicide. With a mother's stubborn willfulness, I will pray my boy into heaven. God knew his brokenness, and is merciful and loving.

I admit that I sometimes fall into despair, so worried that I will not spend eternity with my boy. But recently a good and holy priest brought to my attention a reason for hope. Referencing the Diary of Saint Faustina Kowalska[7], the Polish nun who, in the 1930s, had received ongoing messages from Jesus Himself, resulting in the commissioning of the now infamous image of the Divine Mercy, he provided a lovely passage:

MY 13th STATION

> God's mercy sometimes touches the sinner
> at the last moment in a wondrous
> and mysterious way. Outwardly, it seems as
> if everything were lost, but it is
> not so. The soul, illumined by a ray of God's
> powerful final grace, turns to
> God in that last moment with such a
> power of love that, in an instant,
> it receives from God forgiveness of sin and punishment...
> DIARY ENTRY #1698

Throughout the endeavor of writing this memoir God has had my back, leading me and sustaining me from beginning to end. Each Monday evening during my weekly Adoration hour through the months I wrote the manuscript, I prayed for His input, soliciting guidance and direction and seeking His divine protection as I covered the dark topics. One Monday evening after Adoration, after asking Him, yet again, what He wanted me to convey in the book, I was just beginning my drive home when suddenly I was prompted to pull over and jot down what had popped into my head. God had inspired me to write this:

> The free will, which God allows, can be manipulated by prompts from the devil. By his lies and deceptions, the free will is hijacked and becomes a tool for satisfying the destructive goals of Satan. Without Jesus and the sacraments, we are weak and vulnerable. Without these graces any unrepentant sinful practices become strongholds or gates for the devil to gain entry into our minds, and to slowly destroy us.

Endnotes

1. Gabriele Amorth, *An Exorcist Tells His Story*, (San Francisco, Ignatius Press, 1999), 54.
2. Beverly Conyers, *Addict in the Family*, (Minnesota, Hazelden, 2003), 65-84.
3. Brad Lamm, *How to Help the One You Love*, (New York, St. Martin's Griffin, 2009), 35.
4. *Courage to Change*, Al-anon Family Group Headquarters, 1992, page 27
5. Bill W., *Alcoholics Anonymous, The Story of How Many Thousands of Men and Women Have Recovered from Alcoholism*, (New York, Alcoholics Anonymous World Services, Inc.; Fourth edition, 2001), pages 21-24.
6. Archbishop Fulton Sheen, *Eternal Galilean*, "The War With Temptation," (National Council of Catholic Men, Washington, D.C., 1934), 38.
7. Saint Maria Faustina Kawalska, *Divine Mercy in My Soul: Diary of M. Faustina Kowalska*, (Massachusetts, Marian Press, 2003), 6th notebook, paragraph #1698.

Additional Reference Material:
One Day at a Time. Virginia: Al-Anon Family Group Headquarters, Inc., 2000.
Douey-Rheims New Testament, Catholic Treasures, 1991.
Holy Bible, New American Bible, Catholic Bible Press, 1987.
Anthony DeStefano. *The Invisible World*. New York: Doubleday, 2011.
David Sheff. *Beautiful Boy*. New York: First Mariner Books, Houghton-Mifflin Harcourt Publishing Company, 2008.
Internet sources:
www.auxiliumchristianorum.org
www.castingnetsministries.com/tools/resources/articles/4311-the-dark-backward-demons-in-the-real-world
www.catholicwarriors.com/pages/warfare_prayers.htm
www.cramer-institute.com/how-satan-gets-to-us/
www.ewtn.com/library/answers/isadevil.htm

www.fisheaters.com/praeternaturalworld4.html
www.foreverconscious.com/sense-spirits-house
www.mnnonline.org/news/suicide-spike-reveals-spiritual-battle/
www.religiousdemonology.com
www.saintpiocenter.org
www.supernatural.wikia.com/wiki/Sulfur

About the Author

THERESA ANTHONY is a professional freelance writer of twenty-two years, extensively published in a variety of print and digital publications and on various websites. Since losing her son in 2013, Ms. Anthony has devoted her writing career to focusing on the fields of addiction recovery and mental health. In this capacity she hopes to make a meaningful contribution toward nudging individuals into treatment through compassionate, informative content writing. Ms. Anthony continues to enjoy her beautiful family, her boxer, Rocky, Zumba classes, and continually growing in her Catholic faith.

Thanks for reading *My 13th Station*. If you would be so kind as to leave a review on Amazon, or another platform from which you purchased it, it would be greatly appreciated. I would love to know how, or if, my memoir affected you, personally. Please share the book with youth groups, young adult groups, high school and college counselors, adults in recovery, friends, teachers, priests, pastors, and coworkers—anyone who might benefit from the valuable information contained in this true story.

Our young people are suffering. I am hoping to inspire open and honest dialogue about mental health issues, drug and alcohol addiction, and suicide prevention awareness. It is my hope that the stigma attached to these important issues will soon be a thing of the past, allowing people to feel comfortable about seeking the help they need. But most of all, I hope that hearts will open up and allow a loving God inside.

Please follow me!
My website: www.TheresaAnthony.com
Facebook: https://www.facebook.com/theresaanthonyauthor
Instagram: @theresaanthonyauthor
Twitter: @TheresaA_author

Theresa Anthony has published a new book, *Hope Springs From a Mother's Broken Heart: 11 Mothers Share How They Survived the Loss of a Child*. It is available on Amazon.com.

Made in United States
Orlando, FL
17 April 2023

32182050R00221